Wet.

"In this time of unprecedented crises on al̠ ̠ ̠every level, our challenge is to become aware of and shed the insidious trance of destruction that has come over us. Only as we awaken can we become the spiritual warriors necessary to free ourselves and our world of this life-threatening spell and step into a prophesied golden time. In this powerful book, Paul helps us look within ourselves and this illness to awaken the amazing potential that Creator has given us to thrive as good stewards of this precious home planet and all our relations."

BROOKE MEDICINE EAGLE, EARTHKEEPER, INDIGENOUS WISDOM
TEACHER, AND AUTHOR OF *BUFFALO WOMAN COMES SINGING*
AND *THE LAST GHOST DANCE*

"Never before in human history has there been a time when we so desperately need the insights and profound wisdom that Paul Levy is offering us in this book. As Levy wisely admonishes us, only by developing a conscious, thriving inner spiritual life can we dispel wetiko for good. Otherwise, we will only collude with the darkness we believe we are fighting."

CAROLYN BAKER, PH.D., AUTHOR OF *COLLAPSING CONSCIOUSLY*
AND *LOVE IN THE AGE OF ECOLOGICAL APOCALYPSE*

"Paul Levy's first book, *Dispelling Wetiko,* is a classic and brought an expanded awareness of the dark force that has invaded Western culture. If you are one of those who wonder how we are to deal with it now that the genie is out of the bottle, Levy's new contribution, *Wetiko,* is a compelling read that will provide you with new tools for your toolbox. A most important book!"

HANK WESSELMAN, PH.D., ANTHROPOLOGIST AND AUTHOR OF
THE RE-ENCHANTMENT AND *THE BOWL OF LIGHT*

"*Wetiko* is a gift to the world. Paul Levy brilliantly and beautifully dissects the wetiko illness and shows us how we can break its insidious spell. There are no topics more important than this, and Paul Levy writes exactly what we need to read."

DERRICK JENSEN, ECOPHILOSOPHER AND AUTHOR OF
A LANGUAGE OLDER THAN WORDS

"In *Wetiko,* the power and authenticity of Paul's narrative is in the grounding of his own lived experience of the collective human psychosis of wetiko.

This important and timely book maintains that the 'spirit of healing is hidden within the illness' and exhorts a shamanic journey of re-membering and reintegrating the innate wholeness of our true Self. Urging conscious co-creativity as a healing response and engagement. *Wetiko* invites us to free our imagination to literally embody the imaginal cells of the potential metamorphosis of our species."

JUDE CURRIVAN, PH.D., COSMOLOGIST, HEALER, AUTHOR OF *THE COSMIC HOLOGRAM* AND COFOUNDER OF WHOLEWORLD-VIEW

"This remarkable book, deeply rooted in Jungian psychology and the wisdom traditions, addresses the contagious psychospiritual disease of the soul that constitutes the crisis of humanity. The author brilliantly integrates a broad range of archetypal themes—from mythology, alchemy, religion, and quantum physics—to unearth the deeper meanings of our individual and collective soul-sickness. A must-read for anybody who is interested in a transformation of consciousness."

URSULA WIRTZ, JUNGIAN PSYCHOANALYST AND AUTHOR OF *TRAUMA AND BEYOND*

"Paul Levy has made a life's work out of studying wetiko—dealing with it in himself and shining the light of consciousness on it in the human world. In this book, he examines this mind-virus from multiple angles, helping the reader to achieve a full recognition of wetiko's nature, its terrible dangers, and the secret gift it contains. *Wetiko* is a book of urgent relevance and vital importance for everyone, alerting us to dire dangers and opening our eyes to our astonishing and wondrous potential as we engage with the multiple, simultaneous world crises that we face in these critical times."

ROBERT SIMMONS, AUTHOR OF *THE ALCHEMY OF STONES* AND COAUTHOR OF *THE BOOK OF STONES*

"After reading Paul Levy's work on wetiko, I knew I had to meet him. I drove from Boston, Massachusetts, to Portland, Oregon. This man Paul, he is something. He knows things. He experiences things in ways impossible to explain. All I can say is, that which walks with me knows that Paul Levy has been placed here to help us—to help us mitigate the climate crisis, the sixth extinction, this pandemic, racism, and this wetiko without and within if only we listen. But we must all do this work if our children and our children's children are to experience The Mother. Read this book. Mitakuye Oyasin."

THOMAS BALISTRIERI, ED.D., ASSISTANT TEACHING PROFESSOR OF PSYCHOLOGY AND GLOBAL STUDIES AT WORCESTER POLYTECHNIC INSTITUTE AND LAKOTA YUWIPI (MEDICINE) MAN

Wetiko

Healing the Mind-Virus That Plagues Our World

A Sacred Planet Book

Paul Levy

Inner Traditions
Rochester, Vermont

Inner Traditions
One Park Street
Rochester, Vermont 05767
www.InnerTraditions.com

Text stock is SFI certified

Sacred Planet Books are curated by Richard Grossinger, Inner Traditions editorial board member and cofounder and former publisher of North Atlantic Books. The Sacred Planet collection, published under the umbrella of the Inner Traditions family of imprints, is comprised of works on the themes of consciousness, cosmology, alternative medicine, dreams, climate, permaculture, alchemy, shamanic studies, oracles, astrology, crystals, hyperobjects, locutions, and subtle bodies.

Cataloging-in-Publication Data for this title is available from the Library of Congress

ISBN 978-1-64411-410-0 (print)
ISBN 978-1-64411-411-7 (ebook)

Printed and bound in the United States by Lake Book Manufacturing, Inc. The text stock is SFI certified. The Sustainable Forestry Initiative® program promotes sustainable forest management.

10 9 8 7 6 5 4 3 2 1

Text design and layout by Priscilla Harris Baker
This book was typeset in Garamond Premier Pro, with Barcelona and Optima used as display typefaces

To send correspondence to the author of this book, mail a first-class letter to the author c/o Inner Traditions • Bear & Company, One Park Street, Rochester, VT 05767, and we will forward the communication, or contact the author directly at **www.awakeninthedream.com**.

I want to dedicate this book to Rina Sircar, one of my

primary teachers, whose love could fill the

whole universe and then some.

In addition, this work is dedicated to all of us human

beings who have chosen to incarnate at this particularly

challenging time in history. Let us all be in service,

elevating our species to its proper place in the cosmos

as stewards of our precious home, planet Earth. Being

human is not an easy gig. We all deserve a gold star.

We moderns are faced with the necessity of rediscovering the life of the spirit; we must experience it anew for ourselves. It is the only way in which to break the spell that binds us.

C. G. JUNG

Contents

Foreword

Larry Dossey, M.D.

Wouldn't it be chilling to learn that a "mind-virus" was rapidly spreading throughout the world, infecting our own society and manifesting in people close to us—even in ourselves? It is a madness that has always plagued humanity, but today we are increasingly aware of it and seeing it for what it is. Some call it "evil." Paul Levy calls it "wetiko."

Wetiko is a successor to *Dispelling Wetiko: Breaking the Curse of Evil,* in which Paul Levy amplified the Native American concept of wetiko, a seemingly malignant spirit responsible for a fearsome disease of the soul. Paul Levy expands on this indigenous understanding with his deep study of Jungian psychology and his knowledge of mythology, shamanism, and quantum physics, combined with his original insights and experiences. Whether you are new to Paul Levy or have read his other writings, you are now in for a reading experience that is both fascinating and unsettling.

Wetiko, says Levy, is a psychological force within the unconscious mind that predisposes us toward unwholesome impulses such as the thirst for power and control, greed, and jealousy. People who are possessed by wetiko are deeply selfish; they seldom have any interest in the well-being of others. Wetiko is a stealth factor. We rarely suspect its presence, even when it affects our own behavior.

Wetiko, as Levy shows, is prefigured in psychiatrist C. G. Jung's concept of the shadow, the unsavory part of our unconscious psyche that we reject in our conscious awareness. Many people recoil from the idea that nice, well-behaved citizens could secretly harbor "evil" thoughts and impulses, but these counterforces are present to some degree in everyone. Under certain provocations they surface readily. As I write, wetiko is having a field day across the globe, visible in headlines and the rapidly changing current events that are evoking fear, anger, chaos, and disruption to individual and collective life.

How does this mind-virus spread among us? We are learning the details about how wetiko functions, and what inhibits it. A growing body of evidence from leaders in modern science suggests that our conscious and unconscious thoughts and intentions are not confined to our individual brains and bodies.[1] They can operate in the world "out there," distant from our individual selves, beyond the limitations and constraints of the here and now. This is the domain of *nonlocal mind*—mind that is boundless and boundaryless, infinite in space and time, and therefore connected and united with all other minds in the past, present, and future. Levy's account of how wetiko operates through the nonlocal field outside the constraints of space and time represents a continuation of an articulation of a genuine nonlocal psychology of mind.

Moreover, experiments in distant healing appear to be crucially influenced by love, compassion, and deep caring, just as healers throughout history have maintained.[2] This is one of the greatest lessons of recent experiments: love and compassion, operating through nonlocal mind, can remotely change the state of physical bodies in positive, healthful ways.

But not *just* love. There is a dark side of consciousness—the domain of Jung's concept of the shadow. It is where wetiko lives and operates in our lives, as Paul Levy shows.

Studies in remote influence show also that *harm* can be extended to living things: microbes can be inhibited, cellular function can be retarded, cells can be killed,[3] and the activity of biochemical reactions can be reduced.[4] Negative, nonlocal intentions resemble the curses, hexes, and spells in which perhaps all premodern cultures (and many modern ones) have believed. In acknowledging this tenebrous side of nonlocal mind, these cultures demonstrate a more complex, sophisticated understanding of consciousness than do we. They accept a dark side of consciousness as simply the way things are, and they gracefully devise methods of protecting themselves. It is cultures such as our own, which deny a negative, nonlocal factor of consciousness, that often get blindsided by it, as Paul Levy reveals. In any case, the capacity of humans to extend harm mentally and nonlocally to living things should not be rejected. Instead, this ability can be used for good, for healing—as when human intentions are used to retard or kill cancer cells or invading pathogens.[5]

Consider: If mind is genuinely nonlocal, this implies that individual minds cannot be completely separated and isolated from one another, and are joined in some sense even as they simultaneously experience themselves individually. In some dimension, minds that are nonlocal come together to form a single unitary mind. This recognition is ancient. It is also modern, as many outstanding scientists have realized.[6]

Our nonlocal nature makes wetiko possible—but love, caring, and compassion also stem from that same quality of consciousness. This is an example of what the physicist Niels Bohr called complementarity: the coming together of apparent opposites to produce a more accurate picture of the whole. One is reminded of a maxim from the field of transpersonal psychology: In order to transcend the ego, you must first have one. Thus we can say that wetiko is ultimately redeemed by its opposites: love, empathy, caring, and compassion. For these qualities, like wetiko, also have nonlocal, infinite effects in the world.

Why is it important to acknowledge the nonlocal, negative aspects of wetiko? Because ultimately wetiko is a world-destroyer by virtue of its nonlocal, infectious nature. It spreads globally; it is unconfinable to individual minds. It has the capacity to wreck more than a single individual's life; it can destroy a species—our own.

We are not helpless bystanders against wetiko. The ultimate antidote for it is love, its complementary, nonlocal opposite. But specific antidotes against wetiko have taken many forms in human history. Now read the words of Paul Levy, a true student and scholar in the burgeoning field of wetiko, who has devoted more careful thought to wetiko than anyone I know. Let us see what his explorations have uncovered about the disease and its cure.

LARRY DOSSEY, M.D.
SANTA FE, NEW MEXICO

DR. LARRY DOSSEY earned his medical degree from Southwestern Medical School in Dallas, then served as a battalion surgeon in Vietnam, where he was decorated for valor. He helped establish the Dallas Diagnostic Association and, in 1982, was chief of staff of Medical City Dallas Hospital. Before his book *Healing Words* was published in 1993, only three U.S. medical schools had courses exploring the role of religious practice in health, compared to nearly eighty today. In *Recovering the Soul* (1989) he introduced the concept of "nonlocal mind"—mind unconfined to the brain and body. Since then this model has been adopted by many leading scientists as an emerging image of consciousness. In 2013, he received the prestigious Visionary Award. The author of thirteen books and numerous articles, Dr. Dossey is the former executive editor of the peer-reviewed journal *Alternative Therapies in Health and Medicine*. He is currently executive editor of the peer-reviewed journal *Explore: The Journal of Science and Healing*. Dr. Dossey has lectured all over the world and the impact of his work has been remarkable.

Acknowledgments

It's an unusual experience as a writer to not be able to find words. This is certainly my experience—for I feel a bit speechless, beyond my capacity—in trying to adequately thank the individuals who have played key roles in helping this book come to fruition. Even though I'm its author, I can easily feel like I didn't write this book, but rather, was simply "dreamed up" to be the instrument by the nonlocal field for the words to come through and arrange themselves in a meaningful form on these pages. This creative process couldn't possibly have taken place without the selfless and caring help of countless others who personified the spirit of being in service. Feeling other people's love and support for one's work is invaluable, not quantifiable—truly priceless.

I first want to thank my longtime friend Larry Berry—who has always been there, without fail, in whatever way was needed, for the many years of loving and never-ending support I've received from him in helping to get my work out. I want to express immense gratitude for the incomparable Donna Zerner for freely sharing her many brilliant gifts in helping this book—not to mention myself—see the light. I also want to acknowledge the generous support I've received from Kendra Crossen Burroughs in ways I could only imagine.

I want to give a shout-out of thanks to Robert Simmons, who went out of his way to connect me with Inner Traditions. And I also want to thank Richard Grossinger, who coincidentally enough, was the person who helped publish my previous work on wetiko and then played the same role for this book, albeit in totally different circumstances. My sincere appreciation to my editor, Meghan MacLean, and all of the wonderful people at Inner Traditions for their seemingly never-ending support to help this work see the light of day. I also want to gratefully acknowledge the help of a close friend of mine who for years has endlessly contemplated the idea of wetiko with me, who, for reasons of his own, wishes to remain anonymous—you know who you are.

I also want to thank Matt Cadenelli, Neil Levenson, Damian Thomas, Seth Taylor, Mark Hartley, Alex Aris, David Frenette, Julianna Bright, Richard Daab, Bob Welsh, Cory Parker, Samuel Freni-Rothschild, Bailey Wayton, Michael Ellick, Seth Lorinczi, Gwen Burns, Mertie Pateros, and Karin Gagnon for their loving reflection and support.

INTRODUCTION

Wetiko in a Nutshell

A contagious psycho-spiritual disease of the soul, a parasite of the mind, is currently being acted out en masse on the world stage via an insidious collective psychosis of titanic proportions. This mind-virus—which Native Americans have called "wetiko"—covertly operates through the unconscious blind spots in the human psyche, rendering people oblivious to their own madness and compelling them to act against their own best interests. Wetiko is a psychosis in the true sense of the word, "a sickness of the spirit."

An inner cancer of the soul, wetiko covertly influences our perceptions so as to act itself out through us while simultaneously hiding itself from being seen. Wetiko bewitches our consciousness so that we become blind to the underlying, assumed viewpoint through which we perceive, conjure up, and give meaning to our experience of both the world and ourselves. This psychic virus can be thought of as the bug in "the system" that informs and animates the madness that is playing out in our lives, both individually and collectively, on the world stage.

"Wetiko," to quote author and environmental activist Derrick Jensen, is "spread till it now covers the earth and to a greater or lesser degree infects us all. There are no hospitals for this sickness. If we cannot acknowledge it, how can we attempt to cure it?"[1]

Before being able to treat this sickness that has infected us all, we have to snap out of our denial, see the disease, acknowledge it, name it, and try to understand how it operates so as to ascertain how to deal with it—this is what this book is all about.

Called by many different names throughout history, the spirit of wetiko renders every other issue secondary. Wetiko is the overarching umbrella that contains, subsumes, informs, and underlies every form of destruction, of ourselves and others, that our species is acting out in our world on every scale. If we don't come to terms with what wetiko is revealing to us, nothing else will matter, as there will be no more human species.

Humanity is facing the most important question in our history—whether human life will survive in anything that resembles what we now know it to be. We are answering this question with governmental policies and collective behavior that, for the most part, only increase our acceleration toward multiple disasters—as we madly compete with each other to race off the nearest cliff as quickly as possible. We have fallen blind—as if in a hypnotic trance—while a seemingly demonic force compels our species toward its own self-destruction. To quote eminent theologian David Ray Griffin, "Our battle seems to be against 'flesh and blood' less than against some demonic power to which human civilization is in bondage."[2]

Wetiko follows on from my earlier book on the same topic, *Dispelling Wetiko.* In this new book I am attempting to elucidate how wetiko has been creatively represented and symbolized, not only in various spiritual wisdom traditions from time immemorial, but by creative artists and philosophers throughout the ages as well. In addition, I am contemplating the current goings-on in our world gone mad through a lens that hopefully will help the reader see and get a better handle on wetiko.

In essence I am attempting to translate deep primordial indigenous wisdom into a modern-day psychological idiom that can be more easily understood and taken "online" in our present state of awareness. We are truly at the beginning stages of understanding this elusive and heretofore invisible virus of the mind. My books on wetiko are in the service of helping us to open our eyes and see this deadly virus of the mind before it's too late.

My Personal Experience of Wetiko

When I first directly encountered wetiko, the experience literally drove me "out of my mind" (some people think I haven't yet returned, but that's another story) and destroyed my entire family. I have written a book about this, *Awakened by Darkness: When Evil Becomes Your Father.* One of the gifts of this nightmarish experience is that it has given me an authority to write about such heavy matters as wetiko and evil in a way that no amount of intellectual study could have provided.

Through this traumatic set of experiences I received a direct transmission/transfusion of the wetiko virus into the veins of my soul, which, besides making me sick and almost driving me permanently crazy, changed the trajectory of my entire life. This destined me to commit to healing myself from this ill-fated happenstance and to try and understand this seemingly otherworldly force with which I had come into contact (or which had contacted me).

Fortunately, my "close encounters of the wetiko-kind" have helped me find my voice and discover my work—this book being just one example. If I hadn't connected with my creative nature, I would have been in deep trouble and undoubtedly would have become another one of wetiko's seemingly endless casualties. The point is that I have not written this book as an intellectual, academic, or scholar comfortably sitting in an ivory tower philosophizing or creating theories about wetiko. Rather, I've written it as a way of coming to terms with my own harrowing experience with the subject matter, barely escaping with my life and my sanity intact.

My personal encounters with wetiko have left me in a weird position. I felt convinced of the profound importance of something that many people seem either unaware of, disinterested in, judgmental of, or possessed by. It can be a very lonely experience to see something that many other people aren't seeing. However, I've learned to persevere in my vision and continually refine my ability to transmit what I'm seeing in a way that can be helpful for others.

I've noticed that it is typically people who have really suffered, be it from going through some sort of wounding experience, emotional trauma, abuse, addiction, and so on—and then have done their *inner work*—who recognize what I am talking about when I point to the insidious workings of wetiko. These are usually people who have found that traditional religions no longer satisfy their deeper spiritual needs and that mainstream cultural values no longer speak to their souls. Not contained in a faith, these are people who don't feel that they are in possession of some absolute truth, but are really open to what resonates with their immediate, lived experience.

The Normalization of Wetiko

A few years ago I ran into a friend whom I hadn't seen for a while. He asked me what I had been up to. I answered that I was writing about the collective psychosis (wetiko is a collective psychosis) that our species had fallen into. His response was telling. He asked me what made me think there was a collective psychosis going on. His question left me speechless; I literally didn't know how to respond. What made him think there *wasn't* a collective psychosis going on, I wondered. Could he give me one piece of evidence? Our collective madness had become so normalized that most people—my friend was extremely bright, by the way—didn't even notice.

Many of us have become conditioned to thinking that if we were in the middle of a collective psychosis it would mean that people would be doing all sorts of "crazy" things such as running around naked and screaming, for instance. This ingrained idea, however, gets in the way of recognizing the very real collective insanity in which all of us are—both passively and actively—participating. If we want to envision what a collective psychosis could actually look like, it might be a real eye-opener to realize it would look exactly like what is happening right now in our world.

Where is the voice of the psychiatric establishment in pointing out that our species has fallen prey to a psychic epidemic of massive proportions? In a personal conversation I had with the late Harvard psychiatrist John Mack about exactly this point, he was of the opinion that the psychiatric community doesn't see it as their job to deal with collective psychoses such as we are in today. Such collective psychopathologies are simply not on their radar. They focus and specialize exclusively on psychopathologies of the (seemingly) separate, discrete, individual human being.*

By not recognizing this worldwide, systemic psychological disease that has infected the global body politic (and hence, is informing the pathologies of individuals), the mental health community becomes its unwitting agent, helping the disease to propagate. Whose job is it to shed light on our species-wide illness, I wondered. Cultural anthropologists? Sociologists? Theologians? Maybe, by default, the responsibility falls on each one of us.

The mental health practitioners' blindness to the psychological disease provides important information about the nature of the beast we're dealing with. The disease has subsumed the very agency that should be monitoring and trying to heal it, transforming it into becoming one of its purveyors. Unless we are consciously aware of its covert operations, the disease will usurp our every attempt at healing it so as to further feed its pathology.

Since the publishing of *Dispelling Wetiko,* I've received many emails that have suggested that the ever-increasing madness that has played out in the world has proven my previous writings on wetiko to be prescient, as if, like some sort of prophet, I had predicted the future. I don't feel this way, for from my point of view, all I was doing in bringing wetiko to light was to point out the deeper process that has been informing events in the collective body politic of our world from time immemorial.

---

*It is noteworthy that, ultimately speaking, no such separate individual self exists. The self is relational, in that we only exist relative to others, to the environment, and to the universe at large.

Instead of telling the future, I am trying to shed light on a dynamic happening within the human psyche that has been rendered unconscious—and hence forgotten—a dynamic that will shape this present moment and will produce our future. We won't be able to effectively deal with the horrors that lie in front of us if we can't face the horrors that lie both behind and within us. This deeper dynamic had been happening in, as, and through the whole course of human history for millennia, but in recent times it's becoming more evident and harder to deny. I was—and still am—simply pointing at a deeper longtime pattern that is revealing itself through the behavior of our species. Once we recognize this wetiko-inspired pattern, we cannot "unsee" it; our aptitude for vision expands accordingly.

The Contributions of C. G. Jung

Being ahead of (as well as outside of and an expression of) his time, the great doctor of the soul C. G. Jung, who, it should be noted, considered himself a philosopher in disguise, was tracking wetiko (although not using the indigenous name). He referred to it by a number of different names (for example, oftentimes referring to the dangers of psychic epidemics, collective psychosis, the germ/infection of evil, totalitarian psychosis, imperialistic madness, counterfeiting spirits, powers of darkness, the demon of sickness, etc.). Jung's wisdom and insight on this topic deeply inform this book.

Finding Jung's work was instrumental for me to get a handle on my own personal encounter with the mind-numbing evil of wetiko. I shudder to think where I would be if I hadn't come across his writings. It can be so helpful when we are experiencing something that is not culturally sanctioned or recognized to discover someone who has found the words for our seemingly unspeakable experience.

Other people have described me, to my horror, as a "Jungian." (In this I think of Jung saying, "Thank God I'm Jung and not a Jungian.") I have never even taken a course on Jung. I am simply an independent researcher who follows what inspires me, which Jung does no end. I am totally self-taught regarding Jung. Indeed, he himself felt that his work would more speak to ordinary people than to the scholars and experts. I am a case in point. I am only interested in the parts of his work that speak to my personal experience and help me to alleviate my suffering. It is my hope that at the very least this book will give the reader a deeper appreciation of the genius of Jung and the value of his work for our times, which is immense. I can only imagine what Jung would say if he were alive today. In these pages I feel like I am doing continual "active imagination" with him, both in this book and within my own mind.[3]

A Native American Idea

The way I have interpreted the concept of wetiko is my own, insofar as I have taken a First Nations idea and developed it in and for a Western mind and cultural context. I feel that I am merely a translator, trying to create a bridge so that their profound insights might benefit the neurotic Western psyche. I've never lived in the environments in which the Native American conception of wetiko arose: pre-Columbian woodlands and plains, wild waters full of creatures and their spirit forms, vast herds of game galloping across windblown grasses. I am a child of cities, machines, and Western civilization. As such, I experienced wetiko in a typical dysfunctional American family and a practically insane Western capitalist society. I thus bring new paradigm, Western symbolic logic and intellectual formulations to a construct from another culture.

I do so with humility, respect, and the recognition that from one point of view I could be seen to be appropriating a concept without knowing its original existential basis and phenomenology. From my perspective I am writing about the indigenous idea of wetiko to honor the great native traditions of wisdom. In a sense, my work on wetiko is a collaboration between me and unknown Native American philosophers, psychologists, and shamans. They lived in a world of tight communities and mutual responsibility for daily survival, in harmony with nature. They had no cars or mass weaponry or stock markets or telecommunications.

But they were human like us. They, too, had to deal with the ins and outs of the human psyche. They fought wars and dealt with psychosis, crime, evil, and people of the lie. They had to protect themselves and their societies. When dark forces arose within the group, they had to identify them and know what could be handled and transmuted by the tribe and what was so toxic that it needed to be exiled for the safety of the rest. Their shamans and medicine women and men understood the nature of demons, possession, and evil in a way that could be most instructive for modern humanity. They provide us with a brilliant diagnosis as well as an urgent warning.

The followers of the Buddhist path can't monopolize or copyright the idea of "Buddha-nature"—for they are pointing at something that is intrinsic to the living experience of being a human being. In the same way, what the Native American wisdom-holders are illuminating in their conception of wetiko is a universal, archetypal experience that is an essential aspect of our experience of being human.[4]

The Native American conception of wetiko can add to, complement, and flesh out the articulation of this same malady by other spiritual traditions. In describing wetiko, the Cree describe giants that grow with each human meal, so they are simultaneously huge and emaciated—never able to fill their inner void—searching desperately for their next victim, driven by excess. In coming across the Native American idea and description of wetiko, I recognized it in my own life as well as within my own mind. I have no doubt whatsoever that what the Native Americans refer to as wetiko is a universal condition afflicting everyone; it is something we are all fated to come to terms with in our lives.

What Is Wetiko Really?

Wetiko is a cannibalizing force driven by insatiable greed, appetite without satisfaction, consumption as an end in itself, and war for its own sake, against other tribes, species, and nature, and even against the individual's own humanity. It is a disease of the soul, and being a disease of the soul, we all potentially have wetiko, as it pervades and "in-forms" the underlying field of consciousness. Any one of us at any moment can fall into our unconscious and unwittingly become an instrument for the evil of wetiko to act itself out through us and incarnate in our world. If we see someone who seems to be taken over by wetiko and we think they have the disease and we don't, in seeing them as separate we have fallen under the spell of the virus ourselves.

Wetiko induces in us a proclivity to see the source of our own pathology outside of ourselves—existing in the other. Wetiko feeds off of polarization and fear—and terror—of the other. Seeing the world through a wetiko-inspired lens of separation/otherness enlivens what Jung calls "the God of Terror who dwells in the human soul,"[5] and simultaneously plays itself out both within our soul and in the world at large.

Wetiko subversively turns our "genius" for reality-creation against us in such a way that we become bewitched by the projective tendencies of our own mind. Falling under wetiko's spell, we become entranced by our own intrinsic gifts and talents for dreaming up our world in a way that not only doesn't serve us, but rather is put at the service of wetiko (whose agenda is contrary to our own). Our creativity then boomerangs against us such that we hypnotize ourselves with our creative genius, which cripples our evolutionary potential.

To the extent we are unconsciously possessed by the spirit of wetiko, it is as if a psychic tapeworm or parasite has taken over our brain and tricked us, its host, into thinking we are feeding and empowering ourselves while we are actually nourishing the parasite (a process that will ultimately kill its host—us). In wetiko disease, something that is not us surreptitiously, beneath our conscious awareness, takes the place of and plays the role of who we actually are. Shapeshifting so as to cloak itself in our form, this mercurial predator gets under our skin and "puts us on" as a disguise. Miming ourselves, we become a copy, a false duplicate of our true selves. We are then truly playing out a real version of the imposter syndrome.

The Sickness of Exploitation

Wetiko is powerless to control our true nature, but it can control and manipulate this false identity that it sets up within us. When we fall under the sway of wetiko's illusion, we simultaneously identify with who we are not, while dissociating from and forgetting who we actually are—giving away our power, not to mention ourselves, in the process. To quote radical psychiatrist R. D. Laing, "We have been conned into the illusion that we are separate 'skin-encapsulated egos.' Having at one and the same time lost our *selves* and developed the illusion that we are autonomous egos, we are expected to comply by inner consent with external constraints, to an almost unbelievable extent."[6] Disconnecting from our own intrinsic agency, we open ourselves to be used, manipulated, and exploited by outside forces.

Indigenous author Jack Forbes, who wrote the classic book about wetiko entitled *Columbus and Other Cannibals,* refers to wetiko as "the sickness of exploitation."[7] Wetiko can be conceived of as being an evil, cannibalistic, vampiric spirit that inspires people under its sway to take and consume another's resources and life-force energy solely for their own profit, without giving anything of value back from their own lives. Wetiko thus violates the sacred law of reciprocity in both human affairs and the natural world as a whole.

Wetiko, like any virus, is fundamentally "dead" matter and, like a vampire, it has a thirst for the very thing it lacks—the essence of our soul, our very life force. A member of the "undead," the vampiric wetiko virus "takes on" and mimics life itself. It is only in and through a living being that it acquires a pseudolife. The person so taken over becomes an outpost for wetiko to do its dirty work.

The raison d'etre for viruses like wetiko is to continually reproduce themselves. The wetiko virus isn't able to replicate itself through its own energy, however, so it's compelled to use us to propagate itself so that we can "pass on" and transmit the bug to others. The main channel of wetiko's transmission is *relational*. It exists through our relationships with ourselves, each other, and the world at large. Like a vampire that can't stand the light of day, the wetiko virus can't stand to be illumined. However, in seeing how it covertly operates through our own consciousness, we take away its seeming independence, autonomy, and power over us, while at the same time empowering ourselves.

The way the vampiric wetiko covertly operates within the human psyche is mirrored by the way it works in the outside world. Speaking about the genocide and colonization that the Europeans perpetrated on the Native Americans, indigenous author and therapist Eduardo Duran writes in *Healing the Soul Wound,* "The colonial process experienced by these people [the Native People] can be described as a collective raping process of the psyche/soul of both the land and the people. . . . In essence, the vampire bit the life-world known as Turtle Island [as the Western Hemisphere is known in Native cosmology], and the infection of the poison injected by the vampire has not been eradicated."[8]

Jung never tired of warning us that the greatest danger threatening humanity today is the possibility that millions—even billions—of us can fall into our unconscious together in a collective psychosis, reinforcing each other's madness in such a way that we become unwittingly complicit in creating our own destruction. When this occurs, humanity finds itself in a situation where we are confronted with—and battered by—the primal, primordial, and elemental forces of our own psyche.

The Internal Origins of Wetiko

The most depraved part of falling under the thrall of wetiko is that, ultimately speaking, it involves the assent of our own free will; no one other than ourselves is ultimately responsible for our situation. There is no objective entity called wetiko that exists outside of ourselves that can steal our soul—the dreamed-up phenomenon of wetiko tricks us into giving it away ourselves. People under the sway of wetiko are implicated in and willingly subscribe to their own enslavement. They do this to the point that when offered the way out of the comfort of their prison they oftentimes react violently. They symbolically—and sometimes literally—try to kill the messenger who is showing them the path to freedom.*

Ultimately speaking, in wetiko disease we are not being infected by a physical, objectively existing virus outside of ourselves. Rather, the origin and genesis of the wetiko psychosis is endogenous; its roots are to be found within the human psyche. The fact that wetiko is the expression of something inside of us means that the cure for wetiko is likewise within us. Though not objectively existing, the wetiko pathogen has a "virtual reality" that nevertheless can influence us in such a way that it can potentially destroy our species. The fact that something that only exists as a function of ourselves can destroy us is pointing at—and introducing us to—the incredibly vast, invisible, and yet mostly untapped creative power that is our inherent birthright. If not used consciously, however, this creative power turns destructive.

Wetiko can be likened to the darkness (which in this example can symbolize the ignorance that is characteristic of wetiko), in a room where there is no sunlight. As long as there is no light, this darkness seems like a real "thing." And yet once we open the blinds and sunlight (symbolic of awakening) pours into the room, the dark-

---

*Christ is one of innumerable examples of this.

ness is in that same moment evicted and exists no longer—as if it never existed in the first place. After the light has emerged, we can contemplate the darkness from the point of view of it being nothing other than the absence of light. And yet, before the coming of the light, the darkness had real effects, meeting every criteria for being real in and of itself. (I think of Jung's idea that in the realm of psyche something is real if it "works," i.e., has real effects.) This is the paradox: as compared to existing by virtue of some quality—wetiko only exists by the "lack of virtue" of not realizing our own nature.

Wetiko is nonlocal in that it is an inner disease of the soul that discloses itself through the canvas of the outside world.[9] This mind-virus has the seemingly magical ability to extend itself out into the world and configure outer events to give itself living material form. Not constrained by the conventional laws of third-dimensional space and time, wetiko nonlocally informs events in the world as well as our reactions to them so as to synchronistically express—and reveal—itself.

Just like in a dream, events in the outer world are symbolically reflecting back to us a condition deep within the psyche of each one of us. Recognizing this correlation helps us begin to develop the vision to see wetiko. If we don't understand that our current world crisis has its roots within and is an expression of the human psyche, we are doomed to unconsciously repeat and continually re-create endless suffering and destruction in increasingly amplified forms, as if we are having a recurring nightmare.

In my language, the inner situation within ourselves is getting "dreamed up" into materialized form in, through, and as the world. In waking life we are continually dreaming right beneath the threshold of consciousness, especially when we are under the influence of our unconscious complexes. In other words, when we are "under the influence" of our activated unconscious, we will unknowingly re-create our very inner landscape via the medium of the outside world. What can be more dreamlike than that?

What is happening in the world today is reflecting—and both literally and symbolically revealing to us—something unknown within our own psyche. At the same time, in a nonlinear acausal feedback loop that happens both atemporally (outside of time) and over (linear) time, events in our world are informed and shaped by the very inner psychological process they are reflecting. The inner and outer are simultaneously co-arising and reciprocally co-evoking each other. This is to say that what is happening within us and what is arising in our world have a mysterious interconnection; the inner and the outer are ultimately not separate nor separable.

Recognizing the correlation between the inner and the outer, between the micro and the macro, is the doorway into being able to see wetiko and wake up to the dreamlike nature that wetiko is simultaneously hiding and revealing depending on our point of view and level of awareness. When we realize that we—as microcosms—mirror the macrocosm (the universe at large), this reveals to us that there is a pathway inside of us that leads not to our particular psychological idiosyncrasies, but to what is truly important. Recognizing the connection between what is happening out in the world with what is taking place within our minds becomes a channel or secret doorway that leads beyond our merely personal psychological issues, empowering us to deal with the essential problem of our time.

Dreaming Wetiko

The wetiko psychosis is a *dreamed-up* phenomenon, which is to say that we are all potentially participating in and actively cocreating the wetiko epidemic in each and every moment. Like a collective dream, the wetiko epidemic is the manifestation of something in our shared collective unconscious taking on material form.

Wetiko is literally demanding that we pay attention to the fundamental role that the psyche (the source of our dreams) plays in creating our *experience* of ourselves and of the world. Forgetting the crucial role that the psyche plays in creating our experience, we marginalize our own intrinsic author-ity, tragically dreaming up both internal and external authoritarian forces to limit our freedom and mold our experience for us. Never before in all of human history has our species been forced to confront the numinous, world-transforming powers of the psyche on so vast a scale.

Even with the ongoing multiple catastrophes that are converging in our world, it is not beyond the bounds of possibility that the darkness that is emerging today might become the soil out of which a regenerative age and nobler culture arise. Although the source of humanity's inhumanity to itself, wetiko is at the same time a potential catalyst for our evolution as a species. Recognizing the dreamed-up nature of the wetiko epidemic can become the impetus for us to awaken to the dreamlike nature of the universe itself.

We are wetiko's offspring in that this peculiar disease helps to grow a new part of us, potentially "raising us" to a higher level of our evolution (if it doesn't kill us in the process!). Instead of the perspective of linear causality (where one thing causes another), to wrap our mind around the nature of the situation with which we are dealing necessitates we implement *bi-directional thinking* (thinking simultaneously in two directions). In a circular process without beginning or end, we are being dreamed up by the universe while dreaming up the universe at one and the same time. To see this not only demands that we have an expansion of consciousness, it *is* the very expansion itself.

The less wetiko is recognized, however, the more seemingly powerful and dangerous it becomes. Wetiko can only be seen when we begin to realize the dreamlike nature of our universe, step out of the illusory viewpoint of the separate self, and recognize the deeper underlying field of which we are all expressions, in which we are all contained, and through which we are all interconnected. These are interrelated insights of the same multifaceted realization. The energetic expression of this realization, and the wetiko *dissolver par excellence,* is compassion. Connecting with the compassion that *is* our nature we find ourselves in very good company.

Being the unmediated expression of recognizing the dreamlike nature, compassion reciprocally co-arises with lucidity. In other words, if we're genuinely awakening to the dreamlike nature of reality, both lucidity and compassion will be inseparably united components of our experience.

As if an instrument of a higher intelligence, wetiko literally invites—make that demands—that we become conscious of and step into our intrinsic creative power and agency, or suffer the consequences. Instead of mutating so as to become resistant to our attempts to heal it, the wetiko virus forces us to mutate—to evolve—relative to it.

Wetiko is a quantum phenomenon, in that it contains within itself the potential to be either the deadliest poison or the most healing medicine. Will wetiko destroy us? Or will it catalyze our evolution and wake us up? How wetiko ultimately manifests depends upon nothing other than whether we recognize what it is revealing to us. How dreamlike—the very thing that is potentially killing us is at the same time helping us to remember who we are. How wetiko manifests depends upon how we dream it.

Before discovering the Native term *wetiko,* I was calling this pathological aberration of the psyche *Malignant Egophrenia*—whose acronym is "ME" disease. For when all is said and done, wetiko stems from our mis-identification of who we think we are (our sense of "me-ness"). In a very real sense, we are not who we believe ourselves to be if we experience ourselves as a separate self who exists separate from other (imagined) separate selves—not to mention the whole rest of the universe. From this misguided thought springs a case of mistaken identity, out of which grows the pestilence of wetiko.

Goldsmithing

In writing this book, I've had to navigate the conundrum of not wanting to repeat what was said in my earlier book on the same subject, while still giving the reader a real sense of the profundity of wetiko in case they haven't read that earlier work. Here, with this book, I want to give as much of a picture of wetiko in case this is the only book the reader will ever read on the subject. Each of these volumes stands on its own—not needing the other—while simultaneously complementing and supplementing each other.

Due to wetiko's multichanneled nature, all of its myriad creative expressions are like variations on an underlying theme, which makes some repetition not only hard to avoid, but necessary. These reiterations feel important to the fabric of this book, as if I am circling a center point, reciting an incantation, and emphasizing certain points more than once in order to get the meaning across. I am applying what the author Alan Watts called "the goldsmith technique," striking repeatedly on the same point from slightly different angles so as to help the reader take in and metabolize what I am trying to shed light on.

This brings to mind how when we have recurring dreams, or a recurrent theme in a single dream, it is an expression that our unconscious is again and again—in slightly different forms—bringing something important to our awareness that would behoove us to consciously recognize. I like to think whatever repetition I've purposely left in this book can be seen in the same way.

Or maybe I'm just dreaming.

PART I

Spiritual Traditions and Creative Artists

It should get our attention that every person who has discovered wetiko considers it to be the most important topic to understand in our world today. In this first section, I am attempting to point out that the idea of wetiko is nothing new, but rather, has been creatively envisioned in unique ways by creative visionaries throughout the ages. When these viewpoints are seen together, they provide us with a multiperspectival vision that gives a higher resolution than any one point of view can by itself. This can help us to begin to see this heretofore invisible mind-virus in a way that is wetiko's (instead of our) worst nightmare.

1

It's All in the Psyche

In today's global society, wetiko has turned on the planet itself and is threatening the survival of all human beings as well as other species and the habitability of Earth itself. Though originally a Native American idea structured by Algonquian syntax, wetiko is a universal human disease that, due to our interconnectedness, afflicts all of us, regardless of where we come from. Wetiko's evil flourishes and is going pandemic in the petri dish of the modern industrial world. There is no way to exile this disease anymore. We must continue to diagnose it and try to treat it by facing it head-on within ourselves. That is the only way to make a habitable future for us all.

I think of Jung's contention that nothing really new happens in history. It is as if we are living in an endlessly recurring dream, experiencing "groundhog day" every day of our lives. Humanity seems to be continually, relentlessly, and endlessly reenacting its unhealed, unconscious wounds, traumas, and abuse issues. It was Jung's opinion that we could only talk of something novel happening in the world if the previously *unimaginable* took place: if true reason, genuine humanity, and love won a lasting victory. It is my prayer that this work—supported by the blessings of those throughout history who have dedicated and even sacrificed their lives in order to shed light on this deadly disease—will be in the service of the heretofore unimaginable to prevail.

A Saving Idea

As Jung has pointed out, when it is a question of mass psychosis, nothing but "new symbolic ideas" that embrace, express, and help us recontextualize—and see—the emerging chaos and disorder in a new way can save us from our self-created, collective nightmare. The conventional mind is utterly useless in this capacity. It cannot help us free ourselves from this predicament because it itself is a product of—and created—the very madness from which we need to be liberated. As Albert Einstein famously said, "We can't solve problems by using the same kind of thinking we used when we created them." And "The only genuine ideas," to quote the Spanish philosopher Jose Ortega y Gasset, are "the ideas of the shipwrecked."[1] Here's a new idea: The Savior itself can arrive in the flash of a truly new creative idea.

What Plato calls "the eyes of the soul," ideas can be an expression of—and reveal—the soul itself. In contrast to being abstract, immaterial vaporous nothings that carry no weight and have no substance, ideas have real power. They are the means by which we see the world and creatively envision and give meaning to our lives. New ideas change the way we think about things—and think in general—as well as what we believe. Newly emerging archetypal ideas can activate people's creative imagination. These ideas are expressions of and catalysts for a deeper, more expansive vision of the world and our place in it. A new idea can transform our very state of being and can change our conception of ourselves and our sense of what's happening in the world. Ideas are no mere afterthoughts.

New ideas, emerging like a lotus from the dark depths of the collective unconscious itself, can be conceived of as living psychic organisms that evolve—and concurrently help us evolve—as we come to terms with integrating their deeper meaning. These living ideas are not merely abstract things to passively think about, but involve our active engagement in integrating and unfolding what they're revealing to us. Consciously participating in the formation of these living ideas conjures up a magical effect that can potentially hold the emerging destructive forces of chaos and disorder spellbound.

What can be thought of as a *saving idea* (i.e., novel, creative, redemptive, archetypal conceptions) can protect a people from succumbing to, in Jung's words, "the infection" of a "one-sided idea."[2] It is noteworthy that Jung is describing a one-sided idea as an infection, for it creates an imbalance and dis-ease in the psyche. Becoming possessed by an antiquated, fixed idea is dangerous, as it can create a sclerosis of consciousness that strengthens our inner blindness. If we are unconsciously in the grip of an unreflected upon (and limiting) idea, like puppets on a string, we—without even realizing it—become the idea's instruments for reproducing itself into the world and other people's minds. The idea then "infects" not just our thinking, but everyone else who has likewise installed it into their minds. These confining ideas are unthinkingly passed down through the generations. One of wetiko's main vectors of propagation is conceptual; through the realm of ideas.

Jung was of the opinion that our "especial need" today was to free ourselves from outworn ideas that no longer serve us. Certain ideas (maybe some that we hold to be "self"-evident) have reached their expiration date, holding us back instead of propelling us forward in our evolutionary process. Ideas about who we are (relative to each other), the nature of our world, our place in it, and our creative power (or lack thereof) are being brought into question by the idea of a mind-virus. Jung felt that collectively held delusional ideas were more dangerous than all of the physical dangers we face. To quote psychologist James Hillman, "I think we're sick from ideas."[3]

Humanity has a long history of falling into mass collective delusions. Just because an idea is held by a majority of humanity does not make it true, for people could be reinforcing a mutually agreed upon, shared hallucination. As a matter of fact, due to humanity's unconsciousness combined with its suggestibility, a widespread dogmatic belief is more likely to be wrong or riddled with unseen errors. Strongly held ideas and opinions have killed many more people than the epidemics of bubonic plague or smallpox combined.

It behooves us to not become entrenched in an immovable viewpoint (which limits our freedom to creatively respond to ever-changing circumstances). Rather, we should fluidly contemplate our situation from as many perspectives as we can imagine. If we become fixed in our viewpoint, we suffer from, in psychologist Erich Neumann's words, an "occlusion to revelation,"[4] which is a form of psychic blindness that we ourselves are participating in creating. In other words, if we become dogmatically entrenched in our perspective, we close ourselves off to whatever the world might be disclosing to us.

New, creative living ideas, on the other hand, are psychoactivating (activating the psyche), potentially opening up new streams of cognition in the human psyche. A novel symbolic idea like wetiko can be likened to a symbol arising in a dream, in that, like a symbol, it is a transformer and liberator of psychic energy. New symbolic ideas can be therapeutic and liberating, as if we have lifted a rock that is lying on top of a germinating seed, allowing the shoot to begin its natural growth. In this example, humanity is the germinating seed and our limited and limiting ideas are the rock that is blocking our organic intellectual, emotional, psychological, moral, and spiritual unfoldment. New ideas are meant to be thought about, contemplated, and entertained. The merit of an idea is a function of how it affects us. Does it generate other ideas, make us think, inspire us to reflect upon things in a new way, spark our creativity, and/or awaken something within us? Ideas are related to knowing and consciousness. This is expressed in our day-to-day language. When someone doesn't know what they are doing, we typically say, "They have *no idea* what they are doing."

Ideas can wake us up to what is truly possible or they can blind us, depending on their nature. Wetiko is an ideological virus that can potentially expand our consciousness when taken onboard. The wetiko idea is a form of revelation that can potentially stimulate our lucidity, for it both expands our consciousness while being an expression of an expanded consciousness.

Some thinkers, such as Philip K. Dick (who we shall hear more from later), conceive of ideas as being entities who are alive. Such ideas are not "made" by us any more than dreams are. From Dick's point of view, we don't invent ideas, rather, ideas find us. When the time has come for an idea to come into the world, the idea—which according to Dick's conception, has a life of its own—enlists a receptive mind to be its purveyor. These living ideas can potentially seize people and make use of them to materialize themselves into the stream of human history. Oftentimes a new idea begins to emerge by informing and giving shape to an unconscious behavior in a group or people, and only much later is it recognized and becomes a conscious conception.

Ideas don't belong to their so-called inventor, nor are they the property of that inventor. Ideas spring from something greater than the individual human being. In a very real sense, we don't make our ideas, our ideas make us. And yet if we are afflicted with wetiko, we can think we have a monopoly on our ideas, believing that we own them. We may accuse others of stealing them when, in fact, they might be tuning into the same higher dimensional repository of ideas that we are.

In light of our current world crisis, a creative breakthrough, a new way of looking at things—a saving idea—illuminating fundamentally new insights into the nature of our universe and our place in it, is imperative—an absolute necessity for our survival. Wetiko and all that it stands for is precisely such a new symbolic idea. Wetiko is more than just an idea, however, for it has a living reality all its own that can transform how our experience of the world manifests.

Our ideas about wetiko are not separate from wetiko, in the sense that our ideas either feed the pathological aspect of the disease or help to liberate it (and us as well). An idea like wetiko, due to its empowering and liberating nature, provides us with a different angle and leverage by which to get a handle on evil. Thus, by its very nature, it is subversive, disruptive, and dangerous from the point of view of the status quo of mainstream reality, which is invested in keeping us in the dark.

The danger for a living idea, however, is that if institutionalized, it can be systematically deadened—killed even—by professional teachers of the new idea. And yet if the newly emerging idea is properly tended and cultivated in the right atmosphere, it can grow and multiply—going viral—in a way that can really affect change. As spiritual teacher G. I. Gurdjieff pointed out, humanity is decisively influenced only by ideas that can be shared among—and speak to—its members.

It is extremely rare that someone is willing to abandon their ideas and viewpoint of the world. Once consciousness has claimed a certain resting point, it can barely be moved. Convictions are created and people so easily get stuck in their ideas that anything different is seen as crazy or evil. It oftentimes requires a severe crisis, catastrophe, or an interminable neurosis to dislocate people from their entrenched perspectives on things.

When people become fixed in a viewpoint and hold onto their idea of the way the world works, it is literally dangerous to reflect back to them another way of looking at things. New ideas are usually met with strong resistance and oftentimes violence, as new ideas typically upset the equilibrium of the existing world order, challenging people to their core. It should get our attention that our species presently meets all of the requirements for shaking up our fixed ideas: We are in the middle of converging world crises, we are creating a worldwide catastrophe, as well as being severely neurotic. Because of the extremity of our situation, there is a real possibility in our time that many of humanity's longstanding fixed ideas that no longer serve us are going to be outgrown. New ideas and ways of seeing that are more reflective and in alignment with who we are will emerge to take their place.

The one thing the greatest tyrants in all of history were and are afraid of is a new idea. This is just as true today in our increasingly interconnected digital age, as is evidenced by increasing attempts by the powers that be to censor liberating ideas that are not in line with the mainstream, agreed upon narrative and its underlying agenda. As I conclude in *Dispelling Wetiko,* nothing is more powerful than a magical idea whose time has come. Wetiko is just such an idea. It's as if it had been secreted by the universe into the world—and into our minds—at this time in our history as the very medicine humanity needs to heal what ails our species.

A Higher Dimensional, Nonphysical Phenomenon

Some people, typically cardholders in the agreed upon consensus reality, consider my work on wetiko so "out there" that they are of the opinion that it shouldn't be taken seriously. (I think they see wetiko as some sort of new age delusional gobbledygook.) Viruses of the mind, psycho-spiritual diseases of the soul—to people who subscribe to mainstream culture, what I am writing about sounds paranoid and crazy, as if I am a weird conspiracy theorist. I have to confess—I find this funny (as well as sad). From my point of view, their reaction is an indication that they are afflicted with the very blindness-inducing mind-virus at which I am pointing. Once again, this typical reaction needs to be factored into the equation of how we deal with this perspective-distorting disease of the mind.

The one thing that everyone—on any side of the aisle—can no doubt agree on, however, is that a genuine form of madness is being acted out in our world. And the apparently crazy and far-out thing (at least in some people's eyes) that I am proposing is that the source, as well as the solution, of the interminable madness that is playing out in our world is to be found nowhere other than within the psyche.* Upon close inspection, this is a no-brainer, it could not be more obvious—how could it be otherwise? Our culture is being forced to acknowledge the force and power of the psychic undercurrents that inform all manner of global events.

Because of the human psyche's ability to inform and give shape to world events, Jung calls it "the World Power that vastly exceeds all other powers on earth."[5] The greatest danger to humanity comes from our own psyche, which unfortunately is the part of the empirical world we know the least about. As we search for myriad external causes and solutions to the multiple crises we ourselves are collectively bringing about, the psyche is overlooked or neglected entirely as a source or causal agent of our planetary crisis. These crises issue forth from the one place we, as a species, are most disinclined to look—within ourselves.

The nightmare that is unfolding in the world today is the emergence of the chaotic world of the unconscious that lies hidden under the ordered and seemingly coherent world of consciousness. Jung felt that "the great problem of our time" is that, to put it simply, we don't understand what is actually happening in our world, which is that we are confronted with the darkness of our soul, with the darker forces of the unconscious, with evil. In writing about wetiko—and its psychic origins—I am simply trying to shed light on our little understood darker half that is, more than ever, insisting on being recognized. Evil has become a visible and undeniable Great Power striding across the world stage. If it goes unrecognized, we increasingly

---

*Following in Jung's footsteps, I am using the word *psyche* in an all-inclusive sense, connoting the totality of all psychic processes, both conscious and unconscious. Not reducible to biochemical processes in the brain, it is a mysterious "substanceless substance" that exists between spirit and matter. Being nonlocal, the psyche is not only contained within our skull, but we are surrounded by, and contained within the psyche. In Jung's words, "the world is psyche." This makes sense when we begin to see the dreamlike nature of the universe.

deliver ourselves into its hands, just as a typhus epidemic flourishes best when its source is undiscovered.

As compared to the Christian revelation where a light shone from the heavens above, in our time a divine revelation is emerging from below. The powers of the underworld have been unleashed. The powers of darkness are coming up, and we need to come to terms with what they are revealing—or suffer the consequences. Contrary to solely being a sign of increasing moral degeneracy or decay, the revelation of darkness is a necessary and critically important part of the next stage of humanity's collective psycho-spiritual evolution.

Reason, as is evidenced all around us, has little traction in times like these. The powers of the underworld hide themselves behind our reason and highly sophisticated intellect. Our rationalism has disoriented us to the point of putting us at the mercy of the psychic underworld.

It is an archetypal idea that a divine spirit was imprisoned in matter, and it was humanity's divinely sanctioned role to somehow free this spirit. The Savior doesn't come down from the celestial heavens, but rather, it arises from below, from the depths, from the unconscious. The Savior doesn't come solely from the light, but through the darkness as well. Great discoveries invariably come from the depths, just as trees never grow from the sky downward, but from the Earth upward. No tree, it is said, can grow to heaven unless its roots reach down to hell.

With wetiko we are dealing with a higher dimensional, non-physical phenomenon that informs and gives shape to our world. This situation reminds me of what the founding fathers of quantum physics encountered when they discovered the quantum realm. They described the situation as if they had come across an unfamiliar animal, one that had never been seen before, one that they had confined for inspection within an animal house. They likened their situation to walking around this house and peering in the different windows, trying to combine their fragmentary views so as to assemble a more complete view of what in fact they were dealing with.

The situation with wetiko is similar. It is as if a higher dimensional object is casting a shadow into the third dimension of space and time and the transdimensional hologram of our minds. By putting together these shadow reflections we can begin to conceive of and construct the "out of this world" object that is their source. There is no one definitive model that fully delineates the elusive workings of wetiko disease, but when all of these unique articulations are seen together, a deeper picture begins to come into focus, one that can help us to see it.

Circumambulating Wetiko

In *Dispelling Wetiko* I tried to describe the idea of wetiko—as well as the way it operates—from as many perspectives as I could imagine. I've learned that this is a seemingly never-ending quest. As soon as *Dispelling Wetiko* was published, I continued writing about the elusive workings of this mind-virus, involving new formulations as to how it operates that I hadn't yet imagined.

In my writings on wetiko, I am *circumambulating* (the alchemical stage known as *circumambulatio*) an unknown something. In this it is as if I am going down an ever-descending spiral as the hard to see center becomes more visible. The ritual of circumambulation is a magical rite in which, by intensely concentrating our attention upon the center, we increase the power of the center, adding, in Jung's words, *medicine power* to it. In circling with my words around the same subject, it is as if I am continually and repeatedly circling around myself. Evolution, after all, doesn't progress in a linear way, but rather is a circumambulation of the Self. Paradoxically, it is the process of circumambulating around this center that simultaneously creates it. Or perhaps we could put it the other way round and say that the seemingly unknowable center acts like a magnet that draws the contents and processes of the unconscious into its orbit so as to disclose and reveal itself.

Along the same nonlinear lines, Plotinus writes in the Enneads, "The soul's natural movement is not in a straight line. . . . On the contrary, it circles around something interior, around a center."[6] From this center emerges the soul, which is why the soul will naturally move around and trend toward this center. What we call progress is actually the circling of a central point in order to get gradually closer to it. This center is what Jung calls the Self, the wholeness of the personality. Plotinus continues, "For divinity consists in being attached to the center. . . . Anyone who withdraws from it [the center] is a man who has remained un-unified, or who is a brute."[7]

Our circumambulation of wetiko can be likened to the additional alchemical stages of *iteratio, circulatio,* and *rotatio,* which are all expressions that no position can remain permanently fixed, that no end point is finally, forever and ever, achieved. This is to say that in our attempts to shed light on wetiko we never get to a definitive end of our inquiry.

Writing about wetiko can be likened to a work in progress without end; we are in some mysterious way deriving wetiko as we go. In our wetiko investigations we are, as if exploring a foreign land, cast in the role of a mapmaker and cartographer. This involves connecting dots and recognizing deeper patterns that are informing and giving shape to events in our world. We, as psycho-spiritual diagnosticians, orient ourselves by outlining the ever-morphing contours of this new world. We find ourselves at the cutting edge of a novel universe that had previously both escaped the reach of our imagination while working through it at the same time.

In addition, an intrinsic challenge to our investigation of the wetiko virus is that it is incarnating in and through the very psyche that itself is the means of our inquiry. In our encounter with wetiko, we find ourselves in a situation where we are confronted—practically face-to-face—with the unconscious, both in its personal and archetypal aspects.

A Shape-Shifting Bug

Wetiko is spirit-like in that it is impossible to pin down and say it is this or that, or here or there. As soon as we say wetiko is something, it proves to us that it is not that, but rather, something else. Speaking of the devil (wetiko), Denis de Rougemont, author of *The Devil's Share,* writes, "While remaining *one,* he can assume as many diverse aspects as there are individuals in the world. . . . being everyone, or anyone, he will appear to us as being No One in particular[8]. . . . His quality of not being positively this or that gives him an indefinite freedom of action, of incognito and alibis as far as the eye can see."[9] Being potentially anyone, while at the same time being no one in particular, makes this seeming entity very hard to get into focus and actually see.

The alchemical spirit Mercurius—the god of revelation (among many other things)—is the alchemical equivalent to the spirit of wetiko. Mercurius and wetiko both consist of the most extreme opposites, containing superposed within their very ambivalent nature the highest good and the darkest evil. As Jung points out, Mercurius is akin to the godhead but is found in the sewers. The figure of Mercurius is conceived of as being the workings of the higher powers in the lower, which is pointing at the idea that there are heavenly spiritual powers at work in and through the seeming powers of darkness.

Like Mercurius, wetiko takes on endless forms, none of which by themselves can ever completely characterize its nature. Interestingly, this is also the same quality that the alchemists attributed to the *lapis philosophorum,* the philosopher's stone. All of this is important data to take into account, with the hope that our difficulties don't make us throw up our hands in despair and prematurely abort our inquiry—or worse yet, go out of our minds. Both reactions, it should be noted, are sponsored by wetiko.

Because of the utterly elusive nature of the shape-shifting wetiko virus, it behooves us to step into our creative imagination in dealing with this deadly bug. This makes sense, for if wetiko continues to remain in the dark, it kills the creative imagination. This is to say that in addition to potentially paralyzing and/or disabling our creative imagination, wetiko also places a demand on us to *mobilize* our creative imagination. The awakened imagination is our greatest power over wetiko, which is why it is the very faculty that wetiko seeks to destroy.

This book is meant to ignite people's creative imagination so as to inspire them to give creative expression to their experience of wetiko, as well as anything and everything else. When seen together, all of our creative expressions of wetiko become like a net that, as if fishing in the depths of the ocean, helps us to catch the big one.

Like a multiheaded hydra, wetiko is multichanneled and it thus greatly serves our psycho-spiritual evolution to become aware of all the various ways in which it works—and thereby warps—our world. As we assimilate our own personal realization of wetiko, however, we of necessity make our expression of it uniquely our own, thereby enlarging and creatively altering both the local and nonlocal corpus of studies on the disease. Our individual understanding enriches and gives life to the ongoing collective investigation of this malady.

If, in our wetiko studies, we assume a fixed viewpoint regarding the nature of wetiko, we have become caught by ideological dogma—hooked by an idea—that limits our ability to creatively respond to wetiko's mercurial and ever-changing nature. In essence, we have then become a wetiko fundamentalist—an activity, it should be noted, that is inspired by wetiko itself. We would then be creating a corpse out of something living.

I have encountered some people who have gotten turned onto the idea of wetiko, but then have presented the notion that they have discovered what the wetiko virus looks like, be it amoeba-like, a flying fish, or whatever. Though I appreciate their intention to find the culprit, to think in terms of wetiko looking a certain way, having a specific shape or structure, or being an identifiable object in space-time is fundamentally misguided and is missing the point entirely. When we see one aspect of wetiko, it is important to not fall under the illusion that we have caught the whole. There is no straightforward or spoon-fed description of this force; it doesn't look like a wolf or a hawk or a shark, nor even like shape-shifting dreamtime ones. It doesn't look like a classic poltergeist or an enlarged or miniscule coronavirus. It has infinite shapes and expressions, hypershapes and metashapes, as many as we can imagine and then some.

As I point out again and again, the nature of wetiko is what Buddhism calls "emptiness." In other words, wetiko doesn't have a particular form. However, its nature is such that it can take on and appear in an endless variety of forms, both in the outside world and within our own minds at one and the same (or different) times. If we think that one of wetiko's ephemeral manifestations is its essence, we have then fallen under its spell. We then become rigid in our thinking and will be further away from understanding wetiko and thus more susceptible to its deceptions than before we thought of wetiko in this limited, static, and reductionist way. We have then conflated the transitory image for the thing projecting the image (the thing itself). This creates a state of delusion, which is both the cause and effect of wetiko.

One of the reasons wetiko is so hard to pin down is that it has multiple channels of operation: both covert and overt, inner and outer, and everywhere in between. Wetiko simultaneously operates intrapersonally (within our own mind), interpersonally (through our relationships), and transpersonally (through collective world events). Each of these—our individual, relational, and collective processes—are internested iterations of a deeper fractal. This is to say that these different dimensions of our experience are actually indivisibly interconnected and interreflective of each other. All of these multidimensional processes are informed by wetiko in different yet similar ways.

Other Voices

After *Dispelling Wetiko* came out in 2013, an increasing number of people became interested in the usefulness of amplifying the wetiko concept. They too recognized that wetiko is not a First Nations relic being rehabilitated as a slick trope. Instead wetiko is a summoning of indigenous wisdom to help us through our crises. Leaping from Native American vernacular into our own, in wetiko's crossing of language it continues to transform itself and prove its transcultural authenticity.

Some of my fellow Westerners did exactly what I was hoping—expressing their own creative articulation of this invisible psycho-spiritual bug. Here's what Alnoor Ladha and Martin Kirk, both activists and authors, wrote in an article called "Seeing Wetiko: On Capitalism, Mind Viruses, and Antidotes for a World in Transition":

> What if we told you that humanity is being driven to the brink of extinction by an illness? That all the poverty, the climate devastation, the perpetual war, and consumption fetishism we see all around us have roots in a mass psychological infection? What if we went on to say that this infection is not just highly communicable but also self-replicating, according to the laws of cultural evolution, and that it remains so clandestine in our psyches that most hosts will, as a condition of their infected state, vehemently deny that they are infected? What if we then told you that this "mind virus" can be described as a form of cannibalism. Yes, cannibalism. Not necessarily in the literal flesh-eating sense but rather the idea of consuming others—human and nonhuman—as a means of securing personal wealth and supremacy. . . . *Wetiko* short-circuits the individual's ability to see itself as an enmeshed and inter-dependent part of a balanced environment and raises the self-serving ego to supremacy. It is this false separation of self

from nature that makes this cannibalism, rather than simple murder. It allows—indeed commands—the infected entity to consume far more than it needs in a blind, murderous daze of self-aggrandizement.[10]

I couldn't have said it better myself. Wetiko is also known as cannibal sickness; symbolically speaking, cannibalism has to do with feasting on another's soul, or in our case, the soul of humanity. The point of attack for the struggle against the evil of wetiko is the human soul.

Again, every spiritual wisdom tradition expresses wetiko in their own creative way. This is the very act that promotes them to the ranks of being worthy of being called a wisdom tradition. For example, in the Islamic tradition, wetiko is called Iblis, who is the Islamic equivalent to the figure of Satan. Here is a creative articulation of Iblis/wetiko by Kirsten Roya Azal, an author and artist:

We can identify very clearly by way of the Arabic language the nature of Iblis and of the Wetiko. Iblis is the force that throws us into cowardness, fear of false authority, disbelief in good, intellectual poverty, and consequently into imaginary and real hells on Earth. The force of Iblis is the source of our individual and collective chronic social sickness which separates us from God, who is the pure light of creation, of hope and the divine good. The force of Iblis wants nothing else but to use our intellect, our goodness and intelligence for its own sinister purposes. Like every crafty criminally minded perpetrator and propagandist the Iblis employs our assorted weaknesses to make us his unwitting minions.[11]

I deeply appreciate Azal's description of Iblis. She is rendering into language—in her own words—an experience that we all are fated to come to terms with. She is using her voice to call out the demon, so to speak, so as to help the rest of us see it. She is embodying what I am talking about: that we all need to find our unique voice and articulate our experience of wetiko in our own creative way.

As I was finishing this book, a practitioner of the Sikh faith, inspired by my work on wetiko, let me know that the Sikh holy book, the Siri Guru Granth Sahib, refers to wetiko as ego or the egoic mind. To quote from the Sikh holy book, "Ego is a chronic disease, but it contains its own cure as well."[12] As we shall explore, this is one of the chief features of wetiko disease—it contains within itself its own medicine. If this latent cure hidden within the disease isn't recognized and brought forth, however, the disease will kill us.

2

The Kabbalah's
Remarkable Idea

During the question-and-answer period for the book release of my book *Dispelling Wetiko,* someone asked what was I going to write about next. Without having to blink, I responded "Kabbalah," which is considered to be one of the most profound spiritual and intellectual movements in all of human history. Soon after the publication of my book I had discovered, much to my surprise, that the Kabbalah had a similarly radical view on many of the things I had written about, particularly the nature and role of evil in the cosmic drama.

In *Dispelling Wetiko,* I contemplate how the wisdom traditions of alchemy, Gnosticism, shamanism, Buddhism, mystical Christianity, and the depth psychology of Jung were pointing at and could help us to deepen our understanding of wetiko. However, I hadn't written about the Kabbalah because I hadn't realized that it was pointing at wetiko in an especially unique and creative manner.* In my continued work on the subject I point out, in as many ways as I can imagine, that encoded in the deepest evil of wetiko is actually a blessing in a very convincing disguise to the contrary.

If we recognize what wetiko is revealing to us about ourselves, it

---

*It was particularly Sanford L. Drob's brilliant writings on the Kabbalah that opened my eyes to how the Kabbalah was, through its own divinely inspired creative imagination, describing wetiko in its own unique way.

can help us to wake up. In essence, the Lurianic Kabbalah of Isaac Luria (1534–1572) says the same thing: Evil, which by definition is diametrically opposed to good, is, paradoxically, at the same time its very source.

Kelipot

Upon studying the Lurianic Kabbalah (henceforth referred to simply as Kabbalah), a place of deep recognition stirred within me. In reading its creation myth, it was as if images were being activated within my mind that matched a deep inner experience I'd been having for years. According to the Kabbalah, when it first arose within the divine will to create a universe, there was a contraction (known as the *tzimtzum*). This was a localized withdrawal and concealment of God so as to prepare a space and "make room" for a finite creation—with all of its distinctiveness, multiplicity, and limitation—to be brought about.

At the very moment that God then conceived of the world and poured his* infinite light into the "vessels" that he had prepared for this very event, the vessels were instantaneously filled and shattered by this influx of divine light. This catastrophic event, called the Breaking of the Vessels, shattered the vessels into shards. These shards fell through primordial space, the metaphysical void, while at the same time severing the previously united (and unconscious) opposites that constitute the underlying unified structure of the universe. Each shard entrapped a portion of divine light, seemingly separating these fragments of primordial light from their source.

These shards, known as the *kelipot,*† were likened to husks or

---

*For consistency's sake, I have chosen to use the masculine gender throughout this book when referring to God because this is the gender used to reference God in the Kabbalah, as well as by Jung.

†*kelipot* = k'lee-pote (the plural is *kelipot;* the singular is *kelipah,* pronounced k'lee-pah)

shells that imprisoned within themselves the divine light of God, which, because of their estrangement from their source, turned malevolent, becoming the source of evil and personal suffering. The negation and mirror image of divine holiness and purity, the kelipot were like envelopes that concealed holiness just as a peel hides the fruit within.

The kelipot altered the appearance of the divine light, but didn't, however, change the essence of the light itself. The kelipot are themselves infertile and lifeless, with no independent existence. They are vacuous apparitions sustained in their seeming vitality and existence only by the very divine light that they have captured. The artist, poet, and visionary William Blake could have been describing the kelipot when he wrote, "This is a false Body, an incrustation over my Immortal."[1] According to the Kabbalah, evil has no life of its own. The very source of evil is both intrinsically connected to, generated out of, and yet parasitic in relation to the divine light. From the perspective of the Kabbalah, though parasitically dependent upon the light of God, evil seeks to destroy holiness, which is to ultimately destroy everything, including itself.

In appearing to do the impossible—sever the primary reality from its source of being—the kelipot had assumed an illusory reality, becoming a lethal mirage that, though ultimately not truly existing, could potentially destroy our species. The kelipot were also thought to imprison and bind aspects of human souls as well, feeding parasitically on the divine light within them. This is to say that the Kabbalah's view of cosmic events was also a description of the dynamics taking place within humanity's soul. The entrapped divine sparks of light symbolize each individual's essential but forgotten reality. Significantly, just like the spirit of wetiko, the kelipot contained within themselves the source and very energy for their own undoing, and ultimately, the potential for their own redemption.

Like autonomous complexes within the psyche, the kelipot appeared to obtain a measure of independent existence, as if they had become separated from, and other than, the light of God itself (something that is inherently impossible). For the kabbalists, evil emerges out of separating things that should (and necessarily do) remain united, a "splitting" of a deeper unity. It was as if the universe itself had been subject to a cosmic "dissociative reaction," in which its underlying unity had been fragmented into a multiplicity of selves. Both the kelipot and affect-laden complexes become *relatively* inaccessible to consciousness, having become shrouded in the darkness of the unconscious. Becoming "exiled" from their source, these split-off complexes (due to their disconnection from wholeness) become the source of much suffering in the personal realm. In the same way, the kelipot become the source of evil (due to their disconnection from the wholeness of the universe) on a cosmic scale.

"Evil," Russian philosopher Nicolas Berdyaev writes, is "always a product of consciousness severed from the primary sources of being."[2] Just as the divine light estranged from its source becomes evil, when our psychic energy becomes encapsulated through repression and severed from the wholeness of the psyche from which it arose, we develop all sorts of negative, neurotic, and self-destructive symptoms. Our neurotic complexes, however, are powered by the radiant wholeness of our psyche from which we've become dissociated. This demonstrates that this wholeness is present and available even when we are feeling most estranged from it. Thus instead of feeding our symptoms, the energy of our wholeness can—potentially—be rechanneled to strengthen and support our healthy parts.

Breaking of the Vessels

It was as if in the process of Creation, God (or in psychological terms, "the Self") had become alienated from itself, as if "Being" was in exile from itself. And yet, according to the Kabbalah, this cosmic cataclysm was no accident, but was inherent in the overall scheme of things. It was built into the very design of the universe, as if God had to become estranged from himself in order to become more fully himself. Where would God's wholeness and freedom be if he could not be other than himself? In becoming concealed and eclipsed from himself, the infinite God creates the illusion of finitude, limitation, and separation as a means of bringing forth and experiencing his fullness even more deeply and profoundly than ever before.

As if clothing himself in a garment that is our world, God creates a very convincing illusion that is akin to a dream. According to the Kabbalah, our world is itself like a dream in the infinite mind of God. Dreams themselves are tailor-made so as to help us understand kabbalistic thought in general. As long as we are under the spell of the dream that we are having, all of the people and objects within it seem separate and objectively existing. It is only upon awakening to the dreamlike nature of our situation that we recognize that who we thought we were is nothing other than a model of ourselves being dreamed by something deeper. The dream in which we find ourselves is a display of, and not separate from, who we have discovered ourselves to be. Similarly, it is only when God is differentiated into, and includes within himself, a seemingly boundless expanse of apparently finite entities, that God completes himself as the Infinite All and his full infinity is achieved. This is to say that the deepest unity isn't opposed to multiplicity, but rather, requires and embraces it.

In the same way that God has to become estranged from himself in order to become more fully who he is, according to the Kabbalah it was only after the vessels break that humanity's potential to become fully itself is set in motion. It's as if some form of destruction, deconstruction, or disintegration is a prerequisite for individuation and is necessary for the birth of the Self. Seen symbolically, the Breaking of the Vessels is an expression of the inevitable brokenness that everyone experiences at one point or another within the course of a lifetime. Shattered, our psyches—both individually and collectively—are like pieces of a broken mirror, each of which holds fragments of what was once a complete reflection. It is when things seem most broken—when we hit bottom—that the deeper process of healing, restoration, and transformation can begin.

This same notion is also expressed in the figure of the wounded healer, who accesses the ability to heal by going through and adding consciousness to the process of being wounded. It is an archetypal idea that salvation will come to us through our wounds. This idea is related to how the coming of the Messiah—symbolically speaking, the birth of the Self that brings salvation—always comes through the most despised and rejected parts of ourselves. Indeed, Psalms 22:6 (KJV) reads as follows: "But I [the Messiah] am a worm and no man; a reproach of men, and despised of the people." It is where we are weakest that intercession from a power greater than ourselves takes place. To quote the poet and philosopher Friedrich Holderlin, "Where danger is, there arises salvation also."

In mythology the would-be hero typically suffers a wound of some sort that takes away their innocence (one of the meanings of the Latin word *innocens* means "not yet wounded"). Seen psychologically, the archetype of the wounded healer (who Christ epitomizes) expresses the idea that the ego, if it's to undergo transformation, must be wounded or broken in some way in order to open up to its connection to the healing energies of the unconscious. The encounter with the Self—the greater personality—is always a wounding experience for our ego, an experience in which our naive innocence is taken away.

This idea of being wounded, broken, of experiencing failure and feeling psychologically and spiritually impotent, and going through a symbolic "death" experience is also related to the archetypal dark night of the soul. The dark night is an inner psycho-spiritual experience that involves feeling disconnected from the light and the source of life and descending into the darkness. This is similar to the archetypal descent of the shaman into the underworld, which is the very process through which the light is rediscovered in a deeper way. In alchemy this stage is correlated with the inner state of *melancholia,* which is a healthy response to encountering our own darkness. It definitely should not be medicated with an antimelancholia pill (i.e., an antidepressant), which would prevent one from fully going through this natural process and receiving its gifts.

This is similar to the personal process of spiritual emergence, which almost always looks like a nervous "breakdown"(i.e., a so-called psychotic break). The person who is spiritually awakening is said to be "falling to pieces" as their psyche "melts down" and disintegrates. This potentially leads toward a higher form of integration more in alignment with their deeper, intrinsic wholeness. This process of falling apart is an iteration of the same fractal, a recapitulation on the microcosmic scale of an individual psyche that the Kabbalah describes as initiating the process of divine evolution on a cosmic scale.

The shattering of the vessels can also symbolize moments when life so shakes us up that we snap out of our fixed patterns of thought, rigid beliefs, and assumed ideas about both the world and ourselves. This temporarily suspends the filters and conditioning through which we experience ourselves, such that a pure, unconditioned divine spark of creativity can come through us.

Light Hidden in Darkness

It makes all the difference in the world whether we conceive of the source of evil as being in oneself, other people, the devil, or in the supreme divine being. Where we think the source of evil is to be found, for example, determines our sense of who we are, our place in the universe, and our relationship to both the darkness in the world as well as its shadow within ourselves. Our perspective on evil determines whether we become a conduit for good or an unwitting instrument of evil.

One of the striking features in the Kabbalah's account of the origin of evil is that, unlike the biblical myth, whose notion of the Fall of humanity is attributed to a human act as described in the Garden of Eden story, the Kabbalah sees the origin of evil as an inescapable feature of the very process of cosmogenesis itself. Instead of seeing evil as existing outside of God, the kabbalists saw evil as an essential component of the Deity, woven into the very fabric of Creation. From the point of view of the Kabbalah, evil issues forth from God himself, originating in the very heart of divinity. In the earliest kabbalistic writings it says, "The Holy One praised be He has a trait which is called Evil."[3]

From the Kabbalah's point of view, to deny evil its rightful place in the cosmos is to do away with the good as well. To quote Sanford L. Drob, author of *Symbols of the Kabbalah: Philosophical and Psychological Perspectives,* "Evil is to creation, and the individual finite existence that is creation's very essence, as the outside of a container is to the space it contains."[4] To one-sidedly strive after good and unilaterally reject and exclude evil would be like trying to grasp the container without taking hold of the boundary that defines it. R. D. Laing writes, "It has always been recognized that if you split Being down the middle, if you insist on grabbing *this* without *that,* if you cling to the good without the bad, denying the one for the other, what happens is that the dissociated evil impulse, now evil in a double sense, returns to permeate and possess the good and turn it into itself."[5]

This "crisis in Creation" was built into all things, both human and divine; into the molecular and subatomic structure of the cosmos itself. The dialectical tensions of the cosmos are mirrored in the psyche of each individual. This primordial rupture, which was a form of trauma on a cosmic scale, became the informing force behind human history itself, conditioning the experience of each individual as well as our species as a whole. It is as if our entire species is suffering from a collective form of cosmically induced post-traumatic stress disorder (PTSD). Seen as a whole person, it is as if the wholeness of the universe had split into innumerable cosmic multiple subpersonalities who are dissociated from and seemingly separate from each other. These subpersonalities are desperately in need of recognizing their connection so as to come together and reintegrate.

When Freud was first introduced to the Kabbalah, he was so beside himself with excitement that he exclaimed "This is gold." When Jung, who to my mind has the deepest insight into the nature of evil of anyone I have yet encountered, had his eyes opened to the profundity of the Kabbalah, he realized that his entire psychology had been anticipated by certain of their adepts. In an interview on his eightieth birthday in 1955, Jung declared, "The Hasidic Rabbi Baer from Mesiritz anticipated my entire psychology in the eighteenth century."[6]

I can relate to how Jung must have felt. The more I studied the Kabbalah's cosmology, the more my mind was being blown, feeling as if I had found an alternative—and complementary—rendering of what I had written about in *Dispelling Wetiko*. The Kabbalah provides an ingenious model of how we have become entranced by the spellbinding powers of our own mind. It was as if the kabbalists had been tracking wetiko for centuries. It appeared that they had created their own mythology and symbol system that "captured" it, and in so doing, had presciently realized how to "break the curse of evil." They encoded this liberating wisdom into their sacred texts, offering uniquely ingenious keys for dealing with wetiko, as their spiritual inheritance to future generations.

The Kabbalah had articulated what Jung refers to as "the remarkable idea": that it is humanity's destiny to become God's instrument to restore the broken vessels of the kelipot that resulted from the creation of our world. The Kabbalah was pointing out humanity's cosmic responsibility to be God's helper in repairing the damage wrought by Creation. Jung was appreciating the kabbalists' (r)evolutionary insight that humanity was playing the crucial role of copartnering with God so as to complete the creative act of his incarnation. The radical and taboo thought was, "for the first time," emerging into a monotheistic worldview. To put it into religious language, humanity didn't just depend upon God, but God, as if to complete the circle, depended upon humanity as well. From the Kabbalah's point of view, God did not just create humanity, but in a joint venture, humanity is reciprocally helping to create God as well. Talk about a "cosmic responsibility"!

According to the Kabbalah, divine sparks, psychic/spiritual treasures—threaded throughout the very fabric of both the inner and outer domains—were encoded within us and hidden throughout the physical universe. It is an archetypal notion that the darkness holds the light in thrall, as if it has the light under a magical "spell." This is quite remarkable, considering that, as mentioned earlier, the darkness parasitically requires the energy of the light in order to maintain its seeming existence and appear real. Ultimately speaking, the light has used its own creative energy to constrain its infinite radiance, as if the light has cast a spell upon itself.

Seen as a reflection of a process happening within each of us, this expresses how something so incredibly powerful (i.e., ourselves as the radiant plenum—the boundless luminosity that is the very fabric of our being) can fall under the spell of a nonexistent phantom appearance. This phantom appearance arises from the immense creativity of our own mind such that it entrances the light within us into believing that this imaginary, illusory phantom of darkness is more powerful than the light that we are. These apparition-like "darker forces," the result of a timeless, acausal, nonlinear, and insidious feedback loop within our own mind, only have power over us to the extent that their illusory nature is not seen through. They can only take on a seeming reality by tricking us to enliven them by giving them our own unrecognized creative power.

The idea of sparks of divine light becoming trapped in the dark denseness of matter, and this state of affairs being linked with human salvation, is a quintessentially Gnostic idea. The Gnostic Gospel of Philip says, "I am scattered in all things, and from wherever thou wilt thou canst gather me, but in gathering me thou gatherest together thyself."[7] It was as if sparks of the Divine, of our very Self, were dispersed throughout the manifest world, waiting to be discovered, reunified, and liberated.

Tikkun

To the kabbalists, it was humanity's divinely appointed task to find, extract, and free this light that is hidden in the darkness of the material realm (called the Raising of the Sparks), thereby helping this light return to its divine source. So as to fulfill our part in the healing of the world, it is the mission of each one of us to raise the sparks hidden within those kelipot that reside within our soul or that come our way over the course of a lifetime.

According to the Kabbalah, humanity plays a key role in this repair and restoration of the world, called *tikkun ha-olam* (henceforth *tikkun* for short). Tikkun is a process by which humanity, the world, and God himself become more fully themselves. This is based on the idea that humanity plays a vitally important role in the completion and actualization of the universe, and if we can talk in such human terms, of God himself. The profound viewpoint of tikkun reveals that the purpose and significance of evil in God's plan is to provide a context for humanity's redemption and further evolution. This is to say that the vision provided by tikkun puts evil, humanity, and God himself in their proper places within the cosmos.

This cosmic process is mirrored in humanity through the process of individuation, of becoming an indivisible unity or "whole." This entails a gathering, recollecting, and remembering of all of the split-off, projected parts of the psyche. Etymologically, the root of the word *individuation* means "undivided," as if the process of individuation is the antidote to the *diabolical* (whose etymology means "that which separates and divides") disintegrating effects of evil. Individuation does not separate and shut us out from the world, but rather gathers the world to us, reconnecting us with it. According to Jung, the process of individuation is, paradoxically, the source of evil as well as its antidote.

The individuation process helps us uncover our essence and uniqueness. Everything that is alive secretly dreams of individuation—of becoming who one really is—for everything is continually growing toward its own wholeness. Just as each one of us strives toward the wholeness of our nature, can't we say the same of the universe itself? Can't we say that it too dreams of individuation, of gathering its nature to itself, and remembering all of its split-off parts? Are we all just instruments playing roles in a cosmic process of individuation—a universal awakening—that is mysteriously being revealed and catalyzed through our darker half?

It is an age-old archetypal idea that light is to be found hidden within the darkness, which suggests that evil is connected to the process of redemption and individuation. Most of us religiously avoid exploring whether God might not have invested in the forces of darkness some special and divinely sanctioned purpose that it would greatly behoove us to know. Evil plays a mysterious role in both creating—and in certain cases, delivering humanity from—suffering.

Light that wants to shine needs darkness. The little sliver of divine light never burns more brightly than when it has to fight against the overwhelming darkness. It is as if the darkness gives birth to the light; it kindles the light. It is only out of the deepest and darkest night that the new light (of consciousness) will be born.

According to the Kabbalah, the extraction of the light requires an acknowledgement of, and sojourn into, the realm of darkness. This psychologically speaking can be thought of as making a shamanic descent into the underworld of the unconscious and coming to terms with our base desires. This in Kabbalah is referred to as a "descent on behalf of the ascent." In alchemy the work starts with the descent into the darkness of the unconscious (the *nekyia,* the night sea journey, the journey to Hades). Going inward is going upward in consciousness, dimensionally speaking.

The hidden treasure that suffering humanity is forever seeking is to be found in the depths. A place of great danger, it is the place of primordial unconsciousness. And yet it is the place of healing and redemption, for it contains the precious jewel of our wholeness, where all the split-off parts of ourselves are united.

This descent always involves a coming to terms with the "shadow" of ourselves (which has both a personal as well as transpersonal/ archetypal component). Our totality must include a dark side if we are to be whole. For if there is no shadow there can be no light. By entering the dark realm of the unconscious, we are offered the possibility of refining ourselves as if in a crucible, as if the shadow world of the unconscious is a divine furnace of purification. It is no accident that in alchemy the philosopher's stone is to be found not in a heavenly place but "in *stercore*," in the dung.

It is only when we are compelled by sickness, extremity, or crisis to come to terms with our own nature that the opportunity arises to experience the somber power of the shadow as a messenger from the creative potential that lives within our own psyche. Just as evening gives birth to morning, the light chooses the shadow so as to reveal itself. The figure of the shadow bears the good news of the treasure hidden in the depths, what scholar Erich Neumann refers to as "the herb of healing which grows in the darkness."[8]

The Light and the Shadow Are Inseparable

Just like a seed is contained within the darkness of the Earth, the darkness of our universe carries within itself a germ of light. When one principle reaches the height of its power, the counter-principle is stirring within it like a seedling. The shadow contains within itself the seed of an *enantiodromia,* of a conversion into its opposite. If we fail to take into account the shadow aspect of ourselves, however, we are unwittingly feeding it, increasing its power over us. If we don't acknowledge and see our darkness, we deliver ourselves into its hands.

The kabbalistic idea of finding the light hidden in the darkness is also a basic psychoanalytic idea, having to do with making the unconscious conscious, as well as connecting split-off complexes to the wholeness of the Self. An important discovery of modern psychology is that bringing the light of consciousness to our unconscious, split-off complexes takes away their obsessional power. This is in accord with the spiritual reality of the struggle of the celestial powers against evil. The good can only successfully combat evil by the mere fact of its presence (instead of fighting against it, which only strengthens the evil it is fighting against). This is similar to how the mere presence of sunlight evicts darkness. This points to the importance of bringing evil into the light of day.

If we don't acknowledge and pay our dues to the darkness, like the return of the Freudian repressed, it will take its due on its own terms, with a vengeance. If our darkness is repressed, it will feed our resentment, waiting for an opportunity to take its revenge in the most socially impolite way possible.

In our darkness there is a light secretly hidden that is fated to return to its source, and mythologically speaking, this light actually wanted more than anything to descend into the depths of the darkness in order to free our imprisoned soul. It is a mythological, archetypal idea that light, by its very nature of being light, wants to illumine darkness. For if light doesn't shed itself, penetrate the darkness, and expose what is other than itself, then what is light's ultimate value?

It is no accident that we—each and every one of us—have chosen to incarnate during these dark times. It is as if we have been preparing over multiple lifetimes, maybe even from the beginning of time itself, to fulfill our cosmic mission of freeing the part of the cosmic soul (an aspect of ourselves) that is imprisoned. Who is this enchained one but the part of us that is "in the dark," which is to say the part of us that is unconscious.

When consciousness begins to expand, we typically experience great upheaval (in our lives and within our minds), followed by a broadening outward toward our true wholeness. In alchemy, the *prima materia* is considered the raw material, the primal chaos that includes within itself rejected elements of unrefined negativity and evil. The prima materia is the raw material out of which the philosopher's stone was made.[9]

To put this into contemporary terms, the chaos that characterizes today's world could be seen to be an expression of an expansion of consciousness that is first announcing itself through the darkness of our times. Symbolized by the element of lead (which, interestingly, symbolizes the negative patriarchy), the darkness of the prima materia is necessary and indeed indispensable for the making of the gold (the awakened consciousness) and the completion of the opus. Similar to how encoded within wetiko is the deepest evil or the healing medicine, hidden within the alchemical lead are either demonic forces or the Holy Spirit.

It is an alchemical idea that the microcosm and the macrocosm—what is happening within us and what is happening collectively in the outside world—are not separate, but are interrelated reflections of each other. The German Romantic poet and philosopher Novalis famously wrote, "The seat of the soul is where the inner world and the outer world meet. Where they overlap, it is in every point of the overlap."

Whenever evil appears in an individual person's process, some deeper good almost always comes out of the experience that would not have emerged without the initial manifestation of evil. Could the same thing be true on a collective scale? Might there be a parallel? Just as in a single individual the emergence of darkness calls forth a hidden light, does the manifestation of a more collective darkness call forth a helpful light in the psychic life of a people? Is the dark shadow befalling our planet the harbinger of a great light, a potential awakening that is taking place in the collective psyche of humanity today?

The entire process of tikkun proceeds out of what the Kabbalah refers to as the Other Side (called the Sitra Achra—a nether realm of evil inhabited by and composed of the kelipot). This is to say that, kabbalistically speaking, there is no liberated light except that which issues forth out of the evil realm. The Zohar, the key kabbalistic text, makes this very point when it makes the remarkable statement, "There is no light except that which issues from darkness . . . and no true good except it proceed from evil."[10] According to the Kabbalah, evil is the very condition of good's realization. Evil, at cross purposes to the good at its core, is at the same time, paradoxically, its very foundation. It is only by attending to the darkness within ourselves and making the darkness conscious, that we become secure in the attainment of the good and begin to wake up. Once we become conscious of the darkness in ourselves, the light is not far behind.

Freedom

From the kabbalistic point of view, evil brings into the world the possibility of choosing between sin and virtue. Evil is the very origin of the possibility of the highest good. Having the choice to take an evil path and choosing against it enables goodness to take on a much deeper meaning than it would have otherwise. On a subtle, energetic level, simply appreciating right in contrast to wrong lightens the evil that provided the contrast. Freedom of choice is a necessary postulate for responsibility, morality, and the creation of values. Evil becomes the condition for free choice, and hence the condition for the full realization of good.

The heart of compassion is a precious treasure that, though it is the essence of our true nature (of who we actually are), it is rarely given freely but typically has to be earned. The doorway to actualize this sacred treasure almost always involves a test in which we risk an encounter with evil (be it from within ourselves or outside in the world) and consciously and wholeheartedly choose the good. Since it ultimately can—at least in potential—produce a good that couldn't have been realized without its darker influence, evil can be seen to be an underground agent of God. This is why the mystical Rabbi Baal Shem Tov describes "evil" as "a throne for good."

As if the revelation of everything is through its opposite, an idea is only complete when it reveals its opposite to be inextricably linked to its very significance. In other words, darkness is only known through light, just as light is only known through darkness. According to the Kabbalah, the world and the soul of humanity are partly immersed in the "Other Side," which is to say that the evil impulse can't be banished but needs to be harnessed for the good. Evil can't be rejected, for it is an essential ingredient necessary for the revelation and illumination of the light. We can't simply extract the evil within us like we are pulling a tooth, lest something essential be removed along with it, something meant for life.

If we were able to get rid of all of the evil in the world, we would be taking the salt out of the bread of life, for there is nothing of substance without a shadow. Adding spice to life, the shadow side of existence enables dimensions of growth and development that would not be possible without it. The idea of totally eradicating evil is one of the most dangerous and evil ideas imaginable. The belief that we can build a perfect, utopian world—if we can just destroy those evil people who block our noble efforts—is what animates the Hitlers of the world.

According to the Kabbalah, God could not create true freedom for humanity without providing a choice for evil. This is to say that freedom and evil reciprocally co-arise as two aspects of the same deeper process. Cultural theorist De Rougemont writes in *The Devil's Share*, "We must realize now that the Devil could do nothing without our freedom. For it is through us only that he acts in the world, and it is by provoking the abuse of our freedom that he acts within us and binds us."[11]

It is through the Breaking of the Vessels, the seeming exiling of the divine light, and the production of evil that resulted, that made possible the process by which humanity can attain its autonomy and potential freedom. To quote Jungian analyst Ursula Wirtz, author of *Trauma and Beyond,* "For me, abysmal evil and darkness are part of our *conditio humana,* of the 'drama of human freedom.' It is the risk we take, and the price we pay, for freedom."[12] Freedom is related to consciousness. To the extent that there is consciousness, the possibility of freedom exists. It is only insofar as humanity has consciousness that we are able to save our light from darkness. Freedom cannot be had without limitation, just as consciousness cannot be had without unconsciousness. The Self is not only the light but also the darkness, the good as well as the evil.

Two Sides of the Same Coin

Only in an evil and tragic world can compassion and kindness be most fully developed, brought forth, and realized. The implication is that the evil one is, in the broader sense of the word, part of the holiness of God. This is not to justify, sanction, or condone evil, but rather to properly contextualize it. The darkness is part of our holy and whole nature. The chaos and negativity that resulted from the Breaking of the Vessels was, for the kabbalists, the inevitable result of and the necessary price to be paid for the infinite taking on finite form. It was divine unity giving itself over to distinction and individuality so as to discover freedom. From the kabbalistic point of view, evil is created by and in service to and for freedom. It is only through the realization of our intrinsic freedom that evil can be overcome. It should be added that our freedom extends only as far as our consciousness reaches.

The deeper our psychological acumen, the more we realize that the forces of light and dark, of good and evil, are intimately related and interpenetrate each other. At a certain point the dark and the light become indistinguishable from one another, a *coincidentia oppositorum* ("coincidence of opposites"). The opposites are related to, dependent upon, and only take on their meaning relative to and in contrast to each other.

The attempt to exalt one pole of a binary (e.g., good) and debase its opposite (evil) is a fruitless endeavor that is simply a waste of energy. If we try to latch onto and align with one pole of the opposites we will invariably become ensnared by the other. And yet it is important to call out—and name—evil when we see it. The idea of the interpenetration, interdependence, and the coming together of the opposites is at the root of every wisdom tradition on our planet (including, in the past century, within the field of quantum physics, via the idea of complementarity). This reunification is an idea that underlies, informs, and animates the Kabbalah's entire cosmology.

The principle of coincidentia oppositorum can be considered to be the cornerstone of Jung's entire psychology. In Jung's personal journal, *The Red Book,* whose reflections are the basis of his life's work, he refers to the coincidentia oppositorum as producing the "supreme meaning."[13] The part of us that is having the realization of, in Jung's words, the *mysterium coniunctionis* ("the mystery of the conjunction"—the cojoining of things typically conceived of as being opposites) is the Self, the intrinsic wholeness of our personality. The Self—who we are—is simultaneously the sponsor and result of this realization.

Through its choices, humanity can realize and actualize the values that are only abstractions and ideas in the mind of God. Humanity's actions can instantiate, embody, and make fully real the higher spiritual values of our universe, helping God to see and experience the totality of himself in the process. It is as if humanity is the vessel that God has created in order to complete and incarnate himself. It is the Kabbalah's perspective that the unity and perfection that is provided with humanity's help is of a higher order than the unity that existed before the Breaking of the Vessels and prior to Creation itself.

This is similar to how, in the alchemical operation of *solve et coagula* ("dissolve and synthesize"), an original unity is separated into its opposing parts and then reunited in a process that brings about a superior wholeness. From the Kabbalah's point of view, it is as if God creates the world in order to fully realize himself in it. In a case where the microcosm mirrors the macrocosm, this is similar to how the unconscious manifests itself in a reflective ego in order to complete and know itself as a conscious "Self."

There are times in the world's history—and the times we are living through might be one of them—when something destined to be in the service of a higher good first appears in evil form. It is only a broken and disordered state of affairs—such as we have in the world today—that provides the optimal environment within which humanity may best exercise the greatest spiritual, moral, aesthetic, and intellectual virtues that truly make us a reflection of God. The discordant, unassimilated, and antagonistic effects of both our personal complexes and the kelipot of the Kabbalah all serve to call forth our highest potentialities. This is similar to how a road test for a car involves it being put under the most difficult conditions to push it to its edge and elicit the limits of its performance capabilities. This world is truly a perfect realm for the "road-testing" of our souls. Humanity's highest virtues are called upon when confronted by evil.

The Self, being a coincidentia oppositorum, manifests in the conflict between the opposites. The way to the Self becomes catalyzed by conflict. Conflicting energies exist relative to, by virtue of, and at the expense of each other. Reciprocally co-arising, they belong together precisely insofar as they oppose each other; their antagonism is the very source of their essential unity and oneness. We deprive someone of their best resource if we take away their conflicts. We can truly help them if we assist them to become sufficiently aware of their inner conflicts and help them initiate a *conscious* conflict within themselves. Individuation becomes activated from and arises out of an intense awareness of conflict. We progress along the path of individuation to the extent that we are able to abide in the midst of the conflict but not become absorbed in it, to be in the conflict yet above it. This brings to mind the archetypal idea of being in the world but not of the world.

Stirring up conflict is what Jung calls a "Luciferian virtue" (Lucifer was the light bringer). Conflict gives rise to the fire of affect and emotions, which has two aspects: combustion and/or the creation of light. In other words, the conflict and friction that is the result of the Breaking of the Vessels can potentially create separation, hurt, and misunderstanding—producing more trauma. Or it can create light, the light of consciousness itself. From this metaperspective, the shattering of the vessels allows, potentially, for more light to be revealed and liberated.

Though the kabbalists envision the Breaking of the Vessels (and the kelipot entrapping the divine light and bringing evil into the world) as a cosmic event that happened back at the dawn of time— at the very moment of the creation of our universe—this process is also atemporal. As such it happens outside of time, which is to say that it is happening right now. It is an eternal process that is happening vertically (outside of linear time and space) and also horizontally (unfolding within and through the framework of time and space). The Breaking of the Vessels is a symbolic articulation of a process that is informing our human condition each and every moment.

Re-Turn

Like the prototypical Adam whose situation in the garden is a metaphor for the archetypal human dilemma, as well as for all subsequent human decisions, each one of us stands at a fork in the road—a place of great opportunity—between the paths of tikkun (and life) on the one hand, and feeding the kelipot and evil (and death) on the other. Deuteronomy 30:19 (KJV) reads " . . . I have set before you life and death, blessing and cursing: therefore choose life, that both thou and thy seed may live."

Adam's sin was catastrophic precisely because it was an act of free choice. For this reason it strengthened the kelipot and the power of the Other Side. Similarly, whenever any of us is *unconsciously* taken over by evil in the form of compulsive, addictive behaviors (as compared to "acting out" our compulsions as the way through which we can become conscious of them), we are unwittingly investing in the grip of the kelipot over our soul. One way of conceiving how evil keeps itself in business is when we sin—which we all have done. When we sin and tend to double down, however, refusing to acknowledge that we've sinned, we are investing in the power of evil over our soul.

We are able to choose differently, however. We are able to redirect our psychic energy so as to "re-turn" (a word that, etymologically, has to do with the word *repentance*) to the true spiritual home within ourselves. In this, the energy that was bound up in the compulsive re-creation of our habitual patterns becomes freed up and available for the expression of love and creativity (which, in religious language, would be to serve God). To "turn away" from the destructive evil impulse within ourselves and to "turn toward" and reorient ourselves toward good is to genuinely "repent." Repentance and remorse are directly linked to the discovery of the authentic self. Repentance is the highest expression of humanity's capacity to choose freely; it is a manifestation of the Divine in humanity. Repentance is a living manifestation of the power within us to extricate ourselves from the binding power of the kelipot, from the chains of endless causality that otherwise compel us to follow a path of "no return." The sin to be repented, of course, is unconsciousness.

From the Kabbalah's point of view, a sinner who repents is on a higher level than the saint who has never sinned. To quote Berdyaev, "The good which has triumphed over evil is superior to the good which preceded it."[14] The return to our true nature is all the more exalted after we have passed through the trials, tribulations, and multiplicities of the temporal world. Consciousness of the restored unity is not merely an awareness of the original divine unity but is actually a crucial act that completes and sanctifies this unity. From the kabbalistic point of view, what is true for individuals in this sense is also true for God. A god that passes through a phase of alienation, finitude, and fragmentation but who is then reunited with itself is superior to a god who had never experienced the limitations of our third-dimensional world.

Berdyaev was of the opinion that "The spiritual life is unthinkable without the great mystery of repentance," adding that "the whole value of repentance is the birth into a new life."[15] Repentance is not an end in itself, but a doorway leading to a new birth. The moment of metanoia, of a shift in our attitude, a change in our mind, and a softening of our heart, is a moment in which we are participating in the birth of consciousness. As Jung reminds us, individuation is incarnation.

In this moment of more expansive awareness, the energy that was bound up in the re-creation of the kelipot and their seeming power over us is instantaneously liberated. The holy sparks imprisoned by the kelipot, like iron filings drawn to a magnet, fly back to their divine source. Here they can assist and inspire the process of a universe-wide tikkun even further. The kelipot, which had been parasitic on this sacred light, are then deprived of their vitality and vanish as though they had never existed. It is as if a dream that had seemed real vaporizes into the light of awakening consciousness, reabsorbed into the very divine light from which it arose.

We, by our very choices, are actively participating in creating (in my language, "dreaming up") the archetypal process of either feeding the kelipot and their resultant evil or denying them their food each and every moment by nurturing the growth of awareness instead.

Once we cultivate the compassion that is at the root of this process, the evil impulse—yetzer ha-ra—within us is not, like in the psychological process of sublimation, merely redirected while the underlying drive is left essentially unchanged. Rather, the redirection implied by this process elevates and alchemically transforms the evil urge into yetzer ha-tov—the impulse for good.

It is the creative tension between these two primordial urges within us that supplies the energy for humanity to potentially connect with our true power and exercise the divine gift of genuine freedom. For the kabbalists, the good that we are capable of in our personal life issues forth and is functionally related to the evil inclination within us. Ergo the energy that is animating the evil impulse can potentially be channeled to inspire good. The greater our evil impulse, the greater our potential for good.

At this point, I am left practically speechless, in awe and appreciation for the divine creative imagination as it imagines itself through the kabbalistic cosmology. My life truly feels enriched after finding the gold of the Kabbalah. The kabbalists' vision of the cosmos and the Native American idea of wetiko mutually illuminate and shed light on each other, expanding our vision of who we are in the process. As I become more familiar with the Kabbalah, I am realizing that I have been a "closet kabbalist," and that my inner kabbalistic nature was a secret—hidden and unknown even to myself.

The Coming of the Messiah

For the Kabbalah, the act of Creation itself is an introduction, a mere opening act, a preparation for the process of tikkun. The kabbalistic myth of tikkun, at least in my imagination, is a satisfying myth, as the "mystic" tikkun is the true coming of the Messiah. This, psychologically speaking, is the birth of the Self through humanity. This is the "Second Coming"—the incarnation of the archetype of the Messiah (the Self)—through the expanding awareness and opening heart of our species. Kabbalistically speaking, the Savior does not come to unite humanity with God, but to unite humanity with itself; individuation accomplishes itself out of the practically irresistible urge to become who we are.

The process of tikkun involves seeing through and transcending the illusion of the imaginary *separate* self and recognizing our true Self. This is a self that is interconnected and interdependent with all beings. This is an insight that is not limited to the merely inner domain within our own minds. It requires us to embody its realization and carry its compassion into the world at large. Tikkun doesn't have to do with leaving the world behind and entering our own personal nirvana, nor does it have to do with transcending the world. The vehicle for tikkun's realization is our world as it is.

When we truly become a living representative for the process of tikkun, we realize the synchronistic interreflective dialectic between the outer world and the inner landscape of our mind. The outer and inner worlds, just like a dream, are recognized to be reflections of each other. This is to recognize that the outer world is the medium through which our inner realization is made manifest and given form. One very powerful way to "work on ourselves" and deepen our inner realization is to engage with, fully participate in, and be of service in and to the world. The psychological redemption that is at the heart of tikkun involves a simultaneous turning inward and outward. As practitioners of tikkun we seek to discover the core of divinity that resides within ourselves as well as within the world at large and experience it directly as an indivisible and seamlessly singular presence that unifies the inner with the outer.

From the perspective of the Kabbalah, it is incumbent upon humanity to discover, recognize, bring out, and sanctify the sacramental value of the material world. The world becomes alchemically transfigured in the moment of recognizing that it is, and always has been, a pure spiritual realm. We ourselves become transformed in the process. The process of tikkun will only be complete when the last spark has been raised and the universe, suffused with the inviolable primordial radiance of the Divine, reveals itself—to and through us—to be the dream that it is. As we collectively connect with each other in the profound process of tikkun, we can refresh and restore the world to a state of harmony undreamed of previously.

3

The Masters of Deception

A few days before my interview on the Internet radio show *Why Shamanism Now?* I received an email from the well-known anthropologist, author, and shamanic practitioner Hank Wesselman. He mentioned that what I am calling wetiko the Hawaiian kahuna tradition was also familiar with, calling these mind parasites the *ʻeʻepa*. He let me know that he talks about these entities in his book *The Bowl of Light: Ancestral Wisdom from a Hawaiian Shaman*.

In any event, intrigued by what Wesselman shared with me in his email about his book, I immediately went out and bought it. When I found the section on the ʻeʻepa, my eyes almost fell out of my head. The description of the ʻeʻepa by Wesselman's teacher, an esteemed Hawaiian kahuna shaman, was almost word-for-word what I had written in my book *Dispelling Wetiko*.

Having just finished writing about how the Kabbalah described the evil of wetiko in its own unique way, I had recently started doing research on how a particularly powerful practice in the Islamic tradition was specially crafted so as to dissolve the pernicious effects of wetiko. After learning about the ʻeʻepa, I was left with the feeling that I was fated to continually find an ever-expanding number of wisdom traditions that articulate the wetiko psychosis. It is truly helpful to find other lineages and traditions that illumine wetiko disease in their own creative way. This provides us with a greater scope and capacity to see what no one particular map or model by itself can reveal.

Wesselman's book is an introduction to the profound wisdom teachings of the Hawaiian kahuna elder Hale Makua. To quote Makua's conversation with Wesselman, "The 'e'epa are deceivers. Some call them the masters of deception."[1]

Interestingly, etymologically speaking, one of the inner meanings of *the devil* is "the deceiver." The chief weapon that the devil relies upon to keep the world in his power is deception. Evil, when we get right down to it, seems to always be bound up with illusion. Makua, the wisdom-keeper of an ancient Polynesian lineage, continues, saying that these deceivers "are free-ranging psychic entities, invisible beings who function as mind parasites. As such, they prey on those who are vulnerable to their influence."[2]

We all have a tendency to potentially deceive ourselves via the reality-creating genius of our own mind; the 'e'epa hook into and amplify our seemingly innate propensity for self-deception. Due to our almost unlimited capacity for pulling the wool over our own eyes, R. D. Laing writes that our species has, "tricked ourselves out of our own mind."[3] When we fall under self-deception, as philosopher and political theorist Hannah Arendt reminds us, we lose contact with the real world.

In the classic *War on the Saints* written over a century ago, the Welsh evangelical speaker and author Jessie Penn-Lewis talks about how, when it is reflected back to us that we have allowed ourselves to be deceived, the involuntary response is to feel repulsed by the very idea that we could possibly have let this happen. Penn-Lewis writes that we typically don't know "that the very repulsion is the work of the deceiver, for the purpose of keeping the deceived ones from knowing the truth, and being set free from deception."[4] The multifarious methods of the deceiver are custom designed to fit the particular state of our mind at the moment.

One of the greatest dangers about when we are unconscious is how prone we are to suggestion. People are particularly susceptible to fall under the spell of these "masters of deception" when they are not in touch with the living and self-authenticating reality of their own experience. Not sufficiently knowing the nature of their own minds, they are overly suggestible to taking on other people's perspective of the world and themselves. They therefore easily fall prey to the prevailing groupthink of the herd as well as to the 'e'epa parasite. The proclivity toward hive-mindedness strongly correlates with being susceptible to having our mind manipulated by the 'e'epa/wetiko virus.

Others, who are "sensitive" and have a permeable boundary between the conscious and unconscious—such as intuitives, psychics, and channelers—can, even with the best of intentions, become unwitting instruments for these incorporeal masters of deception in ways that can create havoc in people's lives. To quote Makua, "This is because the deceivers reside in the same realm in which psychics operate—the mental-emotional levels of awareness and experience."[5] Taking on and customizing their very image so as to have the most personal impact, Makua continues, "They can simply pluck them out of the mind of the psychic, then appear to them in that form . . . The 'e'epa then simply tell psychics what they wish to hear."[6] When we are inspired by "spirits," it is always a good idea to check our sources, to discern if they are of the left- or the right-hand path.

"The Devil," to quote de Rougemont, "is the absolute anti-model, his precise essence being disguise, the usurpation of appearances, shameless or subtle bluff—in short, the art of making forms lie.[7] . . . Impelled by the imperative logic of camouflage," this figure (equivalent to 'e'epa/wetiko) has a "borrowed and parasitical existence."[8] In his description of the devil, de Rougemont is describing 'e'epa/wetiko precisely.

Antimimon Pneuma

Makua comments, "The 'e'epa are accomplished shape-shifters who are good at mimicking. They can assume forms that are meaningful to the ones they choose to deceive . . . they are devious, and their motivation is deception. They operate through illusion, and they are masters of this practice." Jung calls this deceiving spirit by the name *antimimos,* which he refers to as "the imitator and evil principle."[9] He equates this figure with the Antichrist.[10] It is a counterfeiting spirit that *apes* the real thing—the *simia dei* (Latin for "God's ape," i.e., the devil). Interestingly, Jung calls the Antichrist "a perverse imitator of Christ's life . . . an imitating spirit of evil who follows in Christ's footsteps like a shadow following the body."[11] This figure corresponds to not merely the personal shadow, but the archetypal shadow, the dark half of the human totality.

The spiritual teacher Gurdjieff pointed out that if we observe ourselves carefully enough, we can see that we are different from who we think we are. We will begin to recognize that there is something inside of us that creates a duplicate of ourselves and then stands in for, takes the place of, and plays the role of the real person. Gurdjieff called this part of ourselves "the machine."

In his teachings, Gurdjieff is in his own way describing the covert workings of the *antimimos/'e'epa/wetiko.* He counsels us to shed light on this deception that is taking place within us such that we develop the capability to distinguish this bogus version of ourselves from the real thing.

Apparently pointing at the same phenomenon, the Sikh holy book describes a person who is blind and living in darkness as someone who "calls the counterfeit genuine, and does not know the value of the genuine."[12] The word *counterfeit* essentially means "the substitution of the false for the true." When we identify with the false, we don't appreciate the value of what is true.

In the *War on the Saints,* Penn-Lewis tracks wetiko in traditional Christian language (calling it "Satan," "evil spirits," "demoniacal forces," "the enemy," "darker powers," etc.). Trying to illumine the workings of "the enemy" upon the mind, Penn-Lewis writes that it works by "counterfeiting the operation of the person's own mind, and trying to insert his suggestions into it as if they were the outcome of the man's own thinking."[13] This is once again an exact description of the working of the wetiko virus upon the mind, which impersonates our mind such that we identify with its impulses, thinking they are our own.

This darker force, by whatever name we call it, can directly communicate with the mind, hiding under the cover of light. It can insert a lie into a person's mind, and if the person's faculty of discernment is sufficiently disabled, they can believe the lie to be true. This leads to the person ultimately becoming deranged and out of touch with the truly real.

Pointing out the danger of being ensnared by these darker forces that mimic the workings of our mind, Lewis-Penn writes that these evil spirits (wetiko) present to the mind "the evil spirit's 'pictures' or visions, which he thinks comes from his own 'imagination'; or very subtly refined suggestions which have no appearance of being supernatural, or even distinct from the person at all . . . the enemy's working is very ordinary—so ordinary that he is unrecognized, and the operations of the supernatural appear so 'natural,' that they are not looked upon as supernatural."[14]

Penn-Lewis is pointing out that though the origin of this process is "supernatural" (i.e., of spiritual origin—from a higher dimension than the physical), instead of manifesting as something otherworldly and awesome, these darker powers blend into our minds so as to appear in the most ordinary and natural way imaginable. This is how they stay invisible.

Archon is the Gnostic equivalent to wetiko. The Gnostic archons' function is in deception. The Greek word for archon is *apaton,* which denotes a willful intent to deceive. Antithetical to the light, antimimos refers to a type of deception that could be thought of as "counter-mimicry." Referred to as the *antimimon pneuma* in the Apocryphon of John (Apoc. John III, 36:17), this counterfeiting spirit imitates something—in this case, *ourselves*—but with the intention to make the copy, the fake version, serve a purpose counter to that of the original. This process ultimately replaces living, self-reflective experience with blind, automated, zombielike behavior.

When what is happening deep within the collective psyche of humanity is not adequately expressed by symbols, the antimimon pneuma steps in to take the place of the real thing. If we fall for the ruse of this snake oil salesman of the spirit, we become disoriented, lose our sense of spiritual vocation, our mission in life, even our very selves. If we identify with the counterfeiting spirit's unreal and limited version of ourselves, to quote the Apocryphon of John (also known as The Secret Book of John and The Secret Revelation of John), we fall into "the tomb of the newly-formed body with which the robbers had clothed the man."[15] We have then lost sight of our divine origins, which is sealed with "the bond of forgetfulness," becoming merely mortal as a result.

Interestingly, the Apocryphon of John, though not widely known, is considered to be one of the most important and influential texts of Gnosticism. It sheds light on the nature and origin of evil (wetiko). This text is gnostic in the true sense of the word, in that it teaches that salvation comes from knowledge, from knowing (gnosis) our true circumstance. The word *apocryphon* means secret or hidden. The apocryphal texts were originally conceived of as being too sacred to be in everyone's hands. These mysterious texts were typically reserved for true initiates of wisdom.

The Apocryphon of John points out that the counterfeiting spirit has a hardening quality, closing and hardening the hearts of those under its thrall.[16] Hardening not just their hearts but their perceptions and their minds, this impure spirit inspires people to solidify not just themselves but the fluid, dreamlike world around them into something that would eventually imprison them in its concreteness. Describing the antimimon pneuma, Jung writes that it is "a false spirit of arrogance, hysteria, woolly-mindedness, criminal amorality, and doctrinaire fanaticism, a purveyor of shoddy spiritual goods, spurious art, philosophical stutterings and Utopian humbug, fit only to be sold wholesale to the mass man of today."[17]

Writer and poet Max Pulver, presenting at the 1943 Eranos Conference, said that "The *antimimon pneuma* [i.e., the 'e'epa/wetiko virus] is the origin and cause of all the evils besetting the human soul."[18] This counterfeiting spirit is the source of humanity's inhuman behavior. The revered Gnostic text Pistis Sophia says that the *antimimon pneuma* has affixed itself to humanity like an "illness."[19] Not having a physical form, this "illness" plays itself out through our minds while at the same time informing, giving shape to, and influencing what manifests in the physical dimension of reality.

Egregores

Makua conceived of the 'e'epa as being "interdimensional demons." What ancient indigenous cultures call "demons" have a psychological reality in that they affect and alter our experience of ourselves. Demons haven't disappeared—they have simply taken on another, more modern form, now being conceived of as unconscious psychic forces.

The genesis and origin of the "wetiko demon" has to do with split-off parts of the psyche, what in psychology-speak are known as "autonomous complexes."* Due to trauma or some other form of transgression of our psychic boundaries, a part of the wholeness of our psyche dissociates, forming a miniature self-contained psyche that can't be educated by the conscious mind. These split-off fragments—like a splinter personality†—develop a seemingly independent and autonomous life of their own. They resist our conscious intentions, abide by their own laws, and come and go as they please.

---

*Interestingly, historian of religion Mircea Eliade calls these demons "the true enemies of humanity."

†These splinter personalities stand in opposition to the conscious ego as an alter ego in the same way that Satan opposes Yahweh in the book of Job.

They may even develop a peculiar fantasy life of their own. They are like unruly, disobedient animals, like a bothersome fly that keeps pestering us.

The person so afflicted, R. D. Laing writes, "has dissociated himself from his own actions. The end product . . . is a person who no longer experiences himself fully as a person, but as a part of a person, invaded by destructive psychopathological 'mechanisms' in the face of which he is a relatively helpless victim."[20] To the extent we are split off from this process, we experience these "mechanisms" happening to us; we have lost our agency and lost touch with the fact that, deep down in our subconscious, we are doing this to ourselves.

These "demons" inhabit the higher (and lower) realms of mind in such a way that, as Makua points out, they are truly "interdimensional." They are easily able to pass through and fluidly operate across the apparently solid boundaries of mind and matter, of inner and outer, of dreaming and waking. The ʻeʻepa/wetiko bug freely exploits the ultimate lack of boundaries between the inner and outer realms. These nonlocal "interdimensional demons" assert themselves by configuring events in the seemingly outside world so as to express themselves.

In his recent book *The Re-enchantment: A Shamanic Path to a Life of Wonder,* Wesselman brings up the unfamiliar word *egregore,* which is another term that can be used to describe ʻeʻepa/wetiko.[21] An egregore is a nonmaterial psychic entity, a collective thought-form that has been created by human beings. It can influence individuals (envisioned as the typical "monkey on our back"), as well as the shared psyche of a group that entertains it. It owes its continued existence to the focused belief of the group. It is important to note that even after the original members who conjured up an egregore leave or pass on, the egregore itself—*as if* it is an autonomous living entity—gets passed down to the next in line.

Egregores are similar to the Tibetan conception of *tulpas,* which are animated thought-forms visualized by a solitary practitioner that actually take on a seemingly autonomous existence and materialize into physical form. As hard as a tulpa is to create, these self-created thought-forms are considered even more difficult—once having taken on form—to uncreate and dissolve. Imagine how much more challenging it would be to dissolve a collectively dreamed-up egregore (a human created, mutually shared thought-form). This challenge, however, starts with each one of us right now, in this moment. Once a critical mass is reached—of people who are dreaming up the tulpa/egregore's dissolution—the tulpa/egregore will indeed dissolve in no time at all. This is an expression of the incredibly potent, mostly untapped power we all have to creatively transform our world when we get in synch with each other.

Evil is, psychologically speaking, terribly real. Today as never before it is important that we not overlook the danger of the potential evil lurking within us. Only someone really asleep, blind, or infantile can pretend that evil is not at work everywhere. The more unconscious we are of the role that evil plays in our world, the more the devil drives us. When we are taken over by the egregore of ʻeʻepa/wetiko, this darker spirit rides us, sitting in the driver's seat of our human vehicle. It's the one calling the shots, all the while convincing us of the exact opposite—making us feel like we are in charge of our lives while we are actually playing the role of a ventriloquist's dummy.

Wesselman is of the opinion that there is an egregore astride our Western society. These egregores encourage us to create false beliefs, distracting and inhibiting us from realizing our true potential so that we cannot be of optimal benefit to humanity. Practically all of our modern social, political, economic, military, and religious institutions have egregores as appendages that have been incorporated into the body of the organization. These egregores are like psychic-energetic attachments that are greatly influencing the institutions off of which they are feeding.

These egregores could not negatively influence us, however, if we didn't have the unconscious potential for darkness latent within us.

This inner darkness becomes easily manipulated and actively mobilized when we stop critically thinking for ourselves and become part of the herd. It is because of our inner connection with the dark side that it is so easy for people who have unthinkingly subscribed to the group-think of the collective to commit the most appalling crimes without thought or reflection.

Programmed for Self-Destruction

The virus of evil at first insinuates itself into the soul in incremental, unnoticed, and insidious steps, but at a certain point this leukemia of the soul becomes seemingly irreversible, leading to its host's destruction. The 'e'epa encourage us to indulge in the negative, darker side of our nature, where we eventually reach the point that we can no longer self-correct. Once we fall into our unconscious, identify with and sufficiently act out our unreflected-upon point of view, our uncorrected error becomes an open door for the 'e'epa/wetiko virus. At this point, it increasingly lends its deviant force to what is increasingly going off course, taking us with it in an ever-downward death spiral. It is then that we ourselves have stepped across a threshold, entering the realm of evil and becoming its victim.

Evil, simply put, is antilife, life turning against itself, *live* spelled backward. In the traumatized soul (and to the extent we are not fully awake, we are all in a state of trauma—the trauma of not being one with ourselves), both Freud and Jung recognized that there is a factor within the psyche that, once it gains a certain momentum and seeming autonomy, continually keeps neurotic, unproductive suffering alive. It certainly seems as if there is a force that is hell-bent on stopping us—both individually and collectively as a species—from reaching our full creative potential.

There is an aggressive anti-wholeness agency within us, as if made out of our disowned, unexpressed, inwardly turned, and inverted aggression twisted back upon ourselves, actively cultivating and breeding dissociation within the psyche. The fluid, ever-flowing, self-reflective/reflexive process of the continually evolving psyche en/unfolding itself over time becomes suspended, rigidified, and frozen. It becomes stuck in time in a seemingly never-ending and self-generating feedback loop. This inertial, entropic, and *thanatic* factor seems actively resistant to and set against us recovering, discovering, and attaining our intrinsic wholeness.

Jung refers to this disintegrative factor as a "morbid" fragment of the personality that inspires a "will to be ill." It is as if there is an unconscious counterforce to the faculty of the will, a "shadow of the will," so to speak. This shadow prohibits the synthesis of the fragments of our experience into the meaningful constructs and perceptions that make up a healthy, wholesome, and coherent psyche. To truly connect with the sacred, we have to become aware of what inside of us is hell-bent on destroying the sacred.

Dark Programming

People who are taken over by the ʻeʻepa/wetiko parasite are unconscious of being taken over, given that this psychic coup takes place through their unconscious blind spots. When we are taken over by more powerful psychic forces, by definition, we don't know that we are possessed by something other than ourselves. This is precisely the way the ʻeʻepa/wetiko virus wants it. The more we do not see the powers of the unconscious, the greater their power over us. They become the directive we are compelled to blindly follow without questioning.

The (worldly) powers that be are themselves lower-level reflections of and instruments for these higher dimensional "masters of deception" that operate within our unconscious psyche. These worldly powers are the people and corporate institutions that are able to influence perception and deceive the masses. Those who are drawn to power are particularly susceptible to being taken over by these deceivers, which feed on their attraction and addiction to power. Having a predilection for power brings with it a self-serving blindness that can easily be seized upon, manipulated, and amplified to malignant extremes by the 'e'epa/wetiko virus.

To a mind so possessed, extending their power in the outside world feels like a natural impulse. The malign aspects of the influence they are spreading is not seen because it takes the same outer form as the deviant qualities of their power-obsessed mind, thus seeming normal to them. This is to say that the maleficent aspects of their influence is rendered invisible to their 'e'epa/wetiko-ridden psyches. The people who find themselves in positions of worldly power and influence are easily able to propagate their pathology far and wide throughout the world at large, thus significantly helping to spread the reach and dominion of this psychic plague.

So many of us seem to have a resistance to seeing and consciously dealing with these darker forces that have insinuated themselves into the greater body politic (as well as our own minds). Our individual and cultural resistance to reflecting upon these darker forces is itself an effect of being programmed by them. This dark programming is the cultural brainwashing, the hypnotic spell that is woven throughout the warp and woof of every aspect of our civilization via the mainstream media and corporate-controlled entertainment industry—the "entrainment industry." Both forms of media can be considered to be the massive propaganda organs of the 'e'epa/wetiko virus. Spread like a net all around us, this dark programming informs our shared collective life through the unquestioned norms and implicitly accepted protocols of our world.

Due to this conditioning we become strongly disinclined to face the dark areas of the human soul. These darker aspects of the soul are always operative and at work in one way or another; the question is whether we notice this or not. There are any number of protective mechanisms within our psyche to protect us from the shock of noticing our dark side. Many of us have unconsciously internalized the dark programming that is being cast all around us, resulting in our protecting the abuser within us. Unable to see the programming within our minds renders us incapable of recognizing this programming as it becomes institutionalized in and incorporated into our world. Our resistance, our looking away, is an avoidance of relationship with a part of ourselves. Our ostrich policy of turning a blind eye to events of enormous negative collective significance is itself nothing other than the 'e'epa/wetiko virus in action.

Vampires

Speaking about the 'e'epa, Makua makes the point, "They could be thought of as psychic vampires. This is who and what vampires really are."[22] As I read Makua's words, the excitement I felt was palpable, for it was like I was reading my own words in someone else's book. Legends and mythologies from time immemorial about vampires—considered the darkest creatures of evil's arsenal—symbolically describe and point at the 'e'epa/wetiko virus. Vampires symbolically represent the will-to-power of the human shadow breaking free of both the wholeness of the human psyche as well as human restraints, as it goes rogue, devotes its allegiance to the dark side, and becomes truly demonic.

Vampires are totally missing eros, the quality of human relatedness. Being predators, they only have the ability to relate to others as sources of food, as objects to be used to satisfy their endless, narcissistic needs. The vampire archetype is the underlying shape-shifting form that informs the dark potential in all human relations.

Casting no reflection in a *mirror* (which reflects back images of the human soul), the soulless vampiric 'e'epa/wetiko can't self-reflect. This means that when someone sees them—reflecting these seeming entities back to themselves—not only is the reflection of their lack of soul invisible to them, but the one who sees and is mirroring their lack of soul becomes invisible to them as well. Having their reflection turned back on themselves renders them both blind, impotent, and for all practical purposes, nonexistent. Interestingly, Hannah Arendt points out that an inability to self-reflectively think about ourselves is one of the primary characteristics of evil.

In addition to casting no reflection, in mythology, vampires cast no shadow. Vampires literally—as well as symbolically—embody the shadow (so there's no need to cast it outside of themselves). To cast a shadow there needs to be light, and vampires are figures in which no light exists. In addition, being shape-shifting creatures, there is no concrete form to reflect back. Not having a soul, vampires are ultimately empty to the core, which is to say that no one is home other than an infinite void, a cavernous and devouring black hole that is ravenously feeding on the universe. Their atrophied soul has been emptied out like a piece of wood hollowed out by psychic termites. Hence, there is nothing to reflect.

Being empty of soul, these figures become mere instruments through which the forces of darkness then act themselves out. This is why Arendt writes, "The greatest evil perpetrated is the evil committed by nobodies, that is, by human beings who refuse to be persons."[23] As if no longer home, the people so possessed become automatons. These people are so disconnected from their authentic selves that something else, of which they are completely unaware, uses them as its unwitting instrument to fulfill its agenda. Dialoguing with them is like talking to a single algorithm that is running in the brains of millions of other people. It is like a computer program has been implanted in their brains to react to stimuli. The people so programmed have no idea of their situation.

Speaking of the mass brainwashing, mind control, and cult-like behavior that took place in Nazi Germany, theologian Dietrich Bonhoeffer (who was executed by the Nazis), wrote about his experience of encountering such people. In describing someone taken over by the wetiko spirit, he characterizes such people as suffering from a form of stupidity. By this I imagine he means that people so afflicted are disconnected from their natural intelligence.

Bonhoeffer writes, "In conversation with him, one virtually feels that one is dealing not at all with him as a person, but with slogans, catchwords, and the like that have taken possession of him. He is under a spell, blinded, misused, and abused in his very being. Having thus become a mindless tool, the stupid person will also be capable of any evil and at the same time incapable of seeing that it is evil. This is where the danger of diabolical misuse lurks, for it is this that can once and for all destroy human beings."[24]

In its full-blown form, wetiko disease turns people into ghosts, demons, zombies, vampires, and members of the living dead. The soul experiences become fixed in an unconscious perspective as a form of living death, for when we become so entrenched in a viewpoint, the possibility of spiritual growth becomes foreclosed. People so taken over become programed like robotic machines in order to spread the infection so as to fulfill the agenda of the darker forces that are driving them.

Being an archetypal, transpersonal energy, wetiko can literally take over, possess, and replace a person with itself. To quote from the article "Seeing Wetiko: On Capitalism, Mind Viruses, and Antidotes for a World in Transition" by Ladha and Kirk, "*Wetiko* can describe both the infection and the body infected; a person can be infected by *wetiko* or, in cases where the infection is very advanced, can personify the disease: 'a wetiko.'"[25] In other words, someone can become so taken over—possessed—by wetiko that they can be said to be the living incarnation of this formless invisible disease in human form.

Along similar unholy veins, professor Jeffrey Burton Russell, author of numerous books on evil, talks about "a fundamental warping of the will that underlies individual actions . . . there are people who have allowed their wills and personalities and lives to be swallowed up by Radical Evil."[26] It can be hard for us to conceive of people who actually intend and "get off" on performing acts of evil, but our difficulty in seeing this is due to our lack of, in Jung's words, an "imagination for evil." Our inability to imagine that such people actually exist serves evil, as it gives them the cover of darkness and obscurity that they desperately crave.

It is completely possible—having happened throughout time to countless people—for the unconscious or an archetype to take over and completely possess a human being. When not in conscious relationship to an activated archetype, the archetype can, to quote Jung's colleague Erich Neumann, "take possession of men and consume them like malevolent demons."[27] The person—or group—unconsciously possessed by the archetype is a cipher of information whose deeper meaning is in need of being deciphered. Embodying the disease in flesh and blood, they are literally and symbolically revealing this previously invisible disease for all who have eyes to see.

When an individual is taken over by an archetype (which is nonlocal; i.e., not limited in or by space and time), their inner circumstance affects and is reflected by the field. Being nonlocal, the archetype extends itself into the outside world in such a way as to arrange the outer world to express, reflect—and reveal—itself. The world—both outer and inner—then takes on archetypal, mythic dimensions. It is in such an atmosphere that synchronistic events occur. The veil between the inner and outer worlds has thinned, become permeable, transparent, and see-through.

The fairy tales of the Fipa people of Tanzania feature horrendous beings called *ifituumbu* who behave and appear like ordinary human beings, but in reality are cannibalistic monsters possessed by and embodying wetiko. The real nature of these vampiric monsters is apparent only when one really gets to know them and sees through their disguise. The extent of their inhuman behavior is so off the map of ordinary people that their evil behavior is literally inconceivable to just about everyone. This is the very thing that allows these monsters to get away with murder.

For years many indigenous people in the Amazon have considered Westerners to be *pishtakos*—"white vampires," a conception based on the historical behavior of nonnative people who have come to the Amazon.*

Acting in a vampiric way, many Westerners have been predatorial, extracting natural and human resources for their own self-enrichment at the cost of human life. These white vampires seemed obsessed with the accumulations of objects. No matter how many material things they possess, they never seem to have enough, always wanting more. What the indigenous people were calling pishtakos was simply another name for wetiko.

The psychological fact of being taken over by something "other" than ourselves finds expression in the belief in demons and their ability to possess humans—a belief found among all peoples from time immemorial. The fact that people attribute at least a pseudodivine origin to these seemingly autonomous entities is an expression of our experience of being overpowered by their superior force. Whether we call these nefarious psychic energies that inspire the worst in people 'e'epa/wetiko, demons, vampires, or ifituumbu, they are clearly something that people all over the world have had to deal with. This is further evidence that "whatever it is we call it" exists in the collective unconscious of humanity.

We become susceptible to falling under the spell of a vampire when we turn a blind eye toward our own darkness, which renders our shadow invisible to us. We can't recognize a vampire if we haven't shed light on our own darkness. Our unillumined darkness means there's a part of us that lives in darkness, just like the vampire. This part of us is just like the vampire who can't see its own reflection, which is why we aren't able to more easily recognize the vampiric aspect of wetiko.

---

*I became familiar with the idea of pishtakos thanks to Jeremy Narby's article "Confessions of a White Vampire."

A Metaphysical Other

To quote Makua again, "The 'e'epa are mental forces that have the ability to intrude into the human mind. . . . They operate through subterfuge and psychic stealth. They are adversaries who are drawn to humans because they wish to acquire our human capacity for creative imagination . . . this they lack completely. Humans are creators, and they are not."[28] The 'e'epa/wetiko virus is an expert at imitation but it has no creativity on its own. Theologically, this same idea is expressed in the notion that the devil's creativity can produce only nonbeing, that he has no power to create, but rather steals from God and can only create a caricature of the real.

If we don't use the divine gift of our creative imagination in the service of life, these adversarial mental forces will use our imagination for (and against) us, with deadly consequences. Once it "puts us on," fooling us into buying into its version of who we are, it can then piggyback onto and plug into our intrinsic creativity. In this, it co-opts *our* creative imagination to serve *its* malevolent, inhumane, and soulless agenda.

In essence, when we are under the thrall of wetiko, the creative spirit within us—the very function that connects us to something beyond ourselves—becomes malnourished and impoverished. We then can't even imagine things being any other way, let alone being able to actively imagine a way out of our dilemma. This points to the profound importance for each of us to intimately connect with the creative spirit living within us as a way of abolishing wetiko's spiritual death sentence.

These deceivers of the mind continually encourage us to indulge in our lower, more base impulses, offering us every justification imaginable for doing so. To the extent we are not awake, the 'e'epa/wetiko virus knows our mind better than we do. With the 'e'epa wetiko virus, it is *as if* an alien, metaphysical "other" is subliminally insinuating its own thought-forms and beliefs into our own mind, which if identified with, compel us to act against our own best interests.

The Gnostics ("the ones who know") are pointing at the 'e'epa/wetiko virus when they describe mind parasites called archons who infiltrate and subvert the workings of our own mind. An expression of its proclivity for wanting to usurp the executive function of any living system it inhabits, the word *archon*, etymologically speaking, means "ruler."

These archons can be conceived of as being delusional nodes in the human mind, quasi-autonomous psychic entities—cosmic imposters who pose simultaneously as gods as well as ourselves. The archons originate from the divine creativity of the universe itself. Operating under the cover of the unconscious, the archons influence humanity by tweaking our perceptions in order to deceive us and lead us astray, which is what they are all about.

The Gnostics were particularly interested in releasing humanity from the dominion of evil that we had fallen under via the archon's subterranean influence on our mind. The 'e'epa/wetiko/archons work in the business of deception. To recognize them is to see through their deception, which is their worst nightmare as they are rendered impotent once they are seen. Recognizing—and then dealing with—their covert psychological operations within our minds is the first stage of a transformational process. This process potentially leads us to cross an event horizon within our minds through which we enter a new world in which nothing is ever the same. Recognizing who and what the 'e'epa are, helps us to more easily recognize who we are, and our potential for spiritual evolution then becomes practically limitless.

Speaking about "the high spiritual guardians who brought us to this world," Makua comments that they knew that "humanity already existed as a dream. We as individuals are the manifested aspects of that dream—aspects that have now grown to the point where we have become creator beings unlike any that have existed on this world before."[29] We ourselves are manifested aspects of the deeper dream who are now being asked—demanded by circumstance—to recognize that we have a hand in creatively dreaming the dream onward.

As creators, we are autopoietic agencies in reciprocal coevolution with ourselves as well as with the universe at large. As Makua points out, once we recognize the ʻeʻepa/wetiko virus for what it is, we can consciously participate in our own evolution and craft both our personal and collective destiny.

Once we see how these masters of deception only have power over us with our unwitting collusion, they are done for, true goners. In a perverse way these forces feed off of our attention. Bringing the light of conscious awareness to bear upon these deceptive pathogens of the psyche, like sunlight evaporating the morning dew, dissolves them back into the empty field of psychic potential out of which they initially arose.

There is a radical difference, however, between ceasing to pay attention to the darker forces out of fear—which is avoidance (and therefore feeds the disease)—as opposed to seeing the darker forces and consciously choosing to place our attention elsewhere. Realizing that we are sovereign beings who get to decide where we place our attention, we can withdraw our attention from the darker forces and focus instead on creating the world we want to live in (which starves the disease into nonexistence). The first impulse—acting out of fear—is avoiding relationship with a part of ourselves. This is an expression of blindness and feeds, supports, and protects the darkness. The latter response is an expression of clear, empowered seeing that nourishes, and is an expression of, the light.

To a person who's entranced by the spell of the collectively agreed upon consensus reality, such talk of demons, vampires, mind-viruses, psychic parasites, and the like sounds utterly ridiculous. Ideas such as the ʻeʻepa/wetiko pathogen are considered to be superstitious dogma, new age spiritual nonsense, and gobbledygook, the ravings of a fevered, paranoid imagination that believes in strange conspiracy theories. It should be pointed out, however, that every one of us experiences the ʻeʻepa/wetiko virus in our own unique way, regardless of what concepts or words we use to describe the experience, or whether we believe in such things or not.

It is sobering to realize that the assumed to be true mainstream perspective that most people unthinkingly subscribe to is a trick, a spell, and a masterful deception cast by the very ʻeʻepa/wetiko mind parasites that are being denied. It is said that the greatest trick of the devil is to convince people that he doesn't exist. Convincing the masses that such malevolent forces don't exist empowers these darker forces to have free reign to manipulate and interfere with myriad human minds on a vast collective scale.

Spurring Evolution

We are all inevitably fated to become aware of the presence of a darkness within ourselves, a darkness into which we have fallen with a little help from these mind deceivers. I would suggest that the sooner we shed light on and become aware of the darkness within ourselves, the better. Postponing dealing with the darkness—just like putting off dealing with an addiction—only strengthens it. As Jung reminded us, we don't become enlightened by imagining figures of light, but by making the darkness conscious. Light is ultimately revealed through darkness; it needs darkness, for otherwise, how could it appear as light and shine? We tend to think of illumination as seeing the light, but seeing the darkness is itself a form of illumination.

Shadows are simultaneously an expression of the absence—as well as the presence—of light, for we can never have a shadow without light nearby. The darker the shadow, the brighter the light. Light informs, gives shape to, and is itself the projector of shadows. Hidden and encoded in the darkness is a higher form of light that transcends the light vs. dark duality: the light of awareness itself. This formless light has the property of not only being invulnerable to the negative forces of darkness, but of touching and transfiguring everyone who "sees" it. This is the light of self-reflective, lucid, primordial awareness that awakens us to the dreamlike nature of reality. The power of darkness has no choice but to immediately yield to the presence of this light.

In illuminating the darkness, we need to rely on a "higher power," a strength in us that is greater than and transcendent to our own ego, which is the Self, our intrinsic wholeness. When we enter into relationship with the Self—what Jung refers to as the god within us—we are connecting with the part of us that is not subject to the distorting influence of the darker forces.

The value of bringing our attention to, putting our awareness on, and contemplating the multifaceted ways that the 'e'epa/wetiko virus deviates the psyche is that, in so doing, we can discover and directly experience the part of ourselves that, being made of this higher-order spiritual light, is incorruptible. This is the very place from which we can bring real and lasting change to both ourselves and the world.

4

Sri Aurobindo and the Hostile Forces

The visionary and teacher Sri Aurobindo, considered to be one of the most highly esteemed spiritual geniuses of recent times, was continually pointing at wetiko by his use of the phrase *the hostile forces*. To quote Aurobindo, "The hostile Forces are Powers of Darkness who are in revolt against the Light and the Truth and want to keep this world under their rule in darkness and ignorance. Whenever anyone wants to reach the Truth, to realize the Divine, they stand in the way as much as possible. . . . So they always try to destroy the work as a whole and to spoil the sadhana [spiritual practice] of each sadhak [practitioner]."[1] These hostile forces, Aurobindo continues, "oppose the divine intention and the evolutionary purpose in the human being,"[2] which he mentions is their "very raison d'etre."

Just as there are forces of light, there are according to Aurobindo, "Forces of the Darkness whose work is to prolong the reign of Ignorance. . . . As there are Forces of Truth, so there are Forces that live by the Falsehood and support it and work for its victory . . . there are Forces whose life is bound up with the existence and the idea and the impulse of Evil."[3] What Aurobindo is pointing at informs the archetypal conception—and lived experience—of the conflict between the powers of light and darkness, between good and evil.

85

It is an archetypal, universal dynamic that as we approach the light, the forces of darkness appear to get stronger and more menacing. Progress in our spiritual path is the very act that stirs up these adversarial forces to attack. Interestingly, Aurobindo refers to these hostile forces as "the Adversary," which is one of the meanings of and monikers for Satan. To quote Aurobindo, "The heaviness of these attacks was due to the fact that you had taken up the sadhana in earnest and were approaching, as one might say, the gates of the Kingdom of Light. That always makes these forces rage and they strain every nerve and use or create every opportunity to turn the sadhak back or, if possible, drive him out of the path altogether by their suggestions."[4] A person entering "the kingdom of light" is the worst nightmare of the hostile forces. This is because entering "the kingdom" takes away the seeming power of the darker forces, rendering them impotent; driving them to the dustbin of the unemployed.

More than taking away their means of (un)gainful employment, establishing ourselves in the kingdom of light reveals the condition of the forces of darkness to be one of nonexistence. This is to say they are actually nonentities possessing no intrinsic, substantial, authentic existence. They only have a pseudophantom-like existence to minds afflicted with ignorance. These are minds under the spell of wetiko, under the thrall to varying degrees of their own darkness.

Speaking about the strategy of the hostile forces, Aurobindo writes, "Their way of testing is to take advantage of any point of weakness and push with all their force at that point to break down the sadhana or else to hurl all the adverse forces on the consciousness while it is still in process of transition and not yet mature so as to shatter all that has been done."[5] If we haven't integrated or stabilized our realization, we are vulnerable to being derailed by the attacks from these hostile forces—who are always on the watch for a weak point in our consciousness.

The Strategy of the Hostile Forces

These hostile forces possess a *malignant cleverness*—their strategy is to mislead by trickery and guile rather than by force. It is noteworthy that Aurobindo's articulation of the hostile forces are precisely the way that the 'e'epa (the masters of deception of the Hawaiian kahuna tradition), the archons (the mind parasites of the Gnostics), and the antimimon pneuma (the counterfeiting spirit of the apocryphal texts) are described. These sinister forces surreptitiously work by subtle suggestions to the mind. These forces create, to quote Aurobindo, "a great depression, discouragement, despair—that is their favorite weapon . . . they put in suggestions to the mind so as to make it also accept the disturbance."[6] Our passive, unresisting, habitual inertia allows the hostile forces to act themselves out through us. Aurobindo comments, "The more unconscious you are and [therefore] their automatic tool, the better they are pleased—for it is unconsciousness that gives them their chance."[7]

Aurobindo elaborates: "The first thing the attack or obstruction does is to try to cloud the mind's intelligence. If it cannot do that it is difficult for it to prevail."[8] Covertly working on and through the person's unconscious, these hostile forces create brain fog, such that it's not a question of what the person does, but, as if under the power of a compulsion, what they couldn't help but do. This is to say that the person so afflicted, regardless of what they think, has no real freedom of choice in their actions, as if something other than themselves is driving them.

These hostile forces, to quote Aurobindo, "prefer to act by influencing human beings, using them as instruments or taking possession of a human mind and body."[9] Aurobindo differentiates between three distinct situations regarding these hostile forces: to be under their attack (where we experience these forces to be separate from ourselves, we resist them, we stand in our power and are not overcome); to be under their influence (where these darker forces can affect our thoughts, feelings, and actions); or to be possessed by them (where, as if becoming their puppet, we become their unknowing minion and instrument).

Aurobindo also distinguishes between our lower nature (that we all naturally have and is what we are called on to transform) and the hostile forces. Aurobindo clarifies, "The hostile forces are anti-divine, not merely undivine; they make use of the lower nature, pervert it, fill it with distorted movements and by that means influence man and even try to enter and possess or at least entirely control him."[10] The hostile forces lend their deviant force to amplify the disorienting force of our untamed lower nature. If there is a subtle violent tendency in our lower nature, for example, the hostile forces will work to feed, strengthen, and exaggerate this violence so that the person will act it out. To quote Aurobindo, "Men are being constantly invaded by the hostiles and there are great numbers of men who are partly or entirely under their influence. Some are possessed by them, others (a few) are incarnations of hostile beings. At the present moment they are very active all over the earth."[11]

Our lower nature, when it occupies its proper place in our psychic ecology, is not in itself evil, for it is part of our wholeness. It is only when our lower nature usurps something within us that is higher than itself—which can only happen with our submission—that it becomes untrue to itself and hence, evil. Enslaved to our lower nature, we become compulsive in our behavior, totally unfree in our actions.

Most people have little or no idea that behind visible events in the world are invisible forces at work. Aurobindo's colleague known simply as "The Mother," writes, "In the universal play there are some, the majority, who are ignorant instruments; they are actors who are moved about like puppets, knowing nothing."[12] Most people are like pawns being moved about without having the slightest inkling that they are fulfilling someone—or something—else's agenda. They become at the mercy of and obedient to a master they do not know.

Speaking about the covert strategies of the hostile forces, The Mother explains, "Their method is to try first to cast their influence upon a man; then they enter slowly into his atmosphere and in the end may get complete possession of him, driving out entirely the real human soul and personality. These creatures, when in possession of an earthly body, may have the human appearance but they have not a human nature. Their habit is to draw upon the life-force of human beings; they attack and capture vital power wherever they can and feed upon it."[13] These are actually vampiric entities that are appearing in, as, and through human beings that are engorging themselves on our vital and precious life force.

Pointing at the same phenomena, spiritual teacher and philosopher Omraam Mikhaël Aïvanhov writes,

The invisible entities in man come and feast themselves, unbeknownst to him. The day we realize this and understand that we have spent our lives working for others, not for our own benefit . . . that our divine Nature is not the one to be enriched, nor fulfilled, it will be too late. Who benefits, who are the "others"? It would take too long to explain now, but many entities feast themselves at our expense! . . . [These entities are] robbing us of our energies. . . . The whole point is to know when you are working for your benefit and when you are working for the lower entities . . . otherwise you are no more than an animal, a domesticated animal.[14]

When we are unwittingly conscripted to work for these entities, our joy, strength, and inspiration will be vampirically sapped from us, as our life force is literally food for these entities, sustaining their very existence.

The Nonlocal Nature of the Hostile Forces

Pointing at the nonlocal nature of these hostile forces (in which they are not bound by third-dimensional space and time—that is to say that their theater of operations is not limited to the person's individual mind), Aurobindo writes, "If they find they cannot carry out an effective aggression into the inner being, they try to shake by outside assaults."[15] Due to their nonlocal connections to the greater field of consciousness, these hostile forces can draft and enlist other people to obstruct us so as to unwittingly implement the dark agenda of the hostile forces. Aurobindo comments, "The hostile forces often take the form of this or that person . . . through the instrumentality of a third person whose movements they control."[16]

Aurobindo writes, "The hostile forces have a certain self-chosen function: it is to test the condition of the individual, of the work, of the earth itself and their readiness for the spiritual descent and fulfillment."[17] These hostile forces test us. They secretly help us to get in touch with a greater strength, a more profound self-knowledge, an unshakable faith, a more intense aspiration to be of help to others. This potentially opens us up to a powerful influx of divine grace-waves. To quote Aurobindo, these tests are "allowed by the Divine because that is part of the soul's training and helps it to know itself."[18] He adds, "Each time these powers attack, if you hold them at bay, you gain an added force for progress . . . each conquest makes the control stronger and brings the full purification nearer."[19] We can't control the world, but the point is to be in control of ourselves.

One of the major ways the hostile forces work is to get us to unconsciously identify with their version of who we are. They seduce us to become overwhelmed, depressed, filled with despair and pessimism in a world seemingly going to hell in a handbasket. It is not just helpful, but crucial, to recognize the attack from the hostile forces as something foreign coming from outside of ourselves that is other than ourselves, and hence, false to our true being. These hostile forces can put suggestions in our minds and, if we are not sufficiently awake in that moment, we can easily believe that these thoughts are our own. This is why it is important to differentiate ourselves from these energies. To quote Aurobindo, "A suggestion is not one's own thought or feeling, but a thought or feeling that comes from outside . . . if it is received, it sticks and acts on the being and is taken to be one's own thought or feeling. If it is recognized as a suggestion, then it can more easily [be] got rid of."[20]

If these external attacks can't be fully rejected, we must try to keep a part of our mind conscious such that we will not take on or identify with the negative suggestions. Instead of becoming absorbed in and identified with the depressing, disempowering, and troubling suggestions of the hostile forces—an image of a devil whispering into our ear comes to mind—it is of the utmost importance to stay connected to the authentic part of ourself and how it sees the world and our place in it.

The Only Way Out

Commenting on the hostile forces, Aurobindo writes, "The concentration in the heart is the way to get rid of them, but there must also be a detachment of the consciousness so that it can stand back from the attack and feel separate from it."[21] In other words, the way to deal with these hostile forces is to cultivate a two-way relationship between the head and heart. We can connect with our heart while simultaneously cultivating the strength of our conscious awareness that is above and beyond the locus of the attack. Thus we don't unthinkingly become unduly influenced by the alien perspective of the hostile forces. Aurobindo concludes, "What has to be attained is not to accept the suggestions, not to admit them as the truth or as one's own thoughts, to see them for what they are and keep oneself separate."[22] In seeing the suggestions of the hostile forces objectively, as separate from ourselves, we differentiate ourselves from them and in so doing are able to avoid falling under their thrall.

The hostile forces work through our unconscious blind spots, which is why it is important to become conscious and recognize them. It is a mistake, however, to overly focus on them. Aurobindo counsels, "It is better not to trouble about the hostile forces. Keep your aspiration strong and sincere and call in the Divine in each thing and at each moment for support. . . . If you begin to concern yourself about the hostile forces, you will only make the path more difficult . . . to think too much of the hostile Powers is to bring in their atmosphere."[23] The idea is that if we become too fascinated with evil, we are conjuring up the very thing on which we are placing our attention in a mind-created feedback loop that codependently entangles us with evil. Fighting the devil is radically different from loving God. True spiritual health doesn't consist of being overly absorbed in fighting evil, but rather, once we recognize evil, we can choose to focus on the good—on what uplifts, inspires, and opens our heart.

Speaking about the hostile forces, Aurobindo continues, "One has to recognize them when they come and repel them, but to think much about them, to fear, to be expecting or looking out for them is a mistake. . . . Fear is the one thing that one must never feel in face of them, for it makes them bold and aggressive."[24] The hostile forces feed off of and into fear. The energy of fear resonates with their frequency and thus entangles us with them.

"The only way out," Aurobindo writes, is through "a consciousness which is not the puppet of these forces but is greater than they are."[25] This is the Self, our intrinsic wholeness, our true nature—who we really are. An intimate familiarity with our true nature—the ground of the human essence—is the never-failing protection against the malevolent influence of the hostile forces. Once we become aware of these darker forces, by connecting to, resting in, and abiding within the radiant luminous presence of our true nature—which is the very part of us that is able to recognize these adversarial forces—wetiko naturally delegitimizes itself. We have no need to do anything other than just be ourselves. Only what is truly oneself, only what belongs to our innermost essence and is most irreducibly who we are, has the power to heal.

Our true nature is inherently invulnerable to these darker powers, just as a mirror is never sullied by even the vilest of reflections. Aurobindo beautifully describes this, "What has to be done is to come to live in the Power that these things, these disturbing elements cannot penetrate, or, if they penetrate, cannot disturb, and to be so purified and strengthened by it that there is in oneself no response to anything hostile."[26] It is noteworthy that these hostile forces introduce us to a power within us that is greater than themselves. The forces of darkness are simultaneously obscuring and revealing our nature. In other words, the darker powers are offering us a unique opportunity to connect with who we really are.

There is no outside force that can ultimately stop us from living in the power that Aurobindo is suggesting is our nature. We can freely choose to turn our attention, the light of our awareness on, in Jung's words, *the germ of unity* that is growing within us.[27] This represents the emergence of the Self into conscious awareness and is thus a place of never-ending creative birth. This power, this germ of unity within us, is nourished by and grows stronger from our attention.

The hostile forces, however, become empowered by our unconscious knee-jerk reactions to them. In trying to avoid them out of fear, they already have us in their grip. In describing the sacred place within us that is untouched by—and nonreactive to—these hostile forces, Aurobindo poetically writes, "There is an internal clarity, a balance, a happy composition in the being reflecting sunlight easily, less amenable to the touch of cloud and tempest, which gives no handle to the hostile forces."[28] This is like being a polished mirror, which effortlessly reflects whatever object is put before it without being affected. Characterized by an unimpeded quality of diamond-like clarity, our mirror-like true nature allows us to not have to unconsciously react to or feel threatened by these negative forces, giving them no handle to get their hooks into us.

Peace as an Antidote

The light of the Self is always with us. Paradoxically, its presence is available to us in its seeming absence. To quote Aurobindo, "The Power with its help and inner working is always there with you and always will be. In the strongest attacks and darkest hours it was covered up and hidden, but it was never absent or withdrawn and never will be."[29] Even on the cloudiest of days the sun is in the sky radiantly shining, its light merely temporarily obscured. One way of conceiving of spiritual practice is that it dispels the clouds that obscure our light so that we can just let our light naturally and effortlessly shine.

Aurobindo considers man to be a transitional being, in the natural process of transitioning from one stage of evolution to another. We will have accomplished a great degree of spiritual realization when we can face the attack of the hostile forces with total confidence in our connection to our true nature. This is similar to how the surface of a mirror simply reflects the object in front of it, but its essence isn't affected—rejecting any influence by—the object it is reflecting.

Aurobindo sums it up quite eloquently, "If you can feel even in these attacks that part in you in which there is constant Peace even amidst the pains and darkness, and if you can keep it always, that is an immense gain."[30] Connecting with the Self means knowing that we can never be other than ourselves. This is to realize that we can never lose ourselves; that we can never be alienated from ourselves.

This is similar to how, in the midst of movement, we are discovering and being in touch with stillness—as if finding and resting in the eye of the hurricane. This is to find within one of the opposites the existence of the other. If in the middle of the most intense, painful, and dark encounter with wetiko we can find the place in us that is not only in touch with the light—but is *itself* the light—then we are truly cooking.

5

The Mind Parasites of Colin Wilson

Fiction or Reality?

Artists throughout the ages have been pointing out wetiko in a multitude of creative ways. In the next two chapters I contemplate the work of authors Philip K. Dick and Colin Wilson to illustrate this. Both Dick and Wilson used the medium of fiction to point out the seemingly fictionalized nature of nonfictional reality, which might be more powerful than straightforward works of nonfiction. Made-up fictions are the most unreal things we can imagine, and yet they have incredible power to effect change in both the psychic and psychophysical realms. Hopefully, to use Dick's phrase, these *fictionalizing philosophers* will inspire the creative artist in each of us to find our unique voice and express wetiko in our own creative way. This may help others to see the darkness, which if left unseen, will overtake our world.

I am continually expanding my articulation of wetiko as I broaden my learning. I never cease to be amazed when I find yet another tradition—or person—pointing at wetiko from their own unique and creative perspective.

To use one example: The renowned writer, philosopher, and novelist Colin Wilson, in "the supernatural metaphysical cult thriller" *The Mind Parasites,* first published in 1967, uses the fictive power of the literary imagination to give living form to this virus of the mind. *"The Mind Parasites,"* to quote from Gary Lachman's foreword, "is really a fable of ideas, philosophical investigations that use the form of the novel—with story, action, characters and dialogue, to embody an exploration of reality."[1] The more I studied Wilson's book, the more I had the overwhelming impression that he was really onto something. I felt that he was tracking the elusive footprints of wetiko. It was clear that he had chosen the form of a fictional narrative to describe, circumscribe, and elucidate the nature of this deadly mind-virus. It is as if Wilson was waking up to the psychic parasites that were within—not only himself, but all of humanity. His activated unconscious was using the vehicle of the literary imagination to express this realization.

Oftentimes creative artists are the canaries in the coal mine of humanity's psyche, presciently giving communicable form to what is emerging within the collective unconscious of our species. Sometimes the work is so informed by the artist's unconscious that the artists themselves aren't consciously aware of the magnitude and implications of what they are revealing. When an artist is bringing in something new, there are usually varying degrees of consciousness around what is coming through them. This is because their work is the result of a creative interaction between their conscious and unconscious minds.

I am so accustomed to writing about wetiko "nonfictionally" that the idea of approaching it through the made-up medium of fiction—through a creative art form that isn't as "serious" as nonfiction—opens up new orders of freedom within my soul. Wetiko can be likened to a "bug" that hampers the creative imagination—potentially even killing it, if it's even possible to talk in such fatalistic terms about imagination. This is to say that it makes sense to use the creative imagination as a way of dealing with its imagination-killing effects. Our imagination, the central prey of wetiko, is in fact our most potent weapon against it. This is the very reason why wetiko works to deviate it.

The Life Cycle of Parasites

Before jumping into Wilson's fictionalized account of mind parasites, it behooves us, in deepening our understanding of the mind parasite called wetiko, to contemplate the life cycle of a typical physical parasite. Actual physical parasites can lodge inside of our brains and manipulate how we think, feel, perceive, and act. Mammals (including humans) so infected can be jerked around, such that we become unwitting instruments to fulfill the parasites' agenda. All the while we believe that we are simply enacting our own impulses. In the literature of how parasites affect our mind, I was amazed to hear such words as *casting a spell, mind control, mesmerizing, bewitching, zombifying,* and *brainwashing* to describe their influence on our consciousness. All are descriptions of wetiko's covert psyops.

Certain parasites seem to have an innate ability to take advantage and exploit the normal propensities of the host, steering the host's behavior in such a way so as to fulfill the parasites' agenda of continuing its life cycle. Once the host is sufficiently taken over, it takes its orders from its invisible passenger (the parasite), and the passenger becomes the pilot who is driving the vehicle (the host). Controlling the host from within, the parasite in effect becomes its new brain, transforming the host into a totally new creature. To quote Carl Zimmer, author of *Parasite Rex: Inside the Bizarre World of Nature's Most Dangerous Creatures,* "It is as if the host itself is simply a puppet, and the parasite is the hand inside . . . a host becomes, genetically speaking, a zombie: one of the undead serving a master."[2]

Once the host is sufficiently entranced, it willingly tolerates the parasite's "abuse." The host will oftentimes compulsively act out in ways that are completely opposite to their own best interests. It should be noted that this is one of the spore prints of wetiko. When this happens, the person loses contact with their intrinsic power. They become like an automaton, having no free will of their own, all the while being convinced that they are freely acting out through their own agency. This is the state of addiction, where we have no choice but to compulsively act out—our (or the parasites'?)—habitual patterns.

Parasites may exhibit a very impressive strategic intelligence. For instance, while lodging inside their current but temporary host, they will sometimes attract the host's predator (by changing the host's fragrance or color, for example) that the parasite next needs to inhabit in order to continue its life cycle. Other times, the parasite will compel its current host to itself be attracted to the very predator that the parasite needs to inhabit to complete the next stage of its life cycle.

In this, parasites have an ability to develop a sense of what their hosts need and want, of what their hosts can and can't live without, for if they kill the host they simultaneously kill themselves. If parasites multiply too quickly in the host, they soon find themselves living inside of a corpse instead of a living host. Needing to keep their host alive, parasites have a full-bodied intelligence that enables them to use the host's immune system to keep themselves in check.

Provocatively, Zimmer concludes his book by suggesting that if we zoom out to a metaperspective and look at the bigger picture, humanity might be the parasites, and Earth might be the host. "Parasites," Zimmer opines in the last paragraph of his book, "are expert at causing only the harm that's necessary, because evolution has taught them that pointless harm will ultimately harm themselves. If we want to succeed as parasites, we need to learn from the masters."[3]

Fictionalized Nonfiction

Now that we know a little bit about parasites, we are more prepared to approach Wilson's book *The Mind Parasites*. In it, Wilson's main character—an archaeologist named Dr. Austin—is stunned to learn of the suicide of his friend and colleague, a psychologist named Karel Weissman. Austin's astonishment is due to his feeling that his friend was the least neurotic, least self-destructive, and most integrated person he had ever known. Austin felt that it was totally impossible that Weissman would ever commit suicide. In his shakily written suicide note, Weissman expressed his wish that Austin take charge of his scientific papers. Austin finds it curious that Weissman wanted Austin to be contacted *immediately* after his death, wondering why the urgency and whether Weissman's papers contained a clue about his friend's suicide. And so the story begins.

When Dr. Austin began searching through his now deceased friend's scientific papers, he was struck by the line, "It has been my conviction for several months now that the human race is being attacked by a sort of mind-cancer."[4] This sounds remarkably like the wetiko virus—which can be conceived to be a cancer of the psyche that slowly metastasizes, gradually subsuming all of the healthy parts of the psyche into itself to serve its nefarious agenda.

At first Austin wasn't taking Weissman's idea literally, but as he read on, he realized that his friend was not speaking metaphorically, but rather was quite serious. In reading Weissman's extensive "cultural history" of the last couple hundred years, it became clear to Austin that Weissman was of the opinion that our species had fallen into an age of darkness, and felt that some sort of darker force had insinuated itself into humanity's mind.

Upon initially encountering Weissman's seemingly paranoid and conspiratorial line of thinking, Austin's knee-jerk reaction was to assume that his brilliant friend had gone truly insane. After reading Weissman's carefully reasoned analysis, however, Austin began to wonder if maybe his friend wasn't crazy after all, but rather, had actually stumbled onto something really profound. Feeling that he would remember this day for the rest of his life, in Austin's words, "If Karel Weissman was not insane, the human race confronted the greatest danger in its history."[5]

Continuing to read his friend's papers, it became clear that Weissman had been doing an exploration inside of his own mind, and he was beginning to realize that there was something "alien"—an "autonomous other"—living inside of him that appeared to have its own independent will that was resisting his inner investigations. To quote Weissman, "I became aware that *certain inner forces* were resisting my researches."[6] It was as if these inner forces didn't want to be illumined. This wasn't a passive form of resistance; whatever these inner forces were, they were involved in *active* resistance.

Weissman was realizing that these negative forces rely on ignorance to keep the human race in chains, and that they not only feed off of our ignorance, they actively promote it. Our psychic blind spots were the open doorway through which these forces insinuated themselves into our psyche. These entities were, like vampires, draining and sucking off people's energy and life force. Humanity, however, had enough innate power to completely vanquish these creatures. But this depended on whether or not we could become aware of our situation and then connect with each other through our lucidity. This was why it was a matter of life-and-death for these darker forces that humanity should not suspect their existence.

Austin Corroborates Weissman's Conclusion

The more Wilson's creative fantasy unfolded on the pages of his novel, the more my ears perked up. I began thinking, *Here is a man after my own heart*—as I recognized that he was pointing at wetiko. In Wilson's novel, Weissman was passing on a precious gift to his friend, transmitting what he had stumbled upon to Austin. Once Austin understood what Weissman had discovered, he continued his deceased friend's investigations by following in his footsteps. Descending into the depths of his own mind, Austin wound up corroborating what Weissman was insistently pointing at by having his own direct experiences of the seemingly "alien" forces that had now taken up residence in his mind.

In reading Weissman's papers, Austin—and the reader—become

aware that Weissman was making an epochal discovery: that these mind parasites had established themselves at a deep level of the human psyche. They had colonized it so that they could, to use Austin's word, *drink* from the deep wellspring of creative, human vitality. The main channel through which these vampires work is consciousness, or more specifically, our lack thereof. It was vital for these vampiric-like entities to keep us in ignorance of their existence, for once we began to wake up to their covert operations within our minds, their jig is up. Weissman wrote, "Once a race becomes aware of these vampires, the battle is already half won."[7]

These darker forces will do everything in their power to avoid being "outed," including trying to inspire the person who is onto them to turn self-destructively upon themselves. These dark forces can obscure that person's connection to their intrinsic life-affirming creativity so that their creative life force turns against itself and gets acted out self-destructively, potentially even resulting, in extreme cases, in suicide. This puts Weissman's suicide in a deeper context, as his act of self-destruction becomes more comprehensible once we see what he was in the process of exposing.

The greater the potential role one is able to play in alerting humanity to the threat posed by the mind parasites, the more of a target one becomes. Not being separate from one's own mind, the mind parasites are capable of sensing when a psyche is onto them, and then make preemptive strikes to ensure the word doesn't get out. Getting closer to the light within ourselves simultaneously illumines these vampiric forces and catalyzes them, as being illumined is their worst nightmare. The closer we get to the light, the more fearsome the forces of darkness can appear.

This can help us to understand the known psychological fact that the greatest danger for someone committing suicide comes right before they are going to have a breakthrough. Demons typically make their worst stink right before they are vanquished. This understanding can also help us to recontextualize when we experience seemingly darker forces manifesting in our mind-streams. When we feel "attacked" by what seem to be the darker forces of the psyche, instead of interpreting this as evidence confirming how screwed up we are, we can realize it is an indication that we are getting closer to the light within ourselves. Shadows are an expression of the presence of light. In other words, the more light there is, the more the darkness becomes activated and visible. Since the darker forces want to derail us from our path, we can learn to understand that their manifestation is a reflection of exactly the opposite—that we are on our right path. It is noteworthy that the point of their worst attack is also when the darker forces are exposing their soft underbelly and are most vulnerable.

Weissman understood that if our species continued to stay asleep to what was actually happening, these negative forces could potentially destroy the human species. He writes, "In some way, the human race has to be made aware of its danger."[8]

Weissman continues, "What I had discovered was, of course, so fantastic that it could not be grasped by the unprepared mind." What Weissman had stumbled onto sounded crazy, absolutely crazy, to people who subscribe to the agreed upon consensus reality—which is unfortunately, most of humanity. Weissman's realization was too much for the "unprepared mind" to take in. What he was pointing at creates too much of a shock—is too traumatic—for most people to process.

Reflecting on the position he found himself in as he tried to communicate his discovery to others, Weissman writes that it is "more probable that people would simply dismiss me as insane."[9] Someone seeing and trying to point out these mind parasites will seem to those who are still blindly afflicted by them as being out of their minds. I can totally relate to Weissman's predicament for it is as if he's describing the situation I've found myself in for much of my life.

In his journal, Weissman wrote about how these energy vampires were capable of completely taking over the human mind so as to use it for their own purposes. In taking over someone's mind, these deceivers—members of "the undead"—replace it with a spurious simulation of their own dead and automated psyche, one devoid of creativity. When these vampires possess someone, the person unwittingly becomes their secret agent—their secret being secret even to themselves. They become the channel through which these higher dimensional forces actually enter into our third-dimensional reality and enact their seemingly counter-evolutionary agenda.

The Devil's Marionette

The person so possessed, not aware of their depraved circumstance in the slightest, becomes a marionette on a string—what Jung calls "the devil's marionette"—a human instrument for these nonhuman darker forces of deception to act themselves out in our world. The devil is considered to be a marionette master; it is his nature to have simultaneous mastery and dependence on a submissive victim.

It is humbling and helpful to realize that any one of us can unwittingly become an instrument for evil if we aren't consciously engaging with ourselves and not connecting with our true nature. Disregarding the numinous powers—the powers of the Self—with which we continually interface becomes the fallow soil out of which the evil of wetiko grows. When the sacred is not honored, it doesn't go away and vanish, but turns into a curse that haunts us.

We are not in control in the way we have been conditioned to imagine we are. Even though we think we are in control of ourselves, we can have the experience of realizing that at certain moments it is not us who chooses what we do, but rather, something inside of us that decides. Is this "something inside us that decides" our inner guide and innate wisdom, or are we being misled and seduced by a deceiving spirit? This is where our ability to discern becomes of the utmost importance.

It takes a strong constitution to genuinely consider such

seemingly outlandish ideas. We can only begin to come to terms with these seemingly autonomous energies within us that can act regardless of our conscious wishes if we go through and come to terms with a terrifying psychic experience that is independent of us. This process is working us, rather than us working it.

Over time these mind parasites become so at home within the person's psyche that their influence seems utterly natural, just part of the person's character, as they assume unhindered sway in and over the person's being. Oftentimes people so possessed have peculiar ideas or unusual habits that, typically, are tolerated by their family and friends. These quirks are written off as part of their eccentric, idiosyncratic nature, instead of being recognized as manifestations of something controlling them from within.

Most of humanity is being influenced by "hidden" (one of the meanings of the word *occult*) forces operating deep within our unconscious minds in ways that profoundly impoverish the quality of our awareness. That the experience of people becoming taken over by a more powerful demonic "intelligence" is so little recognized, and typically belittled, can itself be seen to be the underhanded workings of the very wetiko-inspired energies at the bottom of the whole enterprise.

Having our minds co-opted and taken over by these energy vampires can happen (in small or big ways) to any one of us at any given moment in time. It can happen when any of us unconsciously acts out our unhealed abuse; indulges in our compulsive, addictive behaviors; speaks falsely; or succumbs to group-think, to use just a few examples. Not just capable of taking over an individual's mind, these mind parasites can operate through and possess a group, a nation, or even, to varying degrees, our entire species. Wetiko is, after all, a "collective" psychosis.

Speaking of people who have fallen under the thrall of these sinister forces, Austin comments that they "were moving mechanically—mere chess men in the hands of the mind parasites."[10] If we ask people in the grip of the mind parasites why they are acting out in the unconscious habitual way they are, they will often produce a ready-made rationalization and justification. Their "cover story" unknowingly serves the agenda of the mind parasites. It camouflages the sinister operations of these entities within their own minds so that they continue to remain ignorant of the true source of their own impulses, thoughts, beliefs, and actions.

Austin saw that once a person is programmed by these mind parasites, they become like a clock that is wound up, only requiring attention once a year or so for a tune-up. This is similar to an abusive agent in the family system who typically has to act out their violence only once. The mere *possibility* of them acting it out again gets their message across loud and clear and keeps the family "in line." We then only occasionally need their attention to remind us of the threat we are living under, which becomes internalized within our own minds. Walking on eggshells, becoming hypervigilant, and being on guard around such a person is implicitly to accept—and introject within ourselves—restrictions upon our own authenticity and spontaneity.

Parasites Are Not Separate from Ourselves

Sufficiently programmed by the mind parasites, human beings reinforce each other's conditioning and condition each other, saving the parasites work. Groups of people so programmed can easily enact their inner state of fear and limitation in such a way that they police themselves, acting as their own control system. They then become complicit in keeping each other asleep. Anyone snapping out of the programming is seen as a threat by those still under its spell. Most people become so accustomed to their confinement that it seems normal, just the way things are. Not knowing anything different, these individuals easily become complacent, satisfied, and actually "happy" with their current state of restriction and limitation, confusing it with freedom.

Austin felt that humanity was struggling with something like a multiheaded hydra and was in the grips of an invisible octopus-like creature whose multiple tentacles are separated from its body and can move about as seemingly autonomous and sovereign individual entities. He was experiencing the nonlocal aspect of the tentacles—the arms—of wetiko. These arms, coming through different people or aspects of the environment, seem separated. However, they're actually coordinated and connected parts of a higher dimensional "body" in which they are all contained and of which they are all expressions.

Austin realized that it was a mistake to think of these parasites as separate beings. Something that seemed plural was actually singular in nature. There was one deeper energy—seemingly originating from a higher dimension than the merely physical—that was animating all of the multifarious manifestations of the mind parasites. Though appearing like he was having paranoid delusions, Weissman's realization indicates that he had become aware of the nonlocal nature of these mind parasites. Despite sounding totally "sci-fi" or crazy the fact remains that these vampiric entities are not bound by the conventional laws of third-dimensional space and time.

Weissman apparently was beginning to understand that these mind parasites, not being a localized phenomenon that could be pinned down, were a field phenomenon and could only be seen—and dealt with—once recognized as such. Existing nonlocally throughout the field, the mind parasites existed in a realm that interfaced with and connected both the outside world and our minds. These entities simultaneously operate through our consciousness as well as being able to somehow influence events in the seemingly outer environment so as to enact themselves in embodied form as a way of accomplishing their agenda. They organize themselves—be it through creating inner or outer obstacles—so as to oppose any effort (such as put forth by this very book) that brings attention to their stealth operations to larger circles of people.

It is important to know what we are up against; as the adage goes, "Know your enemy." In Wilson's novel—as well as in the "real" world—what we are up against is not anything explicable in the usual terms we use to talk about history and politics.

It was crucially important for these mind vampires to keep their presence unknown, for if someone vanquishes these vampires in their own mindstream, they become dangerous to these creatures, as this person is then in a position to alert other people to the danger we are all facing. If we do manage to connect with the light within ourselves and try to share our light with others, these nonlocal vampiric entities (what I have in previous writings called "NonLocal Demons," or NLD for short), will, via their connections to the nonlocal field, try to stop us by influencing other people to turn against us. Wetiko will make them think, for example, that we are paranoid, crazy conspiracy theorists.

When someone begins to wake up, it is as if the forces of darkness become alerted and mobilized. They then ensure that the person becoming aware of the operations of these inner adversaries (and who is beginning to remember who they are) gets taken back down, silenced, and put back to sleep.

To people still trapped in their mind-created prison, someone breaking free is a threat, as it reflects back (to their unconscious) and potentially reminds them of their own lack of freedom and their enslaved condition. This is why they oftentimes try to bring the person who is breaking free back into their own locked-down and amnesiac state. In a nightmarish situation, our slavery has become voluntary, in that we ourselves are actively subscribing to our own unfree condition. We no longer need chains to keep us locked up. Gurdjieff was of the opinion that this is the most depraved and terrible thing that can ever happen to a human being.

The mind parasites are able to "draft" unsuspecting others to become portals through which these forces can exert their influence into our world so as to seduce, distract, or obstruct us from our path. A biblical example is when the disciple Peter—with the best of conscious intentions—tried to save Christ from being arrested.

This would have stopped him from being crucified, thereby aborting and derailing the divine plan for humanity's salvation. This is why Christ—who recognized the obstructing force coming through Peter—in response to Peter's attempt to protect him from accomplishing his divinely sanctioned fate said, "Get thee behind me, Satan." Peter had in that moment unwittingly become the conduit for the mind parasites to—if unrecognized—potentially alter the course of human history.

I often wonder how many people who have been diagnosed with some form of mental illness are actually having inchoate experiences of the mind parasites, but haven't developed enough fluency or awareness to be able to deal with their situation. These "mentally ill" people oftentimes complain of feeling strange, alien energies living inside of their own minds and trying to control them.

Well-meaning psychiatrists then pathologize and medicate them—all for their own good. Yet might these psychiatrists be the unwitting instruments through which the mind parasites are able to carry out their dirty work?

As the drama unfolds, Dr. Austin speaks at a press conference in which he tries to alert the people of the Earth to the fact that they face a greater menace than they had ever faced in all of their history. He tried to emphasize that these darker forces are more dangerous than anything previously known to the human race because, being invisible, they insinuate themselves into the human mind. They do this both directly and indirectly, which is how they secretly inspire people to act out their sinister agenda. Thinking of his friend Weissman, he pointed out that these entities are able to destroy the sanity of anyone they attack and cause them to turn on themselves and possibly even commit suicide.

It gets my attention that the very situation that Wilson is describing through his fictional narrative is actually being mirrored by the deeper process currently playing out in our world. Darker forces, covertly operating in the shadows, possess certain people who unwittingly do their bidding as these forces attempt to enslave humanity. This isn't a paranoid conspiracy theory, but something that is hidden in plain sight, visible to all who have developed the (inner) eyes to see. In his papers Weissman wrote that these mind parasites, once they take over an individual's mind, cause that person to become an enemy of life as well as the human race as a whole.

Weissman suspected that these mind vampires, like a heat-seeking missile, specialized in finding races who were on the brink of evolving, and then fed on the creative energy they were tapping into until they had been depleted of their newfound resources. In addition to the weak and defenseless, these psychic vampires seek out people who are on the verge of entering "the kingdom." However, they have not yet fully integrated their realizations and stabilized themselves in the higher, more coherent level of consciousness that they are beginning to access, making them susceptible to be victimized by these vampires.

Jessie Penn-Lewis writes in *War on the Saints* that when someone enters "the heavenly places," where they can attain "union with the Lord," they will find themselves having to confront "the very keenest workings of the wiles of the deceiver."[11] Like moths attracted to the light of a flame, these darker forces are particularly attracted to people who are actively engaged in consciousness-raising activities, seeking truth, and speaking out about it with the intention of helping to awaken others.

From his writings, it was clear that Weissman knew that it wasn't the actual intention of the mind parasites to destroy their host. This is because, as mentioned previously, in doing so, they created the inconvenience for themselves of being forced to find another host. Their intention was to freeload and feed for as long as possible on the immense energies generated by the host's evolutionary struggles. These mind parasites don't want to kill us too soon, before they successfully use us as their instruments to accomplish their nefarious agenda of propagating the virus throughout the field.

As he gleaned the intent of these mind parasites, Weissman continues, "Their purpose, therefore, is to prevent man from discovering the worlds inside himself, to keep his attention directed *outwards*."[12] The strategy of these predators is to distract us so as to keep our attention directed outside of ourselves—"fascinating the outer eye." This stops us from finding and utilizing the immense light, the powerful radiant force of intrinsic awareness within ourselves. This would, if properly wielded, immediately "kill" the vampires by rendering them not only impotent, but assigning them to the realm of nonexistence. Wetiko is only able to flourish when we are in "object-referral," focusing our attention on the outside world—thinking the problem is outside of ourselves—rather than being in "self-referral" (i.e., self-reflection). This is when we are in touch with our immense creative power as observer/participants and use this power to shape our experience of both the world and ourselves in each and every moment.

The Stealth-Like Tactics of the Mind Parasites

According to Austin, these mind parasites, if left unseen, had the ability throw the mind off-balance. Feeding off of the natural potentiality of the psyche to dissociate, they split the mind and compel a one-sidedness wherein we lose touch with not only our intrinsic wholeness but the full spectrum of possibilities that are always available to us. Inspiring and then feeding off of the resultant polarization, the mind parasites exploit, take advantage of, piggyback on, and encourage people's unconscious tendency to project their shadow outside of themselves.

Austin continues, "The chief weapon of the parasites was a kind of 'mind-jamming device' that could be loosely compared to a radar jamming device."[13] It was when the mind parasites knew a person was onto them that they would use whatever measures were at their disposal to obfuscate themselves so as to keep their covert operations hidden. These predators distracted us whenever we got close to real-izing our vast untapped and intrinsic creative power. Interestingly, in the highest spiritual teachings, the one and only instruction is to not get distracted from recognizing and abiding in the true open-ended nature of our always present intrinsic awareness.

Whenever anyone would get too close to discovering their ploy, these parasitic entities would try—through their connections to the person's unconscious mind—to disorient them, diverting them from their path. For example, as we are on the verge of having a transfor-mative and elusive insight, we might get distracted and fail to write it down, thereby not anchoring it to consciousness. Then afterward we forget—and lose—what we had realized. Or we might find our-selves, as we get close to seeing the covert psychological operations of the mind parasites, experiencing our unhealed trauma retriggered, making us feel anxious or afraid. Or, as we begin to see through the subterfuge of these mind parasites, we might start feeling a lot of pain, which can easily cause us to dis-associate (i.e., split), resulting in moving away from our discovery of the mind parasites. Or we might suddenly have an overwhelming impulse to eat, or drink, or go for a walk, or call up a friend—*anything* that would take us away from being present with what is happening in that moment.

As we begin to discover the light within ourselves, instead of cultivating an ever-deepening *relationship* with the radiance we find within, we might fall for a classic ruse of the mind parasites and iden-tify with the light instead. In this we may become inflated and gran-diose, thinking we are someone special. We might even entertain the deluded belief that we have a messianic mission to enlighten others. Jung refers to this resulting state of inflation as a "condition of 'God-Almightiness,'" which always produces, "those qualities which are peculiar to fools and madmen and therefore lead to catastrophe. . . . 'God-Almightiness' does not make man divine, it merely fills him with arrogance and arouses everything evil in him."[14]

The mind parasites are masters of deception, tricksters par

excellence. Though this can sound like the ravings of a paranoid madman, it is actually the opposite—a clear-sighted articulation of what we're up against. The part of us that thinks that any talk about mind parasites is crazy is the very part of us that is taken over by the mind parasites.

In Weissman's writings it was becoming clear to him that these mind parasites weren't just messing with *individual* people's minds, but were wreaking havoc through the collective unconsciousness of our species, a process that was playing out en masse in the world theater. In his papers he wrote that he felt no doubt whatsoever that all of the wars of the twentieth century were a deliberate contrivance of these vampires. It is as if "the beast" of war is a virulent collective incarnation—in living (and dying) flesh and blood—of these mind parasites writ large. If we look at the state of the world today, once we cultivate the eyes to see these psychic vampires, we notice their influence everywhere throughout our planetary "culture" (or lack thereof).

Through his deepening insight into the depth of the darkness that was animating these mind parasites, Weissman also realized that there was a hidden gift secretly encoded within these nefarious entities: Though intending evil, these mind vampires are, contrary to their seeming intentions, the instrument of a higher intelligence. They could, of course, succeed in destroying any race that becomes their host. But if the race happens to become aware of the danger they pose, the result is bound to be the exact opposite of what is intended. This brings to mind Goethe's masterpiece *Faust,* in which Faust asks Mephistopheles (who represents the devil) who he is. Mephistopheles replies that he is the "part of that force which would do evil, yet forever works the good." The idea is that concealed within the darkness is actually a force that would potentially serve the light, if only it is recognized as such. Weissman writes, "The vampires might serve, therefore, to inoculate man against his own indifference and laziness."[15]

Making Light of the Darkness

The mind parasites/wetiko's appearance on the scene is in some mysterious way related to humanity waking up to its true nature as divinely inspired creative beings. These seemingly darker forces are obscuring this nature. At the same time, their deadly challenge is the very thing that is paradoxically helping us to discover, wake up to, and connect with our true nature. For if humanity were to break free and withdraw its fixation on outward appearances and connect with the universe within, to quote Weissman, "He would suddenly realize that he possesses inner-powers that make the hydrogen bomb seem a mere candle."[16]

We think of nuclear physics as having unleashed the incredible power latent in the atom, and yet we have hardly begun to realize—haven't yet dreamed of—the incredible transformative powers of the psyche. The powers of the psyche are mightier, by orders of magnitude, than all of the great military powers of the Earth. The powers hidden within the psyche can transform the culture of our world in ways we can only imagine.

Sometimes we have to try to *imagine* what's happening in order to gain access to reality. By creating a made-up fantasy world, it is as if Wilson, like the proverbial figure of the fool in the king's court, is making light of what is actually taking place as a way of getting the word out and telling the truth. Telling his story as if it's fiction or not true enables Wilson to break the taboo against speaking the truth in a world where to do so is fraught with peril, even criminalized. Sharing his tale as if it's merely a fictional product of his creative imagination skillfully allows him to bypass the flaming editorial swords of the gatekeepers of consensus reality. Ordinarily, his message—if put out as a factual warning to humanity—might be seen as disruptive and the breaking of an unspoken taboo. The powers that be would mock the spokesperson as crazy.

Ironically, if what Wilson is saying is true, by presenting this information as if it's merely fiction, he's protecting himself from a retributive attack from the very mind parasites that he's pretending only exist in his fantasy novel. As if a member of a timeless underground resistance movement, Wilson has managed to sneak "living information" into a world that is unknowingly imprisoned and in desperate need of exactly such knowledge. As Pablo Picasso famously observed, "Art is a lie that makes us realize truth."

Interestingly, while writing about Wilson's book, I felt the mind parasites doing everything they could to stop me from getting this information out. Am I picking something up that's really happening, or is this only my overly activated imagination? Am I awakening to the truth of our situation or am I falling into paranoia and going crazy? In any case, I can easily feel like I am living inside of Colin Wilson's mind parasites novel. Am I just a fictionalized character in Colin Wilson's mind? Or is Wilson, and *The Mind Parasites*, just a projection of my own mind?

The Mind Parasites by Colin Wilson is a beautiful and powerful example of someone giving themselves creative license to express an aspect of our experience that—because it operates in the shadows of the psyche—usually goes unrecognized and thus easily becomes marginalized. The idea of mind parasites invading both our world and our mind sounds completely and utterly crazy, but sometimes an idea is so crazy that it just might be right.

6

The Enlightened Madness of Philip K. Dick

The Black Iron Prison and Wetiko

Recently I was delighted to learn that the science fiction author Philip K. Dick (1928–1982; henceforth PKD) was, in his own unique and "Philip K. Dickian" way, describing wetiko to a *T.* Considered to be one of the preeminent sci-fi writers of his—or any—time, PKD had one of the most unique, creative, unusual, and original minds I have ever come across. Way ahead of his time, he was a true visionary and seer, possibly even a prophet. To say that PKD had an unfettered imagination is an understatement of epic proportions—it is hard to imagine an imagination more unrestrained. Continually questioning everything, he was actually a very subtle thinker whose prime concern was the question, What is reality?

Though mainly a writer of fiction, PKD didn't consider himself a novelist, but rather, a "fictionalizing philosopher," by which he meant that his stories—what have been called "his wacky cauldron of science fiction and metaphysics"[1]—were employed as the medium for him to formulate his perceptions. In other words, his fiction was the way he was trying to figure out what was going on in this crazy world of ours, as well as within his own mind. As the boundary dissolved between what was real and what wasn't, he even wondered whether he had become a character in one of his own novels (in his own words, "I'm a protagonist from one of PKD's books"). Through his writing, PKD tapped into the shamanic powers of language to shape, bend, and alter consciousness, thereby changing our view and experience of reality itself.

From all accounts, it is clear that PKD's life involved deep suffering, which included bungled suicide attempts, self-described psychotic episodes, psychiatric hospitalizations, and abuse of drugs. (He was a "speed writer," in that most of his writing was fueled by speed—amphetamines.) We shouldn't throw the baby out with the bathwater, however, and use these facts to invalidate his insights or dismiss the profundity of his work. Though much of what he wrote came out of whatever extreme state he was in at the moment, he was definitely (in my opinion) plugged into something extremely profound. PKD was a true creative artist who, in wrestling with his demons, left us a testament that can help us illumine our own struggles today.

In early 1974 Dick had—at least from his point of view—an overwhelming mystical experience, which he spent the rest of his life trying to wrap his mind around and make sense of. He was thrown into a "crisis of revelation," feeling a passionate demand to understand, integrate, and articulate what had been revealed to him. I love that he didn't have a fixed point of view in his inquiry but, depending on the day, wondered whether he had become, in his words, a saint or schizophrenic. He continually came up with new theories and viewpoints, depending upon God knows what. There is no psychiatric category yet devised that could do justice to the combination of genius and high weirdness that characterized PKD's process. It is clear from his philosophical writings, letters, and personal journal (his "Exegesis") that whatever it was he experienced in 1974 upended his world and radically changed his whole perception of the universe and his—and our—place in it.

PKD confesses in his letters that the world has always seemed "dreamlike" to him. To quote him, "The universe could turn into a dream because in point of fact our universe is a dream."[2] We are asleep—in a dream state—and mistakenly think we are awake. PKD writes in his journal, "We are forgetful cosmocrators [i.e., rulers], trapped in a universe of our own making without our knowing it."[3] In our state of amnesia, we have forgotten that we are the dream's creators—the dreamers of the dream. As PKD points out, "One of the fundamental aspects of the ontological category of ignorance is ignorance of this very ignorance; he not only does not know, he does not know that he does not know."[4] We ignore—and remain ignorant of—what PKD is pointing at to our own peril.

I imagine that if PKD were here today he would be most pleased to learn that his mind-blowing revelations are helping us to wrap our minds around the over-the-top craziness that is being acted out in every corner of our world. Not only precisely mapping the covert operations of the destructive aspects of wetiko, PKD offers psychoactivating insights into how to deal with its insidious workings. These insights are novel beyond belief, and can therefore add to the ever-growing corpus of studies on wetiko. Like a modern-day shaman, PKD descended into the darkness of the underworld of the unconscious and took on—and into himself—the existential madness that afflicts humanity. In his utterly unique and creative articulations of his experience, he is offering gifts for all the rest of us. For this we should be most grateful.

The Black Iron Prison

PKD writes, "We are in a kind of prison but do not know it."[5] Becoming aware of our imprisonment, however, is the first, crucial step in becoming free of it. One of the main terms PKD coined to describe wetiko is the *Black Iron Prison* (henceforth BIP). PKD writes, "The BIP is a vast complex life form (organism) which protects itself by inducing a negative hallucination of it."[6] By negative hallucination, PKD means that instead of seeing what is *not* there, we cannot see what *is* there. In PKD's words, "The criminal virus controls by occluding (putting us in a sort of half sleep). . . . The occlusion is self-perpetuating; it makes us unaware of it."[7] Being self-perpetuating, this occlusion in our consciousness will not go away of its own accord. It acts as a feedback loop—in PKD's words, "a positive feedback on itself"—that perpetually self-generates until we manage to break free of its spell. PKD writes, "the very occlusion itself prevents us from assessing, overcoming or ever being aware of the occlusion."[8]

An intrinsic challenge to our investigation of wetiko/BIP is that it is incarnating in and through the very psyche that itself is the means of our inquiry. Speaking about the difficulty of seeing wetiko/BIP, PKD writes, "We alter it by perceiving it, since we are not outside it. As our views shift, it shifts. In a sense it is not there at all."[9] Similarly to how an image in a dream doesn't exist apart from the mind of the dreamer, wetiko/BIP does not objectively exist, independent from the mind that is perceiving it. In our encounter with wetiko, we find ourselves in a situation where we are confronted—practically face-to-face—with the unconscious, both in its light and darker halves.

There is another problem with seeing wetiko/BIP. Because it is invisible to most people, seeing it can be an isolating experience. When we see wetiko/BIP, we are seeing what many other people are blind to. Hence, no semantic sign exists to depict what we are seeing, which can potentially break down the natural bond between members of our species. This points to the important role language plays in human life. It is the cardinal instrument through which individual worldviews are linked so that a shared, agreed upon, and for all intents and purposes common reality is constructed. Hence, creating language and finding the name—be it wetiko, the Black Iron Prison, or whatever we call it—is crucial for getting a handle on this elusive mind-virus.

It is as if our species is suffering from a thought disorder. PKD writes, "There is some kind of ubiquitous thinking dysfunction which goes unnoticed especially by the persons themselves, and this is the horrifying part of it: somehow the self-monitoring circuit in the person is fooled by the very dysfunction it is supposed to monitor."[10] When we have fallen under the spell of the wetiko virus, we aren't aware of our affliction. From our point of view we are normal, oftentimes never feeling more ourselves even though the exact opposite is actually true: We have been taken over by something alien to ourselves. We then suffer from what is called *anosognosia,* which is to be afflicted with a disease but to be ignorant of our diseased condition.

PKD makes clear in his writings that he is not making up the idea of the BIP as a clever literary device to serve the weirdness of his science fiction. In his journal PKD comments on his own work, "The reality I discern is the true reality. . . . The core of my writing is not art but *truth*."[11] In writing about the BIP, PKD was really pointing at something to which most of us are blind.

Speaking of the BIP, PKD writes, "We are supposed to combat it phagocyte-wise, but the very valence of the (BIP) stasis warps us into micro-extensions of itself; this is precisely why it is so dangerous. This is the dread thing it does: extending its android thinking (uniformity) more and more extensively. It exerts a dreadful and subtle power, and more and more people fall into its field (power), by means of which it grows."[12] "Android thinking," i.e., robotic, machine-like, standardized group-thinking (with no creativity programmed in), is one of the qualities of a mind taken over by wetiko/BIP. Just as someone bit by a vampire becomes a vampire themselves, if we don't see how wetiko/BIP works through our blind spots—which by nature we are *unconscious* of—it "warps us into micro-extensions of itself." In this, we unwittingly become its purveyors, which is how it propagates itself in the field.

The masses are breeding grounds for this nefarious mind-virus to flourish. Wetiko/BIP is not just something that afflicts individuals— it is a collective psychosis that can only work the full power of its black magic through groups of people. In PKD's book *The Divine*

Invasion, one of the characters says, "Sometimes I think this planet is under a spell. . . . We are asleep or in a trance."[13] Throughout his work PKD writes about our species becoming beguiled, enchanted, enslaved. It is clear that this was an idea that deeply spoke to him about his own circumstance, as well as the existential human condition. He felt that it was as if we were living within a mythic or fairy-tale-like reality, and that our species is under a bewitchment—a seeming curse—of massive proportions.

Contemplating "the basic condition of life," PKD writes that each one of us will "be required to violate your own identity . . . this is the curse at work, the curse that feeds on all life."[14] Violating our own true identity, we identify with a fictitious, made-up version of ourselves. In R. D. Laing's words, we are haunted by the ghost of our own murdered selves. To quote Laing, "Each person, not being himself either to himself or the other, just as the other is not himself to himself or to us, in being another for another neither recognizes himself in the other, or the other in himself."[15] Thankfully, in his writings PKD gives us clues regarding how to break out of this curse called wetiko.

Wetiko According to PKD

We can't break out of the curse, however, without first shedding light on the nature of the darkness we have fallen into that is informing and enabling the curse. Giving a precise description of how wetiko/ BIP works, PKD writes, "This is a sinister life form indeed. First it takes power over us, reducing us to slaves, and then it causes us to forget our former state, and be unable to see or to think straight, and not to know we can't see or think straight, and finally it becomes invisible to us by reason of what it has done to us. We cannot even monitor our own deformity, our own impairment."[16]

Further elaborating the BIP, PKD writes, "It can not only affect our percept systems directly but can alter our memories."[17] We become convinced that our—"its"—memories are objectively real, therefore feeding into the self-limiting and self-defeating narrative the virus wants us to believe about ourselves. We then tell stories—both to others as well as ourselves—about who we are and what happened to us in the past to make us this way in a manner that reifies us into a solidified and afflicted identity. In *The Divine Invasion,* PKD has a character say, "Something causes us to see what it wants us to see and remember and think what it wants us to remember and think."[18] Are these the ravings of a paranoid madman, or insights of someone who is seeing through the illusion, snapping out of the spell, and waking up?

PKD writes, "It is as if the immune system has failed to detect an invader, a pathogen (shades of William Burroughs: a criminal virus!). Yes, the human brain has been invaded, and once invaded, is occluded to the invasion and the damage resulting from the invasion; it has now become an instrument for the pathogen: it winds up serving as its slave, and thus the 'heavy metal speck' [i.e., the BIP] is replicated (spread through linear and lateral time, and through space)."[19]

In his idea of "a criminal virus" (which he connected to language), Burroughs,* an important postmodern author, intuited there was a shadow side to language. Language is an emergent phenomenon arising out of and within the psyche. Besides helping us to communicate (and commune) with each other, it can potentially be co-opted by the wetiko virus to serve its nefarious agenda of creating misunderstanding and separation. As the twentieth-century philosopher Ludwig Wittgenstein pointed out, we can easily bewitch our natural intelligence by the unconscious mis-usage of the magical, reality-shaping power of language. Language is composed of words,

---

*Burroughs had his own personal experience of the wetiko virus, which he referred to as "the invader, the Ugly Spirit." It was helpful for him to objectify it and give it a name. Interestingly, the way he found to deal with it so as not to become fully possessed by it was through the act of writing. He writes, "I have had no choice except to write my way out."

which are made by "spelling." Through our use of words, we can cast either imprisoning or liberating spells. Language isn't merely descriptive, but is invocative, evocative, and creative. As if casting a spell, the power of words calls forth and conjures up a particular universe into existence. As a writer, PKD was intimately familiar with the power of language to create reality, which he did time and again through his various stories.

To quote PKD, "We may not be what we seem even to ourselves."[20] What we seem to be is not who we are; the appearances of things are misleading. We seem to ourselves one way, but are in actuality another. Wetiko/BIP is in competition with us for a share of our own mind. It literally does everything it can to think in our place and occupy our rightful place in the universe. Speaking of this very situation, PKD writes, "A usurper is on the throne."[21]

PKD also writes, "Being without psyche of its own it slays the authentic psyches of those creatures locked into it, and replaces them with a spurious microform of its own dead psyche."[22] Sometimes using the phrase the *Black Iron Prison Police State* (which is mirrored externally in the ever-increasing police state of the world), PKD also describes this state as one where the person so afflicted becomes "frozen" (as in trauma), in a "corpse-state" (i.e., becomes spiritually dead).

Speaking of the part of the psyche that has been captured by the BIP, PKD comments, "This section died. It became fossilized, and merely repeats itself. This is scary; it is like mental illness: 'one day nothing new ever entered his mind—and the last thought just recirculated endlessly.' Thus death rules here . . . The BIP is the form of this death, its embodiment—of what is wrong, here."[23] PKD is describing the endless, self-perpetuating feedback loop that informs the potential black hole aspect of both trauma and addiction.

Commenting on the BIP, PKD continues, "To see it is to see the ailment, the complex which warps all other thoughts to it."[24] To quote PKD, "We're a fucking goddam 'Biosphere' ruled by an entity who—like a hypnotist—can make us not only quack like a duck on cue, but imagine, to boot, that we wanted (decided) to quack."[25] Being ensnared in the BIP induces such a state of blindness regarding our enslaved condition that we believe that *its* impulses are our own, which is the exactly the way the BIP wants it.

PKD continues by saying that "We begin to see what formerly was concealed to us, or from us, and the shock is great, since we have, all our lives, been trading (doing business) with evil."[26] This is one of the reasons it is so hard to see wetiko/BIP. There is a counterincentive built into seeing that we have been in bed with evil. We have to be strong enough to bear the trauma of seeing the extent of our own longstanding collusion with darkness. If we choose to look away from how the BIP occludes us and become resistant to bringing awareness to the actual nature of our situation, we are then being unconsciously complicit in our own imprisonment.

To quote PKD, "So there was a base collusion between us *and* the BIP: it was a kind of pact!"[27] Somewhere along the line, as if signing a contract, we have entered into an agreement with the BIP. He conjectures, "We're sources of psychic/psychological energy to it: we help power it."[28] This is reminiscent of the movie *The Matrix,* where people have fallen asleep and plugged into the matrix (which generates a dreamworld of illusions that they take to be real). They are, however, unwittingly being used as sources of energy to power the very matrix that has entrapped them.

As if we are in a double bind with no exit, PKD points out that "The enslaved people cannot be rescued by departing the Empire [the BIP] because the Empire is worldwide."[29] Existing within the collective unconscious itself, wetiko/BIP/Empire is ubiquitous. Being nonlocal it can't be located within the third-dimensional space-time matrix, and yet, there is no place where it is not. Its very root—as well as the medium through which it operates—is the psyche, which is somehow able to inform, extend itself, and give shape to events in our world. To think that the ultimate source of the horrors that are playing out in our world is to be found somewhere other than within the human psyche is to be truly dis-oriented, looking in the wrong direction.

PKD writes, "The very doctrine of combating the 'hostile world and its power' has to a large extent been ossified *by* and put at the service *of* the Empire."[30] In fighting the seeming demonic power of wetiko/BIP/Empire, we are playing its game and have already lost, as it feeds off of polarization. PKD warns that "the BIP warps every new effort at freedom into the mold of further tyranny."[31] Even our thoughts about how to solve the BIP might potentially "fuel" the seeming reality of the BIP, strengthening its grip over us. The Empire/BIP/wetiko will subvert every attempt at shedding light on its darkness in such a way as to feed the very darkness we are trying to illumine. And yet, if we don't fight it, then we have no chance. What are we to do?

PKD opines, "The idea is to break the BIP's power by revealing more and more about it."[32] Just as a vampire loses its power in the light of day, wetiko/BIP has no power in the light of conscious awareness. To quote PKD, "The Empire is only a phantasm, lingering because we have gone to sleep."[33] It is as if the Empire/BIP/wetiko is an afterimage that we have mistaken for being real. PKD refers to it as a "deceitful corpse" that apes life.[34]

Along similar lines, describing Satan (equivalent to the Empire/BIP/wetiko), William Blake refers to it as an "empire of nothing," and "Satan this Body of Doubt that seems but is Not."[35] Not only is lying the root of evil, but evil itself is a lie. It is always pretending to be that which it is not; its enchanting power lies in deception. Theologically, the devil is considered to be an imposter, having no source of life, existence, or being of his own. His seeming overwhelming power is illusory, part of his deception.

The paradox is that, ultimately speaking, wetiko has no real intrinsic existence on its own (separate from our own mind), and yet, if unrecognized, it can destroy our species. Contemplating this paradox can lead us to many liberating insights about the immense creative power of our mind, a power that can be used to either enslave or liberate us.

The idea is to shed light on darkness—what good is seeing the light if our vision doesn't illumine the darkness? The teachings of the Gnostics point out that evil only has seeming power over us because its nature is not recognized. Being a phantasmal artifact of our lack of awareness, wetiko feeds off of and into our nonrecognition of it. This is analogous to what happens in the psychological realm. If we don't see our unconscious aspects, we are taken over by them and act them out. It is only by becoming aware of these unconscious contents that we can liberate ourselves from being possessed by them. As Berdyaev reminds us, "A person who lives in a world of phantasms is always partially insane."[36]

Throughout history, periods where genuine spiritual realization flourished in our species were also the exact times when the activated invisible forces of darkness were recognized. This is to say that these are not two separate processes but are one and the same process, two sides of the same coin that always go together. Be it in the old or new dispensations (the Hebrew scriptures or the Christian scriptures), both Moses and Jesus recognized—and were demanded to deal with—the powers of evil. Bonhoeffer writes, "Surely we do not wish to accuse Jesus of ignoring the reality and power of evil! Why, the whole of his life was one long conflict with the devil. He calls evil evil."[37] In dealing with evil, we have to be able to recognize it and call it by its right name. Conversely, when these darker powers aren't recognized are the times in history when destruction plays itself out most flagrantly in this world of ours.

Fake Fakes

Wetiko/BIP can be likened to an "anti-information" virus. Not only does it block the reception of information, but it substitutes false and potentially even dangerous information for the real thing (what in previous writings I've called "info-toxins"). PKD writes, "The bombardment of pseudorealities begins to produce inauthentic humans very quickly [in his words 'spurious humans']."[38] PKD writes of the BIP, "It has grown vine-like into our information media; it is an information life form."[39] It is an info life-form (composed of and creating living disinformation) that lies to us; PKD compares this to the figure of *Satan*, who is "the liar." Wetiko/BIP has co-opted the mainstream, corporatized media to be its propaganda organ, which becomes its instrument for creating and delivering fictitious realities into our minds. These institutions have, to quote PKD "an astonishing power: that of creating whole universes, universes of the mind. I ought to know. I do the same thing. It is my job to create universes."[40]

PKD was intensely interested in what makes an authentic human being. He continues, "Fake realities will produce fake humans. Or, fake humans will produce fake realities and then sell them to other humans, turning them, eventually, into forgeries of themselves."[41] PKD realized that authentic human beings, however, cannot be coerced or compelled to be what they are not. No matter how many spurious realities a real human being is confronted with, they are never taken in by them, as the purposely manufactured fakes never penetrate them.

Succinctly stating the problem, PKD writes, "The problem is that a mock creation has filtered in, which must be transubstantiated into the real."[42] Our universe is a collectively shared dream or hallucination that appears real; in PKD's words, "our reality is a cunning counterfeit, mutually shared."[43] To imbue our world with an intrinsic, objective reality that exists separate from the mind that is observing it would be, in PKD's words, "a dreadful intellectual error."

Pointing directly at wetiko/BIP, PKD writes that "There is a vast life form here, that has invaded this world and is camouflaged."[44] He marvels at how it camouflages itself and in his words, it "simulated normal objects and their processes so as to copy them and in such an artful way as to make himself [the BIP] invisible within them."[45]

Through its mimicry of real phenomenal objects, the BIP, according to PKD, "steadily, stealthily replaces them and mimics—assumes their form."[46] PKD's writings might appear "out there," and can easily sound crazy, paranoid, and conspiratorial. However, we should remind ourselves that what he is pointing at in his own quirky, eccentric way is the very counterfeiting spirit that wisdom traditions throughout the ages have been trying to illumine. Wetiko is empty of substantial existence, yet it simultaneously hides and reveals itself—by fleshing out its transcendental nature through the physical forms of our universe.

PKD has articulated wetiko's/BIP's counterfeiting ability, and how the universe responds, in a way that only he can. He has realized that the very ground of being itself—PKD refers to it by various names: "Christ," "God," "the Savior," the "Urgrund" (a German term used by both Meister Eckhart and Jacob Boehme to describe ultimate reality)—is responding to wetiko/BIP in a very unique and revelatory way. As the BIP mimes reality so as to create a counterfeit of the real thing, the ground of reality, in PKD's words, "counterfeits the counterfeit."[47] In PKD's words, "So originally the bogus info mimicked the actual successfully enough to fool us, and now we have a situation in which the actual has returned in a form mimicking the bogus."[48]

Wetiko/BIP has created a counterfeit version of reality, and the ground of reality itself, in response to being forged, imitates the imitation in a radically new ontological category that PKD calls a "fake fake." Delighted by this new idea, PKD asks the question, "Is a fake fake more fake than just a fake, or null-fake?"[49] In other words, if a fake fake is not more fake than a fake, is it the real thing? PDK's idea of a fake fake is cognate to the indeterminacy between originals and simulacra that is the hallmark of the world of virtual reality. To quote PKD, "A fake fake = something *real*. The demiurge [the false God in Gnosticism] unsuccessfully counterfeited the pleroma, and now God/the Savior is mimicking this counterfeit cosmos with a stealthily growing *real* one."[50] In other words, God/the ground of being is assimilating our seemingly counterfeit universe into and as itself in order to transform it so as to once again become one with itself.

The Ground of Being as Our Saving Grace?

Writing about the Savior, PKD writes that "It doesn't want its adversary to know it's here, so it must disguise (randomize) its presence, including by giving out self-discrediting information; as if mimicking a hoax."[51] Just like the BIP tricks us into identifying with its world, the true ground of being tricks the BIP by surreptitiously imitating and becoming it, taking it on (and into itself). It doesn't want to let the BIP know it is doing this. That would defeat the purpose of its counterploy; the Savior does its mimicry on the sly.

PKD comments, "The Urgrund does not advertise to the artifact [i.e., wetiko/BIP] that it is here."[52] Just as the BIP works through our blind spots, the ground of being works through the BIP's blind spots. PKD comments, "The artifact is as occluded as to the nature and existence of the Urgrund as we are to the artifact."[53] Like an underground resistance movement, the Urgrund's activities, in PKD's words, "resemble the covert advance of a secret, determined revolution against a powerful tyranny."[54]

Speaking of Christ as another reference for the ground of being, Dick writes, "Through him the *properly* functioning (living and growing) total brain replicated itself here in microform (seed-like) thereafter branching out farther and farther like a vine, a viable life form taking up residence within a dead, deranged and rigid one [the BIP]. It is the nature of the rigid region to seek to detect and ensnare him, but his discorporate plasmatic nature ensures his escape from the intended imprisonment."[55] In other words, the spirit can't be pinned down or entrapped within dense matter; in PKD's words, "He is everywhere and nowhere."[56]

Describing this deeper process of how the ground of being

potentially saves us—and itself—from wetiko/BIP, PKD comments, "A criminal entity [BIP] has been invaded by life giving cells [Christ, God, the Urgrund] which it can't detect, and so it accepts them into itself, replacing the 'iron' ones."[57] PKD is describing transubstantiation in the flesh. Speaking of the Savior, PKD writes, "like a gas (plasma) he begins invisibly to expand and fill up the whole of BIP."[58]

What I so appreciate about PKD's vision is that he's not just describing the life-destroying workings of wetiko/BIP, but he's also articulating the other half of this process, which is the salvific response from the living intelligence of the universe as a whole. To quote PKD, "The key to everything lies in understanding this mimicking living stuff."[59] This mimicking living stuff, "the key to everything," is none other than wetiko. PKD equates this "form-mimicker" with the *Deus Absconditus,* the dark and hidden God. The idea is that God covertly infiltrates the BIP under the cover provided by Its darker side. God then reveals itself through its darker half.

This makes me think how the unconscious responds to a one-sided situation in our psychic lives by sending compensatory forms—like symbols in a dream—so as to bring us back into balance. To quote PKD, "If the universe is a brain the BIP is a rigid ossified complex, and Zebra [another of PKD's names for the Savior] is metabolic toxin (living info) designed to melt it out of existence by restoring elasticity to it, which means to cause it to cease recirculating the same thought over and over again."[60]

Seen psychologically, the BIP is a rigidified complex that has developed an autonomy and has gone rogue, seemingly having an independent life and a will of its own that is antithetical to and at odds with our own. In psychological-speak, until this "autonomous complex" is dissolved and rejoins the wholeness of the psyche, "the organism," to quote PKD, "is stuck in its cycle, in cybernetic terms; it won't kick over—which fits with my idea that we are memory coils which won't kick over and discharge their contents."[61] We are like malfunctioning memory coils in a quasi-dream state; in PKD's words, "We are an impaired section of the megamind."[62]

These contemplations helped PKD to contextualize, and hopefully integrate his overwhelming spiritual experience of 1974. He writes that his experience is "an achievement by the Urgrund in reaching its objective of reflecting itself back to itself, using me as a point of reflection."[63] In other words, PKD realized that we are all potentially reflecting mirrors for the divine ground of being to wake up to itself. This is to say that we play a crucial role in the deeper archetypal process of the incarnation of the Deity.

Connecting with Christ Within

PKD writes in his journal, "Perhaps the transformation of and in me in 3-74 [i.e., March, 1974] was when this mimicking 'plasma' reached me and replaced me—although I appeared outwardly the same (i.e., my essence changed—a new self replaced the old) . . . my 'me' was covertly replaced by a greater other 'me' I'd never seen or known before."[64]This greater Self—a pneumatic body—that replaced PKD's ego goes by many names: the greater personality, the Self, our true nature, Buddha nature, and Christ, to name but a few. It is as if the guidance of life has passed from our limited conscious ego to an invisible center that is connected to a higher-order intelligence.

PKD was having the archetypal experience in which a higher spiritual being—in his case, Christ—was born inside of him. In this spiritual birth, a new identity is taken on ("put on Christ") like a garment. The subjective "I live" transforms into the objective "It lives me." This occurs when we see through the illusion that we, as ego, are independent and in control, and recognize the authority of the transconscious psyche (i.e., the Self, a.k.a., Christ), in which we, as ego, are contained. In this we, as ego, are contained (as a part to the whole). We dispel our pretention of thinking we exist in a way (as a separate ego) that we do not. This heals our isolation and releases us from the compulsive self-contracting, clinging, and grasping of the ego.

PKD writes, "A human can evolve into Christ if Christ ignites his own self in the human and takes the human over[65] . . . it is at the moment of when the ultimate blow (of pain, murderous injury, humiliation and death) is struck, it is Christ who is there, replacing the victim and taking the blow himself. This is what happened to me in 3-74."[66] He continues, "So flight from suffering inexorably involves a flight from life (reality). . . . But the secret, mysterious opposite from this is a full facing of suffering—a non-flinching—that can lead to a magic alchemy: suddenly it is you/suddenly it is Christ/so you must equal (be) Christ."[67]

In psychological speak, the genuine suffering that PKD went through enabled him to withdraw his unconscious projections from an outward historical or metaphysical figure encrusted with dogma and *wake up* the actual Christ within himself. In other words, he was able to introject this sacred figure and realize that Christ (i.e., the Self) lived in him and was not an external figure separate and different from himself. This brings to mind the quote from Galatians 2:20 (NKJV): "It is no longer I who live, but Christ who lives in me."

In essence, the crucial step in healing wetiko is to open our eyes and look, and to recognize that what we are seeing out there (be it in the outer world or our minds eye, be it demons or God) is reflecting ourselves.

As PKD's writings make clear, he was not able to keep the Christ event outside of himself, but rather was able to personally experience the reality represented by the sacred legend firsthand. His experience wasn't an effortful striving at imitating Christ. Instead it was its opposite: an involuntary experience of assimilating the Christ-image to his own self. In a real sense it was not PKD who suffered. Stepping out of personally identifying with his torturous ordeal, it was the arcane, esoteric substance of the Higher Self—the God within—that suffered these tortures for and through him. Through this process, the eternal substance passes through death and rises again in a new human form.

Dreamlike Cosmology

According to PKD's cosmology, it is as if God the Creator has allowed himself to become captured, enslaved by, and hostage to his own Creation (images of the kelipot from the Kabbalah come to mind). PKD is pointing out that the living Creator God is at the mercy of the mechanical, a circumstance where the master and servant have switched roles. PKD's words have a particular ring of truth in this technological age of ours. Today many people think that one of the greatest dangers that faces humanity is that artificial intelligence (AI) can potentially enslave its human creators. PKD was realizing, however, that the artifact is teaching us to remember who we are and our place in the universe. In other words, the servant-become-master is attempting to help the master remember his or her true identity.

PKD's contemplations shed light on what might be the hidden purpose of the emergence of wetiko/BIP in our world. PKD comments, "The artifact enslaves us, but on the other hand it is attempting to teach us to throw off its enslavement."[68] Wetiko/BIP tests us so as to make sure that we will make optimal use of our divine endowment. As PKD points out, the fundamental dialectic at work is liberation vs. enslavement.

Interestingly, one of the meanings of the word *Satan* is one who creates obstacles. During a recent visit to Portland, one of my teachers pointed out that all of the great realized beings of Tibet didn't attain realization because things were going great in their lives, but because they met with great hardship and obstacles. They were able to alchemically transform these difficulties into opportunities that expanded their consciousness. These challenging events became the catalysts that snapped them out of their habitual patterns, helping them attain realization. In other words, the very obstacles that appeared to oppose their enlightenment were secretly helping them—like undercover allies—to attain their goal.

PKD has created a parable in which a fallen and amnesiac God has fallen prey to its own creation and is in need of redemption. Lest we think that PKD's cosmological imaginings are the ravings of a madman, it should be pointed out that his theories are fully resonant with those found in the profound wisdom traditions of Alchemy, Gnosticism, Kabbalah, Buddhism, and Christianity. Evoking "Christ as the *salvator salvandus* [the saved Savior]," PKD writes of "the savior who must be saved and who is in a certain real sense identical with those he saves."[69]

In PKD's words,

The creator can afford to descend into his own creation. He can afford to shed his memories (of his identity) and his supernatural powers. . . . The creator deliberately plants clues in his irreal creation—clues which he cunningly knows in time (eventually) will restore his memory (anamnesis) of who he is. . . . So he has a fail-safe system built in. No chance he won't eventually remember. Makes himself subject to spurious space, time and world (and death, pain, loss, decay, etc.), but has these disinhibiting clues or stimuli distributed deliberately strategically in time and space. So it is he himself who sends himself the letter which restores his memory (Legend of the Pearl). No fool he![70]

It is as if we, or more accurately, our true identity as the Self (which is whole, never separate from, and connected with the whole) plants alarm clocks in the waking dream. PKD calls this "a perturbation in the reality field."[71] These alarm clocks are set to go off at just the right time, acting as a catalyst to wake us up. In PKD's words, "The megamind is attempting to stimulate us back to being in touch with itself."[72] Once these clues—which can be conceived of as a higher dimension of our being signaling to us—are deciphered, we can discover, as PKD suggests, that we've composed them ourselves. What PKD calls "disinhibiting clues" (what he also calls "Logos triggering agents," and what I call "lucidity stimulators") are like keys that open up the lock encasing our minds so that we can remember who we are and our life's mission: what we are here to do. PKD writes, "Zebra is trying to find—reach—us and make us aware of it—more primarily, it seeks to free us from the BIP, to break the BIP's power over us."[73]

Our classical, materialist mechanistic worldview is, as PKD rightfully points out, "shabby and cracking apart and fading away."[74] PKD writes that there is a "universe lying behind ours, concealed within—yes, actually concealed within ours!"[75] The universe we see conceals and simultaneously reveals the universe lying behind ours. It is PKD's opinion that in order to construct a new worldview to replace the one that is cracking apart, we need to see—to re-cognize—this universe that is concealed within ours. "The world is not merely counterfeit," PKD writes, "there is more: it is counterfeit, but under it lies another world, and it is this other world, this Logos world, which filters or breaks through."[76]

PKD continues, "But in truth, in very truth, this is a shadow universe we see, a reflection in the mirror of another universe behind it, and that other universe can be reached by an individual directly, without the help of any priest."[77] This other universe—a universe that we are not separate from and is not separate from our consciousness—doesn't need an external mediator to be accessed, but can be reached through direct experience. In the allegory of Plato's cave, people looking at shadows reflected on the wall of the cave believed the shadows to be reality itself. In the same way, quantum physics—considered the greatest intellectual achievement of the twentieth century—has discovered that with the physical world we are dealing with a lower-dimensional shadow projection of reality, not reality itself.

I call this other, higher dimensional world that underlies and is concealed within ours (borrowing a term from physics) *the nonlocal field,* which is a field that contains, pervades, and expresses itself through our third-dimensional world (while at the same time not being constrained by the third-dimensional laws of space and time). The nonlocal field connects us with everything. When the nonlocal field, or in PKD's words, *the Logos world,* breaks through consensus reality and reveals itself, we experience synchronicities—which can be thought of as momentary fissures in the fabric of reality that allow for an ephemeral glimpse into the underlying unity of our cosmos.

Synchronicity and the underlying synchronic order are the more fundamental nature of reality and it is our linear-time-based and classically conditioned mindset that act as bars in the BIP, creating an artificial mental overlay that obscures and prevents our noticing the ever-present, atemporal ground of being.

Just like the BIP/artifact/Empire/wetiko will co-opt and subvert any of our attempts at illumining it to feed into and serve its nefarious agenda, God/Christ/Zebra/Urgrund/Savior will use the BIP/artifact/Empire/wetiko's attempts at imprisonment to ultimately serve our freedom. Speaking of the artifact's agenda of "enslavement, deception and spiritual death" PKD writes, "even this is utilized by the Urgrund, which utilizes everything, [this] is a sacred secret."[78] PKD points out that one way of expressing the fundamental dialectic is information vs. anti-information (remember: wetiko is an anti-information virus). To quote PKD, "The Empire, which by suppressing information is therefore in a sense the anti-Christ, is put to work as half of the dialectic; Christ uses everything (as was revealed to me): in its very act of suppressing information, the Empire aids in the building of the soma of the Cosmic Christ (which the Empire does not realize)."[79] This is to say that the Cosmic Christ is, in essence, generated and served by its antithesis (the Antichrist).

Bodhisattvic Madness

Speaking from his own experience, PKD writes, "The only question is, which kind of madness will we choose?. . . . We are, then, *all* mad, but I, uniquely, choose to go mad while facing pain, not mad while denying pain."[80] PKD is delineating two different ways of facing the pain of reality. In his writings he makes it clear that his ("non-flinching") way of facing pain "is not necessarily better" (which is a questionable statement, as in the long run facing our pain is better than avoiding it), it just "hurts more." Avoiding our pain, in PKD's words, "would be evil madness."[81] Liberation comes not from avoiding, glossing over, or repressing painful feelings, but only from experiencing them to the full.

From his writings it is clear that PKD was having the realization that the pain that he—as well as all of us—are feeling is the pain of waking up. The intense pressure of this pain motivates us to seek a solution, which is to say it mobilizes us toward greater consciousness. PKD is professing a point of view that can help us to recontextualize what seems to be meaningless suffering. One of the things that's hardest for human beings to bear are experiences bereft of meaning. If we have a sense of meaning with which to make sense of our pain it become much easier to endure. "The artifact," PKD explains, speaking of and from his own experience, "by inflicting too much pain on me it had, in a certain real sense, awakened me."[82]

In his novel *Valis,* PKD writes, "It is sometimes an appropriate response to reality to go insane." PKD writes, "My insanity, facing an insane world, is, paradoxically, a facing of reality, and this is sane; I refuse to close my eyes and ears."[83] Paradoxically, PKD's form of insanity is the sanest response of all. This is similar to how post-traumatic stress disorder (a form of mental illness), is the sanest response to an insane situation. PKD wonders, "Perhaps if you know you are insane you are not insane." He elaborates, "The distinction between sanity and insanity is narrower than a razor's edge, sharper than a hound's tooth, more agile than a mule deer. It is more elusive than the merest phantom. Perhaps it does not even exist; perhaps it is a phantom."[84]

Never one to shy away from the tough questions, PKD asks, "So, then, in what sense am I insane? I am insane in that I continue to face the truth without the ability to come up with a workable answer. . . . I really do not know anything in terms of the solution; I can only state the problem. No other thinker has ever stated a problem and so miserably failed to solve it in human histories; human thought is, basically, problem-solving, not problem stating."[85] Oftentimes, however, accurately stating the problem and asking the right question is more important than finding the right answer.

I personally don't think PKD is giving himself enough credit. For in fact, it is clear in his writings that he did come up with a workable answer, one that is universal and is common to all wisdom traditions. PKD likened our existential situation to being in a maze, what he refers to as "one colossal and absolute Chinese finger trap." The harder we try to get out, the more trapped we become. This is to say that we are not able to find our way out through ordinary means. Seemingly alive and sentient, the maze has a peculiar nature of shifting as we become aware of it. It is *as if* it is aware of—and responds to—our awareness of it. This is because the maze exists within and is created by our own mind, and thus is aware of the efforts we make to escape from it.

One only escapes from the maze, to quote PKD, "when he decides voluntarily to return (to resubject himself to the power of the maze) for the sake of these others, still in it. That is, you can never leave alone, to leave you must elect to take the others out . . . the ultimate paradox of the maze, its quintessential ingenuity of construction, is that the only real way out is a voluntary way back in (into it and its power), which is the path of the bodhisattva."[86] We would only voluntarily return to help others if we recognize that they are not separate from ourselves, which is to realize that we are all fundamentally interdependent and interconnected aspects of one singular indivisible being. This is the very realization that simultaneously enlivens compassion and dissolves wetiko.

PKD writes, "When you think you are out of the maze—i.e., saved—*you are in fact still in it.*"[87] This brings to mind the insight that if we think we are free of wetiko and it is only "others" who are afflicted with it, this very perspective is, paradoxically, a symptom of having fallen under the spell of wetiko. To quote PKD, "If there is to be happiness it must come in a voluntary relinquishing of self in exchange for aware participation in the destiny of the total one."[88]

In a very real sense, PKD did find the solution to humanity's existential dilemma. He writes, "Compassion's highest power is the only power capable of solving the maze."[89]As he points out, "The true measure of a man is not his intelligence or how high he rises in this freak establishment. No, the true measure of a man is this: how quickly can he respond to the needs of others and how much of himself he can give."

PKD concludes, "If the final paradox of the maze is that the only way you can escape it is voluntarily to go back in (into it), then maybe we are here voluntarily; we came back in."[90] In other words, perhaps we have chosen to incarnate at this very moment in time. Perhaps we have already solved the problem of the maze and simply have to recognize this fact. This is true anamnesis—a loss of forgetfulness—which is a remembering, a re-collection of our dissociated members, as we remember our membership in the greater whole, connected to and one with all that is. "Anamnesis," to quote PKD from a 1976 interview, "was the loss of amnesia. You remembered your origins, and they were from beyond the stars."[91]

PART II

Wetiko in the World and in Our Minds

In this section I am trying to shed light on how the wetiko mind-virus is giving shape to social, political, and economic events in our world. Metastasizing through our body politic like a form of cancer, wetiko is a peculiar form of blindness that doesn't realize it is blind. This mind-virus underlies the processes of addiction and trauma and has its psychological roots in projecting our own shadow outside of ourselves.

7

Are We Humans Terminally Insane or Just Waking Up?

The world today hangs by a thin thread, and that thread is the psyche of man.

C. G. JUNG, *PSYCHOLOGICAL REFLECTIONS*

We are truly living in dark times. More accurately, we are living in times where the darkness is emerging from its hiding place in the shadows and is becoming visible. Have psychopathic qualities ever been more obvious than in our modern-day political situation? It is easy and very seductive to become overwhelmed with pessimism, despair, and depression during these times of darkness, which, sadly, would be to unwittingly feed and collude with the darkness. Our situation is dire but there is no need for pessimism. To quote a popular saying on the French left, "The hour calls for optimism; we'll save pessimism for better times."

How does anyone possibly express in words the state of collective madness that humanity has fallen into at this time in our history? What modern-day humanity is confronted with is a genuine crisis of sanity first and foremost. We are truly at a choice-point of human evolution. The question is: Are we going to continue killing ourselves, or are we going to shed light on what inside of us is killing us? The state of our collective insanity is hard to fathom. As Sir Isaac Newton, one of the greatest scientists of all time, is widely quoted, "I can calculate the motion of heavenly bodies, but I cannot understand the madness of men." It is impossible to wrap our rational minds around the irrational insanity that we are all playing out.

Our madness, however, is not happening in a void. Having incarnated on this planet at this present time, we are born into involuntary servitude within a complex web of interlocking institutions. Many of these were conceived and built before we were born by asleep human beings. These institutions coerce and mandate us to live in unnatural ways contrary to our innate creative impulses. Like sorcerers' apprentices who have unwittingly imprisoned themselves by their own magic, we have constrained and seemingly trapped ourselves within an insane, abusive, and corrupt system of our species' own making. This is forcing us to act in ways that are out of integrity for our soul and are truly crazy-making.

As if in a hypnotic trance, our species is enacting a mass ritual suicide on a global scale, rushing as fast as we can toward our own self-destruction. We are building our own funeral pyre. We are destroying the biospheric life-support systems of the planet as well as attacking the continued viability of continued human life on Earth in so many different ways that it is as if we are determined to make this suicide attempt work. In this we are using a multitude of methods as a perverse insurance policy, in case a couple of them don't do the job.

In trying to find a way to write about this state of affairs, I find myself going "off-planet," imagining what it would look like if some highly evolved enlightened aliens, in their travels throughout the universe, came upon Earth. Observing from a distance, they would naturally see all the various living beings who call planet Earth home as related members of one larger organism—a single ecosystem—who literally depend upon each other for survival. From this vantage point,

I imagine, they would be utterly baffled at why human beings—the seemingly most intelligent species ever to appear on planet Earth—are acting out their destructive impulses. These impulses are being enacted practically without restraint and are executed through a wide variety of methods in every corner of the globe. Contemplating the state of humanity, I imagine these awakened beings wondering, "What in the world has gotten into them?"

I imagine that these illumined aliens would quickly conclude that human beings had become afflicted with some sort of psychological illness, a disease of the mind and soul that has caused us to turn destructively upon ourselves and others. Apparently in a "fallen state," we have lost our way, become disoriented and, in our confusion, become quite deranged. It is as if our collective madness is so overwhelming—and by now so familiar and so normalized—that most of us, its sufferers, have no idea how to even think about it, let alone how to deal with it. Not knowing what to do, many of us inwardly dissociate—which only exacerbates the madness. In our fragmented and disempowered state we go about our lives in a numbed-out, zombie-like trance, making the best of what seems to be a bad situation.

The question naturally arises: How would these enlightened beings conspire with us to help wake us up? We can only imagine. For our part it seems essential that we ask questions such as, What is the nature of this madness? How can we intervene and consciously engage with it so that humanity can get back on the right track?

Seen as a single organism, there is a systemic psycho-spiritual disease (a.k.a. wetiko) that has infected the whole body politic of humanity. At present we are having an acute—and potentially deadly—inflammation of this illness. As with any disease, in order to cure the pathology that afflicts us we must come up with the right diagnosis. Under the present circumstances, it is a healthy response for us to have an appropriate level of alarm. If we aren't "alarmed" at what is happening in our world, we are still sleeping. The multiple crises going on in our world are the cosmic alarm clocks going off in our world, trying to wake us up.

Economy

It's difficult to appreciate how our behavior might appear strange—let alone completely insane—to an impartial observer. But engaging in a "benign onlooker" thought experiment—in this case, through the imagined insights of enlightened aliens—affords us some much-needed perspective. Even from this vantage point, though, the collective madness that humanity is acting out is hard to fathom, as if the inmates are running the asylum.

The first thing these aliens might perceive is a single living organism in crisis. What makes life itself possible is that every cell and organ of a living organism plays a uniquely vital role to the life and health of the greater organism. Each part works together synergistically as an aspect of an integrated and interdependent, whole system. Our planet and its biosphere are a seamlessly interconnected whole system that operates as a macroorganism. And yet, its supposedly most intelligent species has set up a global system for managing its rich diversity of natural resources that would kill a living organism in no time if it were implemented within the individual bodies of any of its members. If the human body was organized and operated in a similar way to the global economy—where certain parts of the system demand disproportionate and ever-increasing shares of the existing resources—the body would die in hardly any time at all.

At the heart of this reality is the fact that the way the global economic system has been crafted primarily serves the interests of the very few. Machine-like, "the system" relentlessly, and increasingly, sucks, drains, and redistributes wealth. The wealth is largely extracted from the majority of the populace—who become increasingly impoverished and practically enslaved—and then given over into the hands of the already inconceivably wealthy. The powers that be use coercive power to not only undermine people's means to make even a subsistence living, but even denies them, on a massive scale, the basic human right to life. This system doesn't just passively allow people to fall below the poverty line. It actively pushes them under, as if poor people are being intentionally "left behind."

These illumined aliens, with their clairvoyant vision, would surely find it revealing that the ones who own the wealth are—like vampires—energetically "feeding" off of the ones who barely have enough to eat. It's as if these enormously wealthy people can never get enough, no matter how much they consume. This indicates that the uber-wealthy, though over their heads in endless material riches, do not have an authentic and direct connection to the source of life itself. They must deep down believe, evidence to the contrary, that they are not living in an abundant universe where everyone can flourish, but reside in a scarcity-based universe of winners and losers.

According to recent figures, the eight richest people on the planet have more wealth than the poorest half of the global population combined, and over time this imbalance is increasingly getting even worse. When I first wrote about this a few years ago, instead of eight the number was sixty-two. When we amplify this dynamic, we are on a trajectory where one day one person might have more wealth than the entire rest of the population. This is globalization at work. One of the most dangerous things in the world is when billions of human beings are being manipulated by the few. This is exactly the situation we're seeing today. Such extremes of inequality are as dangerous to democracy as cancer is to a living being. This is because such wide disparities in the distribution of resources invariably lead to social breakdown and violence, a process that greases the skids toward fascism.

Much of this rising inequality is a direct result of the fact that globalization is the process by which multinational corporations are taking over sovereign governments—of the one hundred largest economies in the world, over half are corporations. It should also be pointed out that this is an out-picturing of how the wetiko bug works within the human psyche. It gradually incorporates and does a "hostile takeover" of increasingly larger parts of the human psyche, compelling it to serve *its* agenda.

These challenging economic times we live in are simultaneously the times of the greatest profits *in all of history* for certain select corporate conglomerates. Those at the top of the economic pyramid then use this ever-increasing gap between the rich and the poor to further game and rig the system in their favor. The United States government, in particular, instead of being a "government of the people, by the people, for the people," has become a plutocracy—a government "of the rich, by the rich, for the rich." It should get our attention that such economic stratification into the have and have-nots has historically always played a crucial role in the collapse of civilizations.

These aliens would recognize that Earth's current way of "doing business" is unsustainable. Instead of creating value and wealth for the good of all, the way business is now done on planet Earth is actually destroying the genuine wealth and health of the whole system. People, communities, and the environment are considered nothing more than collateral damage—all for the benefit of a small minority. If humanity is viewed as a family, abuse of power is being perpetrated within the family system for the simple reason that those in the positions of power can act with total impunity and, in a case of "moral insanity," can—and do—literally get away with murder.

Many of the institutions in our world are embodiments of the formless wetiko virus taking on corporeal—and incorporated—form. As priest and philosopher Ivan Illich said, once a living revelation is institutionalized, what could be the repository for the highest good suffers an inversion. It becomes instead the nesting place for the *mystery of evil*—what Paul (in his second letter to the Thessalonians) calls the *mysterium iniquitatis*—to take root. As Illich points out, what could be the best has a unique potentiality for becoming the worst. This is to say that the greatest good opens the door for its own extinction if not tended carefully.

Being a priest, Illich uses the example of the institutionalized church to make his point, but any institution formed around something of value has the same potential to serve the opposite of its original intentions. The counterfeiting spirit of wetiko, a true imposter, imitates something—in the aforementioned process known as countermimicry. And yet it does so with the intention of distorting the original intention. Any one of us *consciously* bearing witness to the mystery of evil, however, opens the door for the incarnation of the light to further manifest.

For example, the entity of the global economic system itself is a living symbol of wetiko disease "in business." A "real" economy has to do with the production and distribution of goods and services— *generating* wealth for the whole system in the process. The virtual bubble economy that we're living in today is mainly an exercise in which an extremely small percentage of people profit from the manipulation of money and the money system—*draining* real wealth from the whole system in the process. It is as if wetiko has managed to create a simulation of the real economy, replacing the real thing with a copycat version (what I call the "wetikonomy")[1] that has inverted its original purpose. This is a reflection in the outer world of the covert operations of wetiko within our minds.

These benign aliens would find it revealing that such an unnecessarily large percentage of Earth's resources—including humanity's intrinsic ingenuity—instead of being used to care for each other and enrich life, are being used to create more potent and deadly weapons of mass destruction. In other words, a good portion of humanity's divinely inspired genius is being channeled into ever-more efficient ways of murdering each other! Seen as cells in a greater organism, it is as if our species is suffering from an auto-immune disease of the psyche. We are infected with a cancer of the mind that has turned us against each other so that we are literally attacking and destroying ourselves.

We have become conditioned to accept that the astonishing cruelty and destruction that pervades our world is normal. We spend trillions of dollars to sustain a state of endless war against God knows whom. At the same time innumerable of our fellow brothers and sisters are impoverished and dying of starvation every day. These spiritually awake beings would realize that the destruction that humanity is playing out in the world is an unmediated reflection of a serious imbalance—a blindness—deep within the collective human psyche.

Blindness

How strange a situation we find ourselves in. Every spiritual wisdom tradition since time immemorial, in addition to many of the most creative and visionary artists, have been pointing at wetiko. And yet what they are trying to illumine is the very thing that most of us are refusing to look at (which I guess is why they are so insistently pointing at it). There is a peculiar form of blindness that comes into play that prevents us from seeing our blindness. And this specific type of psychic blindness *is* the very thing being pointed at—wetiko.

Our collective psychosis is invisible to us, manifesting itself both in the way we are looking at the world as well as the unspoken ways we have been conditioned—in other words, programmed—to *not* perceive. Wetiko has the power to induce—both individually and en masse—Philip K. Dick's aforementioned "negative hallucination." Instead of seeing what is *not* there, we cannot see what *is* there. This looking away, this "conspiracy of denial" that is endemic to our culture, is a form of blindness, which is simultaneously both the cause and effect of wetiko.

"Our age," Jung writes, "is afflicted with a blindness that has no parallel."[2] Not being able to see what is there, combined with seeing what is not there—such as, for example, thinking that there is an objective universe outside of ourselves*—becomes a toxic brew that makes us doubly blind. Our all-around blindness conveniently absolves us from any sense of responsibility for whatever predicament we find ourselves in. On top of this is the fact that wetiko disables our discernment. Add to the mix how shocking—literally traumatizing—it is to realize that we've been blind; not seeing reality. Due to the painful shattering—and dis-illusioning—nature of the realization of our blindness, there is a disincentive to open our eyes and see. Oftentimes the inertia of staying blind is more comfortable and tranquilizing than becoming awake.

It is an unconscious human tendency to believe comfortable lies rather than to confront uncomfortable truths. When, for example, people want a politician's lies to be true more than they want to know what's true, it's hard to change their mind with facts and help them see the truth. Commenting about people who know that what they believe are lies, Jose Ortega y Gasset writes, "It does not worry him that his 'ideas' are not true, he uses them as trenches for the defense of his existence, as scarecrows to frighten away reality."[3]

Many people would do just about anything to keep themselves from having to deal with the pain of facing reality. There is a magical, primitive tendency in humanity whereby we think that not seeing a danger will somehow remove it. A great number of protective mechanisms within our psyche prevent us from noticing our dark side. In dealing with the problem of evil, we have to become aware of and prevent the unconscious, instinctive reaction that typically happens when we encounter evil, whereby our consciousness becomes diminished and loses its ability for discernment.

On the one hand, we don't see our powerlessness. We think we are in control in a way we are not. If we identify with our ego—with a reference point in time and space—we think we have an agency that simply isn't ours. We are like a kid turning our toy steering

---

*I wrote a book about this—The Quantum Revelation.

wheel affixed to the dashboard of a car, imagining we are steering the car. On the other hand, we are also blind to the incredible intrinsic power that we actually do have to create our experience. We have creative power beyond belief that we don't realize.* Paradoxically, we are blind to both our powerlessness and our powerfulness simultaneously.

Our creative power is getting turned against us to literally hypnotize us into a state of endlessly self-generating blindness upon blindness. Like wizards who don't know our own power, we have a hand (or two) in conjuring up and reinforcing our own blindness each and every moment. We are complicit in the moment by moment refreshing of our blind state, whether we know it or not.

When we've been hoodwinked long enough, we tend to reject any evidence of the fact that we've been bamboozled. This is to say that we then no longer prioritize finding out the truth, which ensures the continuation of our blindness. In addition, in our culture to see things a certain way is rewarded with cash. To unsubscribe from the collectively agreed upon view of things can adversely affect our pocketbooks. On top of everything else, if there's any attraction—or worse yet, addiction—to power, this makes us susceptible to falling into a self-serving blindness that feeds our unconscious dreams of power.

All of these multiple factors conspire to keep us (both happily and unhappily) entrenched in our blindness. It takes real courage to open our eyes and look. There is no other way to heal the blindness from which we are suffering than to actually use our capacity for vision, which has atrophied due to disuse.

Wetiko isn't just a psychic form of blindness. It both actively and passively *induces* blindness in those who are afflicted, as well as—due to its contagious nature—being able to extend itself into the surrounding environment. It does this via people's unconscious

---

*But this power is not ours in the sense that we don't own, possess, or control it. It is a power that is beyond us. This power comes from and is itself the spontaneous creativity of the quantum realm that pervades the whole universe as well as our very being.

reactions to this blindness, creating a dissociative, polarized "field of blindness" that engenders more blindness in the process. Those suffering in this way see their own blindness reflected in others, but don't recognize it as their own. They have become entranced by the projection of their own mind, seeing their own inner condition as if it exists outside of themselves in the external world.

Wetiko does not exist in sole individuals separate from their environment. Being a field phenomenon, wetiko's medium of operation is the nonlocal field of consciousness that pervades everything and then some. This is to say that wetiko doesn't exist in separate individuals for the simple reason that, ultimately speaking, there are no separate individuals. Each of us only exist in relation to each other, each of whom in turn don't exist as isolated, self-existing, independent individuals—no one exists on their own.

Seeing our interrelation to the world in this way is to be connecting with the transpersonal viewpoint of the Self. Seeing through the "trans-personalizing" lens of the Self allows us to not personalize or solidify ourselves as a separate and seemingly concrete individual. Rather, it helps us to open our heart and experience our interconnectedness with all other beings. This opens up the door for love and compassion—our true nature—to flow through us toward the world.

We can only see wetiko when we snap out of the spell of thinking we exist as a separate discrete entity alien to other discrete entities. Thinking we exist as a separate self is a form of blindness that concurrently blinds us, both to wetiko and to seeing—and thereby being—our true selves. Thinking that we are a separate self *is* wetiko (hence wetiko's other name: ME disease). Conceiving of ourselves as a separate self is wetiko's main act.

Hiding in Plain Sight

Wetiko influences not only what we do and don't see, but *how* we see as well. Wetiko hides in the shadows, but it hides in the light too.

It hides in plain sight, both in front of our eyes and behind them, as well as in between. It hides everywhere and nowhere in particular. Wetiko disables our discernment, dumbs us down, blinds us, and propagates itself through the contagious nature of our shared styles of unconsciousness.

Psychology, the study of the human psyche, can be helpful in illuminating wetiko, for psychology is fundamentally concerned with the act of seeing. When an unconscious content is available to be seen and we make the choice to turn away and not to see it, choosing to remain artificially unconscious when the natural flow of events is inviting us to become conscious, we are unknowingly feeding the forces of evil.

Wetiko is a semantic syndrome in that it influences the meanings we place on our experiences. If we interpret our experience literally, for example, taking things at face value, we would be strengthening our bondage to the physical world. We thereby invest in wetiko's hold over us, which would be increasing our blindness. If we recognize the dreamlike nature of life and interpret our experience symbolically, however, our life force becomes channeled so as to get us in touch with the true spirit of our experience. Life itself is a spiritual experience that is inviting our creative participation to begin to heal our literal-minded blindness.

Erich Neumann writes, "Those who saw but failed to act, those who looked away because they did not want to see, those who did not see although they could have seen, and those, too, whose eyes were unable to see—each and every one of these is actually in alliance with evil."[4] In turning a blind eye to evil, we become complicit with the very evil we are refusing to see. To connect with our destiny, we must surmount our preference of living in illusion and our unwillingness to face the darker side of reality. Our looking away—a form of blindness—is itself wetiko in action.

When we fall under wetiko's spell, we become blind to our blindness, literally unaware that we are blind. Having become habituated to our blindness, we are unaware of what it is to be truly seeing, as we have no reference point for comparison. The source of our experience of blindness is not coming from outside, but is to be found within the very mind that is suffering from the blindness. In essence, we are blinding ourselves.

Wetiko's blindness has two distinct but complementary aspects. On the one hand, we are blind to the underlying sickness—wetiko—and the darkness that it casts both within and outside of us. Wetiko blinds us so that we don't see its covert operations in both the world and our minds. In other words, wetiko keeps the dark in the dark, both keeping us in the dark and blinding us to the dark in the process.

On the other hand, wetiko induces in us a blindness such that we don't recognize, and hence, become blind to, the light of our true nature as well. There is a "systemic blindness" in which we have been conditioned to see the divine outside of and other than ourselves, instead of recognizing it within. It is an archetypal conception that the light is right in front of our eyes and we simply don't see it.

Notice the similarity to Christ's famous statement that the kingdom is spread all over earth and people just *don't see it*. Wetiko's blindness is a comprehensive, all-around blindness, in that it obscures us from seeing both the darkness as well as the light, leaving nothing untouched and the most important things completely unseen.

Wetiko induces a blindness on many levels; some of its forms of blindness are quite common. Many of us are familiar, from our own day-to-day lives, of being in a twilight state of "knowing but not knowing." This condition is typical in situations where there is abuse going on in a family system (or a world) that is too shattering to our sense of the way things are to fully see and take in. We are all experiencing this right now on the macro scale by inescapably being participants—whether we know it or not—in the collective body politic gone mad. The evil that is getting played out in our world on a daily basis is so over the top that, practically speaking, it has to be denied to some extent for us to go on with our seemingly normal lives and not go totally out of our minds.

When the darkness of the shadow comes onto the scene, it brings with it an energy that makes us want to look away. If we do turn away from the shadow, what could have been seen is then not cognitively apprehended, contextualized, given meaning, or symbolized within our personal map of reality. Instead, the experienced but not perceived content is held in a borderland between the conscious and the unconscious. This results in a state of inner dissociation between what one part of us knows to be true, but which another part of us can't fully admit to or integrate. To keep this borderland area safely encased, we then develop a need not to know. This further strengthens our blindness. The outcome is that in our looking away we are unwittingly feeding and are complicit in the genesis of wetiko, both within ourselves and in the world at large.

In a perverse inversion of the compartmentalization that is characteristic of the pyramid-like corporate, global power structure (in which people are only given information on a "need to know" basis and are otherwise kept in the dark), wetiko's power structure also works through creating a subconscious "need not to know" system. In this, *not knowing* is incentivized while the natural desire to know is made so difficult as to be practically disabled. In their state of not knowing, people are once again left in the dark. Becoming disempowered, their lack of knowledge prevents them from attaining a proper orientation to the world they live in. Both the "need to know" and "need not to know" models—along with the lack of transparency and the secrecy that is endemic to both systems—feed wetiko.

In a sense, our choosing not to know is to be inwardly lying to ourselves. Lying to ourselves and then convincing ourselves that we are not doing so, is an extreme form of self-deception that is to be (unconsciously) hiding from ourselves. This is to choose to live in what the philosopher Jean Paul Sartre calls "bad faith." The one to whom the lie is told and the one who is telling the lie are one and the same person. This means that deep down, in our role of deceiver, we must know the truth (in order to be hiding it), which is hidden from the part of us that is deceived. One part tells a lie to another part that believes it. This not only splits our consciousness, but renders us incapable of recognizing the truth.

Playing the divine fool and trickster on our very selves, we have fooled ourselves then forgotten we have done so. Once we sufficiently pull the wool over our own eyes like this, however, our consciousness, as philosopher Herbert Marcuse puts it, becomes inured to its own falsity. As if in the throes of an addiction, we then become compulsively driven to sustain the denial and the lie that underlies our blindness. We do this by whatever means necessary, lest we snap out of our self-generated cycle of self-deception and confront the lie that we have been perpetrating on ourselves. Once our denial becomes airtight, however, it continually doubles down on itself without end so as to avoid both the light and the dark. This process creates a safe haven for the wetiko pathogen to work its black magic.

The insidious blindness of wetiko typically grows in small increments composed of seemingly innocent and innocuous decisions that we make on a day-to-day basis. C. S. Lewis writes in *The Screwtape Letters,* "Indeed, the safest road to Hell is the gradual one—the gentle slope, soft underfoot, without sudden turnings, without milestones, without signposts."[5] So often we open the door to wetiko to further lodge itself in us by our internal dialogue. Indulging an addictive, habitual pattern, we think, "This one time won't matter (for I deserve it, I worked hard today) . . . I'll break my habit starting tomorrow." If we stepped out of our blindness and saw where we were headed when we indulge in this way, we would immediately turn around. Yet, there is something inside of us that doesn't want us to see what we are doing.

Strangely, as we see less and less, we typically feel more comfort and greater certainty. There is a built-in paradox to the blindness of wetiko—the person so afflicted makes themselves blind thinking it will make them safe. Paradoxically, though, the powerlessness that results actually puts them in danger. As well, it increases the likelihood of them becoming a danger to others. It is a type of blindness that continually gets in its own way and blocks its own light.

Biblical Mind Blindness

The Bible can be seen to be a self-revelation of the psyche itself. The Bible is continually pointing at wetiko in a myriad of ways. It is replete with references to spiritual blindness: to eyes that do not see, of seeing but not perceiving ("seeing they do not see," Matthew 13:13 [NIV]), to people who are blind but don't know they're blind. The Bible talks about "the darkness" blinding people's eyes (1 John 2:11 [NIV]). Gnosticism likewise refers to a darkness that anesthetizes our natural intelligence and spreads the cancer of mind blindness. The Bible makes clear that Satan (the biblical personification of wetiko), "who is the god of this world, has blinded the minds . . . to keep them from seeing the light" (2 Corinthians 4:3–4 [NLT]).

Many biblical references make clear that this blindness isn't a physical blindness, but a blinding of the mind. To again quote the Bible, "But if your eye is bad, your whole body will be full of darkness" (Matthew 6:23 [ESV]). In other words, if we suffer from mind blindness, we will be taken over by—and embody—darkness.

The Bible is continually correlating eyes that are blind to darkness and darker powers. However, if our eyes are good, healthy, and sound (and "single," i.e., in phase with our true being), in the words of the Bible, our whole body will be "filled with light." Christ is conceived of coming into the world in order to help blind people "recover" their sight, to open people's eyes. Our situation is of blind people who do not know that their eyes could see. It is clear that the Bible is using eyes as a symbol of consciousness, of being awake. The Bible explicitly describes eyes that are open and able to see as being blessed. We as a species are desperately in need of vision. To quote

Proverbs 29:18 (KJV), "Where there is no vision the people perish."

The Bible also connects spiritual blindness with a closed heart ("He has blinded their eyes, and hardened their heart; that they should not see with their eyes, nor understand with their heart," John 12:40 [KJV]).* There are numerous biblical references to people in this state of blindness being as if intoxicated, in prison, in a stupor, or in a state of forgetfulness and being asleep. (For example, "I found them all drunk . . . they are blind in their hearts and do not see," Gospel of Thomas—Logion 28.) It should get our attention that the Bible itself is pointing at an equivalency between the act of seeing and having an open heart that is filled with love and compassion. Seeing in its fullest sense requires feeling, a function typically associated with the heart. In blinding us, wetiko gives us a cold unfeeling heart, turning it to stone, draining our psychic lifeblood and warmth in the process.

Certain biblical references make clear that it is not solely some external force that is blinding us. For example, in the Bible it says, "For the hearts of these people are hardened, and their ears cannot hear, and they have closed their eyes so their eyes cannot see" (Acts 28:27 [NLT]). Even though the powers of darkness have a hand in making— and keeping—us blind, we are unconsciously participating in the creation of our own blindness (having closed our own eyes), which is an expression that the source of our blindness is to be found within us.

The Bible points out that even though "the light has come into the world," that people "loved the darkness" (John 3:19–21 [NKJV]). When people are still unconsciously identified with (and taken over by) darkness, the light is experienced as a threat, as it will expose their own evil. This impulse to avoid the light is the very workings of evil within them. This is illumining our own complicity in keeping the darkness alive (within ourselves, and hence, out in the world). The devil, after all, shuns the light like the plague.

---

*The Qur'an, the holy book of Islam, says exactly the same thing.

As if inverted mirror images of each other, wetiko has a shadow equivalence to Christ's "kingdom of God." To quote Christ, "God's kingdom cometh not with observation [it's not something you can see]. Nor shall people say, Lo here! or, lo there! For behold, the kingdom of God is within you" (Luke 17:20–21 [NKJV]).

Christ also points out that the kingdom is spread all over the Earth, that it is everywhere, but people just don't see it. The mysterious kingdom (which is "not of this world") can't be seen and yet paradoxically it's omnipresent, already here and staring us in the face. The kingdom can't be seen objectively (as an object outside of ourselves) that's located here or there (found in the third dimension of space-time); it is to be found within and everywhere (there is no place where it is not). In the same way wetiko can't be reified as an object (though we can momentarily objectify it to help us to get a handle on it). Yet it is to be found, just like the kingdom, both deep within us as well as appearing all around us. It should get our attention when such transcendental realities as Christ's kingdom and wetiko share the same articulation. At the very least, it suggests that these two opposites might be related, that the highest light and deepest darkness have something—maybe everything—to do with each other.

Seeing

Because wetiko is a psychic blindness, the cure for wetiko starts with seeing it—both seeing how it operates in the world and also tracking how it covertly operates within our own being. There is nothing in the way that is stopping us from seeing wetiko—other than our own mind. Those childhood puzzles in magazines where we have to find the faces hidden in the picture come to mind—we don't have to add or create the faces, we simply have to change our focus and recognize them. They are literally staring us in the face. Wetiko, however, modifies and influences what we pay attention to and how we do so.

In the medical model we describe the various pathogens that

make us sick as cancers, bacilli, parasites, plagues, and viruses, for instance. Due to the materialistic culture we live in, we are attached to the idea that for something to have "reality" it must be made of a material substance capable of being measured. The implication of this perspective is that if something is not physical or quantifiable it is not real. This limiting materialist bias disables our capacity to see wetiko. This misbegotten belief, by giving cover to wetiko, is itself none other than wetiko in action. Though immaterial, wetiko is as real as we are.

I struggle with how to get our blindness across to people who are suffering from the very blindness that I am pointing at in a way that will be understood. From their standpoint, which has its own self-justifying internal logic, they are seeing clearly. Anyone reflecting anything different is deemed a threat or dismissed as crazy. It is of no use to preach the light to people whose eyes are blind, rather, it is much more productive to teach the art of seeing. In a sense all of my work is to try to teach people—including most especially myself—the art of seeing: to simply open our eyes and look. I am continually amazed at how many people have eyes but do not see. Sadly, we have become accustomed to our blindness.

If I am trying to convince people that they're blind, I'm wasting my energy. For if what I am saying is *true*—that the people I'm talking to are blind—they are, by definition, in no position to see that they are blind. In my misguided attempt to show them the light, the one who is truly blind is myself, which is to say that I am then contributing to the blindness in the field. I am then complicit in an ever-deepening all-around blindness that pervades everything and then some.

We start becoming acquainted with our soul when we overcome our tendency to look away from all the things we do not wish to see in ourselves. In overcoming our reticence to see unflattering truths about ourselves and courageously shedding the light of our consciousness onto the darker corners of our psyche, we initiate an inner process of transformation. Re-connecting with our soul in this way is the very thing that creates the circumstance that begins to dispell wetiko, which is, after all, a disease of the soul.

We can conceive of the soul as being a perspective rather than a substance. It is an attitude that informs our way of seeing rather than being something seen. In our modern-day encounter with the problem of evil, the issue is the long-forgotten soul of humanity.

Part of the blindness is focusing on the external and marginalizing—and becoming blind to—the world within ourselves. Materialistic science embodies this tendency to focus on the world outside of us at the expense of our soul. In our one-sided focus on the things of a (two-sided) world, we prevent ourselves from recognizing the synchronistic correlation between the inner and the outer worlds. This results in disconnecting from our true self as well, which is to be found within. We too easily become absorbed and entranced—spellbound—by the forms of the waking dream. We then dissociate from and forget who we actually are as we play out—and give living form to—our unconscious in the world theater by the choices we make (paradoxically, as a way to *potentially* remember who we are). As Jung famously writes in a letter, "Who looks outside dreams;* who looks inside awakens."[6]

Distracting Us Outside of Ourselves

Wetiko covertly works through the projective tendencies of the mind to distract us, keeping our attention directed outside of ourselves. It thereby obstructs us from finding and utilizing the immense light of intrinsic awareness within. This light of awareness would, if accessed, dispell wetiko's curse in no time, rendering it impotent.

And yet, humanity is always seeking outside ourselves. We remain unaware that no matter how many possessions we acquire,

*Please note that Jung is using the word *dreams* in a nonlucid sense.

no matter how great our outer success, we remain inwardly the same. Our inner being incessantly raises its claim, a cry that can't be satis-fied by any outer acquisitions. Humanity's insatiability is, according to Jung, "the sickness of Western man, and he will not rest until he has infected the whole world with his own greedy restlessness."[7] Our all-consuming hunger, a hunger that can never be filled, is our main export to the rest of the world and is none other than wetiko.

The "Buddha" means one who has woken up to the dreamlike nature of reality. The Buddha was a true physician of the soul who discovered the cure for the sickness of humanity, a sickness that was at the very root of human suffering. He realized in his enlighten-ment that the solution to the human predicament could never be found externally, but had to be discovered within the very nature of our own mind. By shedding light on the darkness within him he cured his own blindness, which was a reflection, an instantiation of humanity's blindness. It is the very light of consciousness itself seeing the malady within our mind that provides the radiant healing force that begins to undermine and dissolve the disease.

We are being invited to heal our own blindness. We are being asked to open our eyes and look. We are being prompted—make that demanded—to shed the light of our consciousness onto the darkness within ourselves. Shedding light on our own darkness magically empowers us to be able to effectively deal with the evil in the outside world.

Wetiko, however, can easily trick and deceive us by materializing itself in, as, and through the medium of the outside world, which we then assume—as if entranced—is distinct from our psyche. Once the ever-increasing sociopolitical insanity plays itself out on the world stage, for example, we have all the proof we need that the conflict is outside of ourselves. The psyche has then become exteriorized, as an internal psychic conflict takes place by way of projection (get-ting *dreamed up*) in the outside world in living (and dying) flesh and blood. In addition to and as a result of disconnecting from ourselves and the true source of our power within, we are then unable to engage with the real power lines that actively underlie and inform what is manifesting in our world. In so doing, we give away our intrinsic power to affect real change, both in ourselves and in the world at large. The sponsor of the whole project(ion), the wetiko bug remains behind the scenes, invisible and unnoticed.

When our awareness becomes too fascinated on external situations, it can block the way to accessing the wellspring of unconditioned, immediate, and unmediated inner experience. Again, we typically think that the source of our problems is to be found in the outside world, and that the fundamental solution is through political or social change. In this we are wrongly hoping and assuming that this would solve the much deeper problem of our inner dissociation. As long as the underlying source of the dissociation within the psyche is untouched, however, over time a variant of the previously existing political and social conditions arise, which bring the same ills back again in an altered form.

While *collective* external events could potentially activate and unleash the demons of the unconscious, the sole resolution lies within the individual. An aberration of the psyche, wetiko cannot be ultimately healed by merely bringing about external reforms (although such reforms are welcome and needed). In other words, wetiko can't be legislated out of existence. It must be dealt with where it originates—within the human psyche of each individual—what Jung refers to as "that individual unit on whom a whole world depends."[8]

Everything begins with the individual, who is the real carrier of life. The great events that determine world history ultimately spring from the life of the individual. In reality only a change in the individual can catalyze a transformation and renewal in the spirit of the collective. A complete spiritual renewal is needed, and we are the vessels through which this process happens.

It is the most sensitive individuals who are inwardly affected by the greater collective problem. They are the ones who are called to respond and contribute to its solution by confronting it in their own lives by wrestling with it within themselves. And yet, one individual by themselves is not enough to really change things in the collective. We are social creatures who exist in community and ultimately speaking, do not exist separately from each other, but are interdependent. The question then becomes, How does one individual's realization become transmitted to the collective in a way that makes a difference?

We live in a thoroughly quantum universe, which is to say that our universe is not made up of separate parts, but is one interconnected and interdependent, whole system. This means that when any of us has a realization, it immediately registers throughout the whole universe. Because an individual's shadow is invariably bound up with the collective shadow, when any one of us metabolizes a bit of the darkness within us that gets triggered by the darkness of the world, a fragment of the collective evil is simultaneously digested and decontaminated throughout space and time.

Clinging

To fall prey to wetiko (ME disease) is to mistakenly identify with a fictitious identity, a false and limited version of ourselves. At the heart of wetiko is our identification with and subsequent grasping onto this illusory "me." This is a seemingly separate, independent self that doesn't actually exist in the way we think it does. Clinging onto this false sense of self becomes a self-perpetuating addictive process with a life of its own. Our life force then gets continually invested in protecting, defending, and maintaining an illusion. Identifying with a self-constructed illusion while being blind to its illusory nature as well as its origin within ourselves is a recipe for both madness and disaster.

Reciprocally co-arising with the subjectively convincing and self-validating feeling of a separate "I" is the feeling of "mine," the sense that this "I" can possess and own things. Modern humanity is, in Walt Whitman's phrase, "demented with the mania of owning things." We insanely devote so much of our time and energy—our precious human life—in trying to obtain material goods that we really don't need and that bring no real benefit to us. Speaking of the white man, Sitting Bull said, "The love of possession is a disease in them."[9] This love of possessing things to fill a void that can never be filled is wetiko disease in a nutshell.

There is a terrible spiritual famine in our world. Savaged by the ferocity of their unending hunger, people who are sufficiently infected by the wetiko virus, like the hungry ghosts of Buddhist cosmology, have become possessed by an insatiable craving that can never be filled. Not in possession of their true selves, they try to possess something outside of themselves to both escape from and fill the void within—the result is a futile and never-ending grasping. As Berdyaev would say, they are condemned to "the bad infinity of insatiable longing."[10] Just like an addiction can never be satiated and an illusion can never be satisfied, attempting to secure a self that by its very nature is illusory is doomed to failure. The modern disease of acquisitiveness has spread like wildfire, crossing over from the material to the spiritual realm (through the ever-prevalent "spiritual materialism").

At the collective level, this perverse inner process is mirrored in the outer world by the consumer society in which we live. This is a culture that continually fans the flames of never-ending and mostly unnecessary desires, conditioning us to always want *more.* Our shared collective sickness is to be infected with, in Jung's words, "the leprosy of desirousness."[11] As if starving, we are in an endless feeding frenzy, trying to fill a bottomless spiritual void. We endlessly consume things while deriving little true nourishment for our souls.

Our cavalier, cruel treatment of our brother and sister animals is wetiko—their incarceration and murder in factory farms, slaughterhouses, recreational hunting, as well as the poisoning of their sea homes and coral reefs as collateral for our lifestyle. We regard other life-forms, their niches too, as objects to be possessed, resources to be used, and products to be consumed. We do not "see" them at all, so we do not recognize ourselves—we have become the cannibals, ogres, and demons of our own myths and fairy tales.

Jung comments, "What is behind all this desirousness? A thirsting for the eternal, which as you see can never be satisfied with the best because it is 'Hades' in whose honour the desirous 'go mad and rave.'"[12] Instead of connecting with the eternal, we try to satisfy our thirst for the sacred in a profane and perverse way that lands us up in hell, a place where our desire will never be fulfilled. This ultimately is a cause, as well as an expression of—and results in—wetiko madness.

The Medicine Within

Wetiko is a collectively "dreamed-up" phenomena in which we are all ultimately implicated. This means that—at least in theory if not in practice—we have the capacity to dream it differently. In other words, because we've created wetiko, we can un-create it.

Our unconscious process of dreaming up wetiko in all its full-blown destructiveness is the way we are teaching ourselves how to *not* destroy ourselves. We evidently haven't yet learned this, or we wouldn't be destroying ourselves. Implicit in this logic is that there is a lesson *encoded*—in need of being *decoded*—within the very acting out of our insanity that we evidently could not have learned any other way. If we recognize what is being revealed to us through the acting out of our insanity, we can snap out of our self-induced hypnotic spell and choose to stop our insane behavior in which we are killing ourselves—what a radical idea! We can then invest our creativity and resources in building the world we want to live in, or so I imagine. It is important to realize that this is within the realm of the possible, and as such, demands the engagement of our imagination to get on board. If we are not imagining this, why not?

The fact that we wouldn't have realized how to not destroy ourselves without wetiko's arrival on the scene is to say that the seeming curse of wetiko actually has a blessing secretly hidden within it. This is analogous to the underlying structure of trauma, which, it should be pointed out, is fueled by wetiko. Similar to someone under the thrall of wetiko, our attempts to heal our trauma are typically the very actions that create more of the very trauma from which we are trying to heal. Like wetiko, trauma is a quantum phenomenon that contains superposed within it both illness and cure.

The traumatized soul continually, compulsively re-creates the trauma (through what is called the "repetition compulsion"), which is the very symptom and pathology of trauma. And yet, encoded within this unconscious re-enactment of the trauma is its own potential resolution. The compulsive repeating of the trauma is not only pathological but is at the same time an attempt at re-membering; putting our disparate and dissociated members (parts) back together. In other words, we are unconsciously reconstituting the trauma in order to give ourselves the opportunity to re-experience it differently so as to assimilate it, thereby liberating ourselves from it. From this more expanded vantage point, the endless repetition of the traumatized behavior is orchestrated from behind the scenes by the Self, whose interest is nothing other than for us to re-establish the wholeness intrinsic to our nature.

Native American oral tradition observes, "The medicine is already within the pain and suffering. You just have to look deeply and quietly. Then you realize it has been there the whole time." It is an archetypal idea that the spirit of healing is hidden within the illness. There is a fundamental relationship between symptoms and healing, as if the symptomology of an illness is at the same time a natural attempt at healing. This is because the symptoms contain within themselves the signature of—and the doorway into—the underlying unresolved unconscious issue that is at the root of the illness.

In order to see wetiko, it can be very helpful to objectify—give shape and form to—and then name our demons. Wetiko has, ultimately speaking, no independent intrinsic identity or existence separate from our own consciousness. Nevertheless, it can be helpful to view wetiko *as if* it's a living, conscious entity with a distinct purpose. Though not ultimately objectively existing outside of ourselves, we *subjectively experience* wetiko *as if* it is an entity other than ourselves. Naming the disease helps to restore our relationship to the energy of the sickness. Seen as a conscious being, wetiko can be seen to be teaching us something, potentially bringing us back to a deeper wholeness that was unattainable before the disease's emergence.

From this point of view, instead of being seen as an obscuration to our wholeness, wetiko can be realized to be a doorway into and disguised expression of the very wholeness it seems to be obscuring. Recognizing this creates the space for wetiko to reveal its heretofore hidden positive side. This is another example that hidden within one of the opposites is the seed of the other.

It is as if through the instrument of wetiko, a higher intelligence is revealing to us the wholeness of our totality through our darker side. This darkness is revealing light by contrast to itself. We can potentially recognize that the evil we see playing out in the world is a reflection of our own darkness. As we do so, we notice that, paradoxically, with our increase in consciousness, the good and positive features within us come to light more, too. Seeing the darkness within us serves as a reference point to help us more consciously experience and connect with our light.

As we more and more recognize the correlation between the outer world with what is going on deep within our soul, the enlightened aliens, who have been signaling to us the dreamlike nature of our situation by synchronistically arranging events in the world to reflect back what's going on deep within us, hide behind the scenes, laughing.

8

A Cancer of the Soul

In these uncertain, crazy, polarizing, and scary times we live in, one thing I think everyone can agree on is this: If viewed as a single macro-organism, humanity has fallen ill. There is a sickness, a type of madness—wetiko—existing deep within the soul of humanity that for many years—perhaps even from the beginning of our appearance on this planet—has been brewing in the cauldron of the collective unconscious and is infecting the global body politic. The obvious question: What is the real nature of this deeper sickness that is pulsing through the veins of humanity?

In contemplating this very question, philosopher John McMurtry, author of the brilliant book *The Cancer Stage of Capitalism,* refers to the "Great Sickness" that pervades our modern-day capitalist system as having all of the hallmark qualities of cancer. He is pointing out that the diagnosis of cancer precisely maps onto a macroanalysis of our current body politic. McMurtry's diagnosis supports, complements, and precisely describes wetiko disease—which has been called the greatest epidemic sickness known to humanity. Wetiko can be likened to a form of mind-cancer that has been metastasizing through the global politic for as long as anyone can remember.

Professor McMurtry is taking a whole systems approach as he analyzes what is happening in our world from a metaperspective. In this he is pointing at the deeper fundamental process that connects, informs, and gives shape to the events that are happening in our world today. Without taking sides, in the following pages I will simply be contemplating the nature of this deeper pathology. I will leave it to the reader to recognize how this might help make sense of the seemingly ever-amplifying contagious madness that is playing out in our current political and psycho-social landscape.

The Public Sector

In diagnosing our global disorder as being cancerous, Professor McMurtry is not speaking metaphorically, but rather is offering an explanatory model. What other disease exponentially metastasizes so as to increasingly capture the resources of the life-host it is invading so as to foster its own proliferation? It is as if cancer, a disease of the human body, has changed channels and is propagating itself in society as a whole.

If humanity and the biosphere are seen as a single organism, this carcinogenic *seeming-entity** continually degrades our social and natural life-support systems. It depredates the productive life of societies at every level. It itself is devoid of any productive life function, other than creating ever more wealth for the already unthinkably wealthy in a process that McMurtry describes as "incarnate evil."

The cancer sponsors a never-ending attack on the public sector, which it is continually trying to defund, dismantle, and privatize. Public treasuries are hollowed out on all levels, which generates the direct blood flow to the cancer system. The carcinogenic agent pollutes, strips, depletes, and despoils the Earth ever more deeply

---

*I choose my words carefully. I write *seeming-entity* because although we subjectively experience the carcinogenic agent *as if* it is an actual entity outside of us, ultimately (as I point out in my book *Dispelling Wetiko*), it has no independent, objective existence separate from our own consciousness. The mystery is that although this entity doesn't objectively exist, it can potentially destroy our species. This points to the incredible, untapped creative (or destructive) power that exists within our unconscious psyche.

and widely at every level, all the while accepting no accountability. It expropriates and rechannels revenues that should be devoted to people's life sustenance to feed its own private financial circuits at every turn. The cancer infiltrates and subjugates increasing amounts of public resources to take control of and privatize them so as to ultimately monetize them, in other words, turn them into money. And one thing we can be sure about: Most of us—in modern parlance, the 99 percent—are not the ones seeing this money.

Public money is continually injected to sustain the carcinogenic circuits. These are funds that are not only taken out of citizens' lives—now and in the future—but are being myopically extracted from the lives of those yet to be born. As the system collapses, the financial liabilities are transferred to taxpayers to hold as their debts or toxic assets. In an inversion that is typical of abusive family systems, blame is placed on the victims, who are accused of, for example, "spending beyond their means." The more the cancer invades the host and metastasizes, the more public money is allocated to its growth. This only furthers the ever-deepening downward spiral, feeding what McMurtry calls the "publicly subsidized transnational oligopoly."

To put it simply: The entire carcinogenic process is financed by and paid for by the public. To the extent that we are unaware of the cancer and think and act as if everything is normal, we are buying into and colluding with its growth. Recognizing our complicity is a crucial step in accessing our power in order to stop being part of the problem and start becoming part of the solution.

Immune System

The key to succumbing to cancer is the immune system's failure to recognize and respond to the rogue code of what is attacking it. McMurtry writes that "The ultimate problem is that the disorder has not been recognized for what it is."[1] Without recognizing what McMurtry also calls "the great disorder," we remain lost in its symptoms, distracted from the root of the problem, as the pathology endlessly deepens. When what attacks an organism is not recognized, a malignant systems mutation has occurred. We know that a civilization is breaking down when it excludes recognition of and social response to its own degenerate trends.

The carcinogenic invasive agent avoids detection, as it suppresses, disables, and eventually hijacks the immune system of the host. The disease incessantly attacks all systems and institutions that can successfully respond to and overcome it. When the social immune system recognizes the invasive element and corrective feedback loops begin to respond to the disorder, they are invariably targeted, invaded, and diverted to instead feed the pathology, deepening the global disorder rather than resolving it. The fact that the immune system is compromised to the point that the disease isn't even recognized tells us that one of the fundamental channels of the cancer's operations is the human psyche.

Official policies keep feeding the metastasizing cancer, even while the system is in the process of bankrupting (i.e., killing) itself. This is the telltale sign of life-host capture by the carcinogen. In a financial and corporate global coup d'etat, the ravenous appetite of the financial juggernaut (Matt Taibbi's infamous and aptly named "vampire squid") continually subjugates governments and the rule of law to protect itself from any accountability. Individuals, political movements, and institutions can unwittingly become mere instruments of these deeper, more powerful forces. Like a body's immune system being co-opted and turned into an accomplice of the very disease that it is supposed to monitor, instead of governments and courts reigning in the carcinogenic invader, many of them have become its primary enforcers, subsumed by and operating as active agents of the disease. Though taken over to a large degree, our judiciary (in the U.S.) is still slightly independent, which is one of the few remaining safeguards left against full takeover by the cancer.

Cancer usually exists long before it is diagnosed; the current outbreak has been a long time coming. This carcinogenic process can take many years to bypass the organism's (be it a person or a society's) immune system. The cancer spreads not only without any regulators to stop it, but with continual deregulation of the rules that could potentially stop it. It makes sure to remove all existing defenses against it. This points to the fact that the forces behind deregulation—be they Big Oil, the financial industry, the military-industrial complex, or any number of other private interests—are all facets of the disease.

The Greatest Epidemic Sickness Known to Humanity

In a psychic coup d'état, the wetiko bug can usurp and supplant a person, who becomes its puppet and marionette. Once the wetiko virus becomes sufficiently entrenched within the psyche, the prime directive coordinating a person's behavior comes from the disease, as it is now the one in the driver's seat. It commandeers and colonizes the psyche—centralizing power and control in the process. As it does so, wetiko eventually incorporates a seemingly autonomous regime that establishes a brutal hegemony over the healthy parts of the personality. It becomes a parasitic autocracy within the greater body politic of the psyche. Once it gains a sufficient sovereignty, wetiko forms something like a totalitarian regime—what Jung calls "a shadow-government of the ego"[2]—within the psyche that then *dictates* to the ego.

The internal landscape of the wetiko-ized psyche is mirrored in the external world through the "shadow government" (by whatever name we call it)—with its ever-increasing centralization of power and control—that has taken over our seeming democracy. Both within our psyche and in our alleged democracy, we are allowed our "freedom," but only so long as it doesn't threaten the sovereignty and dominance of the archonic ruling power.

The more I study McMurtry's work, the more it has become clear that what he is referring to as the great sickness is a full-bodied, incarnate manifestation of wetiko disease acting itself out in the social, political, and economic realms. In other words, McMurtry's cancer is an expression and creation of a wetiko-ized collective psyche writ large on the world stage. The corruption and malfeasance endemic to the global financial system is one of the main vectors through which the wetiko virus is going pandemic in our world.

What is happening politically in our world is a manifestation of an unconscious psychological problem in millions of individuals—because people are unaware of this is what makes it so dangerous. If we don't realize that our current world crisis has its roots within, and is an externalized expression of the *human psyche* then, as if having a recurring dream, we are fated—doomed—to unconsciously, compulsively, and repeatedly re-create endless destruction in an increasingly amplified form. Our waking dream will then be destined to continue with ever-alarming intensity, becoming a nightmare until we receive its message and take appropriate action.

The Lie

This cancer of the psyche can be likened to, as previously mentioned, an "anti-information virus," in that not only does it block the reception of information, it substitutes false information for the real thing. Whether it's fake news, alternative facts, mainstream media propaganda, or our government's lies, it is getting increasingly harder in this Orwellian world of ours to discern what is in fact actually happening. A lie, if skillfully wielded, can be a more potent weapon than the bare and simple truth. For a lie can be molded to match and resonate with people's unmet psychological needs and their will to believe; the truth is less malleable. One of the most important abilities in confronting the forces of evil is to cultivate an unwavering discernment between truth and deception.

Our culture doesn't supply the adequate vocabulary necessary to describe, express, and thereby expose evil. Speaking of evil, de Rougemont writes, "It is emptying all words of their meaning, turning them inside out and reading them backwards, according to the custom of the black mass. It is inverting and ruining from within the very criteria of truth."[3] The sacred mass is about communion with the Divine. De Rougemont points out that, as if in a black mass, the darker forces co-opt words, the medium of communication, to have the opposite of their desired effect. This works to cut us off from our communion with the Divine, as well as separate and divide us from each other.

The rules of narrative do not apply well to describing ruptures of the moral order or radical breaks in the shared social consensus. Experiences of evil destroy the threads of narrative the moment we try to weave them. Evil seems to have a magic power that ensures that whatever words we do use will be psychic flypaper for projections and endless misunderstandings. It is as if evil has dumbed us down—we no longer seem able to talk intelligently about the subject. Evil's inability to be articulated is one of the things that allows it to get away with the murder it does.

From the spiritual point of view, lies are a murder at the level of soul. According to Buddhism, lying in one form or another—be they big or small lies of commission or omission, to oneself or others—is the root of all evil.* And as former dissident Vaclav Havel who eventually became the first president of the Czech Republic famously said, "Lying can never save us from another lie." In other words, once we step on the path of lying, lies feed on and off of themselves, weaving a never-ending web of evil and deceit in which we become caught.

---

*As the Buddhist Maharatnakuta Sutra says, "A liar lies to himself as well as to the gods. Lying is the origin of all evils." (Maharatnakuta Sutra 27, Bodhisattva's Surata's Discourse)

One way we are all geniuses is our incredible ability to deceive ourselves. When someone lies and falls into the perverse situation of believing their own lies, they can develop a type of charisma such that their lies, through psychic contagion, become very convincing to others. Nothing has such a convincing effect on others as a lie that we believe ourselves.

In order to navigate a world filled with lies and be able to differentiate lies from truth, we need to shed light on and dismantle all of the different ways we lie to ourselves. Fyodor Dostoyevsky, in the classic *The Brothers Karamazov,* writes, "Above all, don't lie to yourself. The man who lies to himself and listens to his own lie comes to such a pass that he cannot distinguish the truth within him, or around him, and so loses all respect for himself and for others. And having no respect he ceases to love."[4] When we lie to ourselves we lose the ability to discern truth from falsehood, both within ourselves and out in the world. This ultimately leads to a lack of self-esteem and even self-loathing, which results in losing our ability to truly love—the greatest tragedy of all.

Evil has been likened to a disease. From this point of view, when people in positions of power intentionally spread untruth and lies, it is spreading the disease of evil. This is because it disables people's capacity to distinguish what is true and what is not. When the power of the word ("In the beginning was the Word, and the Word was with God, and the Word was God"—John 1:1 [NKJV]), which is the power of the logos itself, is severed from its connection with the Divine, the shadow side of the word comes to the fore. The word itself can become an infernal slogan of propaganda—a logo—that is capable of any and every kind of deception. Instead of its original intent to unite humanity, the word in the wrong hands and minds can polarize people and pit them against each other, creating endless destruction.

The danger is when the pathological liar is in a position of power and is taken seriously by the wider public. Like Faust, the liar is bound to make a pact with the devil and slip off the straight path. In this, he takes those who are enabling him, as well as anyone under his sphere of influence, into the abyss too. To quote clairvoyant and spiritual teacher Rudolf Steiner, "This effect of 'untruth as truth' contains an enormous force of evil. And this force of evil is made full use of in various ways and by different interests."[5] The result of the systemic institutionalization of lies and untruths is a disabling of our discernment and a deadening of awareness, which serves the forces of darkness. Lying has become an accepted means of discourse among us the likes of which has never been known. Lying has gone pandemic in our world.

McMurtry writes, "This collapse of the distinction between truth and fiction opens the way to totalitarian occupation of consciousness."[6] Instead of occupying national territories, the cancer and its tumors occupy and feed off of public consciousness. Hannah Arendt pointed out long ago that *the big lie* (what McMurtry refers to as the *omnipervasive lie*)—takes hold when the line between fact and fiction becomes overridden as a matter of normalized routine. This "big lie" is why totalitarian regimes depend on keeping knowledge and free public discourse silenced and repressed. As soon as enough people start seeing through the lies, however, recognize what is in fact actually happening, and become able to creatively transmit their lucidity to others, the collective spell is broken.

If we turn a blind eye toward the lying that has become normalized all around us, in our looking away we have become unwittingly complicit in the evil of the lie. In his Nobel Prize acceptance speech, Russian novelist and philosopher Aleksandr Solzhenitsyn said, "Anyone who has once taken up the WORD can never again evade it; a writer is not the detached judge of his compatriots and contemporaries, he is an accomplice to all the evil committed in his native land or by his countrymen."[7] In other words, once we, as someone with open eyes, see evil, it is our moral and spiritual responsibility to speak out against it.

Solzhenitsyn continues,

> But let us not forget that violence does not live alone and is
> not capable of living alone: it is necessarily interwoven with
> falsehood. Between them lies the most intimate, the deepest
> of natural bonds. Violence finds its only refuge in falsehood,
> falsehood its only support in violence. Any man who has
> once acclaimed violence as his METHOD must inexorably
> choose falsehood as his PRINCIPLE . . . [Violence] does not
> always, not necessarily, openly throttle the throat, more often
> it demands from its subjects only an oath of allegiance to false-
> hood, only complicity in falsehood.[8]

Lying is a form of violence in that it subtly coerces and interferes
with people's decision-making process—and hence, their free will.
This potentially causes them to make choices that they would not
have made if they had more truthful information. Lying and violence
feed off of and into each other. They are two sides of the same (counterfeit) coin. For a lie to gain currency all that's needed is for enough
people who see through the lie to lack the moral courage to call it
out. Silence in the presence of a lie is to be in collusion with evil.

Solzhenitsyn points out, "And the simple step of a simple courageous man is not to partake in falsehood, not to support false actions!
Let THAT enter the world, let it even reign in the world—but not
with [only] my help. But writers and artists can achieve more: they
can CONQUER FALSEHOOD! In the struggle with falsehood art
always did win and it always does win! Openly, irrefutably for everyone! Falsehood can hold out against much in this world, but not
against art . . . . ONE WORD OF TRUTH SHALL OUTWEIGH
THE WHOLE WORLD."[9] A totalitarian state depends upon people being cowed into lying to themselves, which invariably results in
the subjects being inauthentic, out of integrity with their very souls
(and hence, disconnected from their true creative power). In his

masterpiece *The Gulag Archipelago,* Solzhenitsyn writes, "One man who stopped lying could bring down a tyranny."[10]

Totalitarian Psychosis

Jung, though obviously not familiar with either McMurtry's great sickness or with the notion of wetiko disease, referred to a similar idea by using the phrase *totalitarian psychosis,* which he described in terms of being a deadly germ or infection. "Fascism," to quote Henry A. Wallace, vice-president under Franklin Delano Roosevelt, "is a worldwide disease."[11] There is something about the disease metaphor that so precisely maps onto what is actually happening in our world that indicates that it is not mere metaphor. Mainstream media has even been using the term *the authoritarianism virus* to point to the trend toward totalitarianism that is happening both in the United States and around the world.

Unless we are lost in denial, it is clear that we are living at a time in which totalitarian forces have reemerged onto the political landscape. Fascism is the result of corporate economic power merging with the political power of the state—a corporate tyranny. It takes willful blindness to not see the parallels between the rise of fascism and our current political nightmare. This marriage of wealth and power can transform a democracy into a totalitarian state in no time.

Arendt warns us in her classic study *The Origins of Totalitarianism,* that totalitarianism is "an ever-present danger" grounded in "the endless process of capital and power accumulation."[12] This is a process, it is worth noting, very much at work in today's world. She was keenly aware that a culture of fear, the dismantling of civil and political rights, the projection of the shadow onto another, the ongoing militarization of society, the centralization of power and control, the relentless attacks on labor, an obsession with national security, human rights abuses, the emergence of a police state, ever-increasing surveillance, a deeply rooted racism, and the attempts by demagogues to undermine education so as to dumb down the citizenry—all happening in America today—are undeniable characteristics of a society trending toward fascism.

Wannabe fascists invariably use the same playbook—playing on people's fear of different groups while appealing to and stoking people's prejudice so as to create division and polarization. To quote Wallace, "It is no coincidence that the growth of modern tyrants has in every case been heralded by the growth of prejudice."[13] And that prejudice will be exploited by those in power to divide the populace so as to further extort even more wealth and power.

Wallace writes, "Still another danger is represented by those who, paying lip service to democracy and the common welfare, in their insatiable greed for money and the power which money gives, do not hesitate surreptitiously to evade the laws designed to safeguard the public."[14] It should be noted that one of the chief features of wetiko is insatiable greed. It always wants more. Wallace chillingly comments, "They claim to be super-patriots, but they would destroy every liberty guaranteed by the Constitution. They demand free enterprise, but are the spokesmen for monopoly and vested interest. Their final objective, toward which all their deceit is directed, is to capture political power so that using the power of the State and the power of the market simultaneously they may keep the common man in eternal subjection."[15] Keep in mind these aren't the words of a paranoid conspiracy theorist, but of the vice-president of the United States who had real insight into how the levers of power work.

Fascism's "greatest threat to the United States," Wallace continues, will manifest "within the United States itself."[16] In other words, the greatest threat to our democracy will not come from external forces, but from forces originating within our own body politic. This is a reflection of how the greatest threat from wetiko is not from outside, but arises within ourselves.

Janus-like, fascism has two faces—one overtly mean, cruel, and sadistic, the other hidden behind a mask of benevolence ("soft totalitarianism"). This second friendlier face presents itself to a captive public as a force for good and moral renewal, promising protection against enemies real and imagined. But this friendly face is truly a velvet glove hiding an iron fist. Let someone speak truth to power to find out that the benevolent persona is a mere marketing campaign, an illusion and cover for what's really going on behind the scenes. Its true intentions are revealed not by its words but by its actions. As we see today, we are being stripped of power, shorn of our most cherished rights, and systematically impoverished.

Wallace continues, stating that the American fascist's method "is to poison the channels of public information."[17] The whole purpose of totalitarian-style propaganda is to destroy our ability to perceive reality. In a nation trending toward totalitarianism, it gets harder and harder to discern truth from fiction. Wallace concludes, "With a fascist the problem is never how best to present the truth to the public but how best to use the news to deceive the public into giving the fascist and his group more money or more power. . . . The American fascists are most easily recognized by their deliberate perversion of truth and fact."[18] I will leave it to the reader to connect the dots as to how this same dynamic applies to our current political situation.

Money

The built-in, unquestioned highest value of our capitalist system is money-value, as compared to and distinct from life-value. This is to say our economic system values profits over everything else, including living beings and the environment. Spiritual leaders of today have pointed out that in the prevailing ethos of our current system, money is more important than people. Our value system is a modern-day version of worshipping the golden calf. The number one priority of our system is to maximize profits so as to make as much money for the stockholders as possible, regardless of the social and environmental costs. As market participants, the underlying philosophy is that there is no need to be concerned with the consequences of our actions. Turning money into more money becomes an end in itself (a pathology that Aristotle called *chremastatik*), justified by any means possible. Having no meta-awareness of the long-term and whole systems implications of their rapacious actions is an expression of having no felt sense of being interconnected with the whole of life.

It is not only the insatiable greed for more and more money that is the sole problem—the disease has taken over the very creation and design of money itself. The fiat money that is produced in a wetikoized system is not backed by real assets but is made out of thin air, created by decree of an elite cabal of people who control the levers of power of the system. The nature of this "funny money" has been denatured, generated in a way that is decoupled from the material world. This funny money is not connected to anything of real value other than itself (which has no intrinsic value). This money can then be continually generated in practically unlimited amounts and can be used to buy up real assets so as to exert pathological control over the world and its inhabitants.

From the point of view of the disease, it makes no difference if the cost of doing business is wrecking economies, making people homeless, dispossessing formerly sovereign governments, or destroying the environment—these are all considered just collateral damage. This sounds like the textbook definition of psychopathy: deliberate and willful disregard of the impact of one's actions on the well-being of others. According to the prevailing logic of our current psychopathic capitalist system, it is a rational imperative to maximize one's private interests in money-value terms at the expense of everything else.

The corollary to this is that it is seen as good and justifiable to override all public protections and regulations that are barriers to optimizing one's profits. From this perspective, for example, environmentalism obstructs business, as it gets in the way of corporations' "opportunity to profit." The insanity of the underlying logic that drives this system is revealed when we extrapolate what would—and is—happening over time when the system is followed to its logical conclusion. A quote attributed to Alanis Obomsawin comes to mind: "When the last tree is cut, the last fish is caught, the last river is polluted; when to breathe the air is sickening, you will realize, too late, that wealth is not in bank accounts and that you can't eat money." As the gospel says, "For what shall it profit a man, if he shall gain the whole world, and lose his own soul?" (Mark 8:36 [KJV]).

Cancer grows at the expense of the life-host, which over time experiences more of its life-supporting systems melting down. This carcinogenic entity requires ever-more resources from the life-host in order to continue spreading. The metaprogram of the cancer system is structured to relentlessly consume and despoil without end. The cancer always wants *more,* which is to say it becomes addicted to ever-increasing growth and never-ending consumption as an end in itself. People under the thrall of the disease exhibit the mindset of a junkie, always thinking of where they are going to get their next fix.

The disease insidiously eats sovereign governments and the life of societies from within. De-regulated corporate globalization is eating the world alive. Native tribes have a prophecy about the cannibalistic spirit of wetiko (sometimes called wendigo, one of its other names). During the Native American protests at Standing Rock, they envisioned the oil pipeline as being like a black snake, which represented the spirit of wetiko/wendigo devouring Mother Earth.

Any living network that becomes sufficiently complex will become self-organizing and will demonstrate an instinct to perpetuate itself, to survive. In practical terms, this means that the pathological system will distribute its resources to support behavior that mirrors its own internal logic and thus ensures its survival. Unless the illness is accurately diagnosed and properly treated, the prognosis is always fatal. This is to say that we are called to confront the destructive effects of our relationship to money and power.

In creating an economic system that *has* to keep making more money, at a certain point the system develops a seeming autonomy such that it has no choice. It is *forced* to do as programmed, developing an artificial intelligence all its own. We have then unwittingly tapped into suprahuman forces—the Bible's "powers and principalities"—which, as if developing a life of their own, can become, Golem-like, an irremediable Frankenstein monster out of control. We—even those lucky among us who seem to be the winners (the 1 percent)—become captives of this force that's got us all by the throats. The ones who are the most amply compensated by this pathological system are, except in the rarest of cases, the least free of all. The rulers and financiers of this system are themselves mere puppets in the clutches of the self-perpetuating momentum of the pathological system that is being informed by far more powerful archetypal forces.

"Genocide," McMurtry writes, is the "leading edge of the cancer system."[19] He points out that the disease "is mass-homicidal by its nature."[20] A living death sentence, it is a self-devouring operating system, ultimately destroying everything within its sphere of influence, including itself. Turning a blind eye toward the cancer is how we become complicit in our own genocide. It should be noted that there is no counterevidence to the cancer diagnosis, only denial, blindness, and ignorance.

Like a parasite that tricks its host, the cancer has to deceive the host organism into believing that the intruder is actually a healthy part of the body politic that needs to be supported, nurtured, and taken care of. In a reversal of meaning that creates a cognitive dissonance within our minds, the cancerously fueled invasions are always portrayed to be in the name of freedom and against terror.

In our war against terrorism, however, human rights are overridden, social programs stripped, taxes on the rich reduced, financial fraud multiplied, endless wars of aggression to capture resources for private corporations are increased, and ever-more terrorists are created. Our air, soil, forests, and water cumulatively degrade, the climate destabilizes, more species become extinct by the day, economic inequality increases, the forces of fascism grow, and every life system on the planet is pushed into further decline. All of this with no evident action other than more "war against the terrorists." War itself *is* terrorism—the idea that terrorism can be defeated by more terrorism is a pathological concept that is itself a reflection of the very madness for which it benightedly claims to be the cure. In any case, the war on terror spreads like a plague.

This systemic devastation of all life-support systems on our planet is without historical precedent. This is to say that the cancer that McMurtry is pointing at presents a greater danger than any prior threat to the human species in all of our history. This is not an exaggeration. Nor is it overly alarmist, paranoid, or conspiratorial, but rather, is an open-eyed, sober assessment of our current situation, supported by ever-increasing data.

The Machine

In describing "the wetiko nature of modern capitalism" in their article "Seeing Wetiko," Ladha and Kirk refer to modern-day capitalism and its "insatiable hunger for finite resources; its disregard for the pain of groups and cultures it consumes; its belief in consumption as savior; its overriding obsession with its own material growth; and its viral spread across the surface of the planet. It is wholly accurate to describe neoliberal capitalism as cannibalizing life on this planet. It is not the only truth—capitalism has also facilitated an explosion of human life and ingenuity—but when taken as a whole, capitalism is certainly eating through the life force of this planet in service of its own growth."[21]

It is noteworthy that we live in a "consumer society." It is the perfect laboratory in which wetiko may propagate itself. Notice how the image of eating—*consuming* (which has a double meaning: to eat and to buy)—is continually used in describing this malady. Wetiko can be envisioned as being a psychic eating disorder informed by a ravenous hunger that can never be satiated. Interestingly, a term that describes the devil is *the devourer,* which also has connotations of eating (as well as destroying).

It is important to differentiate the lifeblood of society from the cancerous money-sequencing that consumes it. The unchallenged *predatory capitalism* practiced in our world today—which it should be pointed out, is a perversion of genuine capitalism*—is a modern form of the vampire, feeding on the soul of living humanity through the rigged money and economic system. The archetypal figure of the vampire sinking its fangs into the greater body politic of living humanity, unless stopped, always leads to fascism. This is to say that wetiko, which is fundamentally vampiric in nature, is related to fascism—hence, Jung's term *totalitarian psychosis.*

This cancerous, vampiric entity is neither alive nor dead, but exists in an inorganic intermediate state between existence and nonexistence. It is death taking living form so as to take life. It is not human in nature, but rather, is machine-like—inhuman—in its operations. People sufficiently taken over—possessed—become efficient zombie-like automatons, cogs in the wheel of "the machine," programmed to unthinkingly serve the state. They become conditioned to react to certain stimuli like a compulsory reflex; no creativity, freethinking, or self-reflection is programmed in. Such people don't control their own minds, and thus are not free to initiate their own actions (having abdicated their free will). They can only do what their programming tells them to do.

This predatory form of capitalism is also known as the *megamachine,* a term coined by sociologist Lewis Mumford more than fifty years ago. This inhuman economic machine, fueled by endless money-making, is potentially enlisting us—through our complicity—

---

*From this point of view in the modern world we have never had real capitalism, only a distorted—and perverted—form.

into the destruction of everything we love. Amoral and indifferent to life, this vampiric carcinogenic entity has no soul or conscience. Individually, a conscience corrupted and sickened by wetiko has a vested and vital interest in not getting over its sickness. Instead it develops a perverse self-perpetuating autonomy so as to keep itself in business. A conscience so sickened cannot allow itself to consciously feel guilt or shame even though this is what is at the bottom of its perverse condition; it is propelled by a single imperative—it seeks only to replicate itself.

It is noteworthy that the system's response to the disease is a call for "more growth," which demands ever-more public resources to feed the very pathological dynamic that is animating the disease in the first place. To quote McMurtry, "The programme is insane to the extent that it seeks always to resolve the problems it causes by more pervasive implementation of the economic policies that generate them."[22] This sounds like trauma and/or addiction, wherein our reaction to the disturbance creates more of the very trauma to which we are reacting in a self-generated feedback loop. McMurtry's point should be highlighted—the underlying program that structures how we do business with each other is *insane*. This also is reminiscent of a mind taken over by wetiko. In this scenario, we double down on the very behavior that is killing us in reaction to our self-destructive behavior, a process that inevitably leads to our demise.

The Great Delusion

The cancer's modes of advance operate like a subtle and brilliant military tactician. When one route of its resource-hijacking invasion is blocked, like a multiheaded hydra, it opportunistically switches to an alternative one. Societies so invaded lay pillaged as if subjugated and held captive by a foreign occupying army. To extend the military metaphor even further, people or countries who don't buy into the cancerous system run the risk of being coerced into compliance by overwhelming force.

In societies where the disease is deeply entrenched, individuals have fewer and fewer rights relative to multinational corporations and their investors, which ironically—and horrifically—are now recognized as "persons" under the law. And yet, these corporate entities actually have *suprapersonal* rights, employing teams of lawyers backed by nearly limitless wealth set to overrun all real persons. This is to say that only the rights of the supranational "investors" are protected. To the extent that governments are infected by the disease, they are typically only concerned with reassuring financial markets and foreign investors at the expense of everything—and everyone—else.

Many analyses have recognized that something is undeniably amiss in our world, but it is rare to see an analysis that searches for the root cause and source of the problem. McMurtry writes that no analysis "connects the degenerate trends across ecological, social and organic life-support systems, nor defines the underlying disorder driving them."[23] A second-order meta-understanding of the underlying disease is lacking. If the pathways of metastases are seen at all, it is in isolation without a connective whole systems diagnosis. For example, "planetary ecological crisis, growing inequality, greed of the 1 percent," are all important aspects of the underlying disorder, but few analyses connect the dots back to the underlying source, which is to be found within the human psyche.

Speaking about "the underlying common cause of the world's greatest cause of disease and death," McMurtry writes that it "remains blinkered out."[24] It is as if the disease itself sponsors a taboo against recognizing, thinking, or talking about it. Just like Philip K. Dick wrote, the disease occludes us in such a way that our occlusion becomes habitual and self-perpetuating, the result being that we can't even tell we are occluded. Psychologically speaking, this is one of the most invisible experiences we can have.

Over time the systemic disorder becomes normalized (even

praiseworthy), and considered to be just the way things are. The life-blind logic of the reigning economic model remains undecoded. The inner logic is presupposed and thus not reflected upon or identified. A system contaminated by the disease loses the ability to recognize its own disordered state, a blindness that continually feeds the disease's genesis.

The disorder's ill-logic, to quote McMurtry "is a closed and unfalsifiable belief system" steeped in magical thinking, what he refers to as "an infallibilist circle of meaning."[25] People bound by the disease will be unwittingly conditioned to attack, with group-mind certitude, whatever exposes their self-hypnotic delusion. In fact, McMurtry sometimes refers to this disease as "the great delusion."[26] Self-referential in nature, the ruling principle of the cancer system is "life-blind"—it can't think itself through, which is to say that it is blind to its life-destroying consequences. As this mind-lock spreads, a collective psychic epidemic such as we see today is the result—what McMurtry calls "a kind of collective delirium in which the mind is submerged as in a dream."[27] In captivating the mind into a closed, self-limiting, and insular form of thinking, the disorder cultivates an inability to even *imagine* how things could be different. It dispels any remaining faith that real positive systemic change is even possible. The disease cannot correct itself; it needs outside intervention. This is where we come in.

Human T-Cells

In describing the impact that this systemic cancer is having on us, words such as *insanity, psychosis, delusion, denial, deception, blindness, unawareness, lack of recognition, belief systems steeped in magical thinking, distortion of our perceptions, programming, negative hallucinations, anti-information viruses, brainwashing,* and *hypnotic spells* are often used. The one thing that all of these phrases have in common is that they all point to processes that are taking place in consciousness itself. This is the source and fundamental arena in and through which the great sickness covertly operates. This is to say that the cancer cannot simply be legislated out of existence by the stroke of a lawmaker's pen. It needs to be dealt with at its source, which is the human psyche.

The mind-cancer is demanding that we recognize it, or we will perish. Recognizing the cancer is the crucial first step that opens up the door for potentially healing the disease. Merely recognizing the disease that is threatening us isn't enough, however. We have to activate our collective immune system's response in the world. Seeing without action is a partial and incomplete response. These two avenues—recognizing the cancer (an inner process) and taking action (an outer process)—are not separate, but rather, are complementary and necessary aspects of a whole systems response.*

To extend the cancer metaphor one step further, once we recognize the threat that the disease poses, our realization deputizes us to become active agents of the collective immune system's response. When a living body is invaded by cancer it sends out "killer T-cells" that isolate, surround, and dismantle the pathogen. As if stepping into a role that evolution has been preparing us for from time immemorial, we are being asked to become living human T-cells—antipsychotic agents—to combat the spreading psychosis that is ravaging the greater body politic of humanity. As anticancer T-cells, we can come together so as to create the necessary external structures to contain the carcinogen, keeping it from going rogue, and going out of control. Connecting with each other through our shared lucidity, we can collaboratively help each other to stabilize and deepen our mutual awakening. How this would look in our collective body politic as we wake up together we can only imagine.

---

*I call this sacred form of activism "spiritually informed political activism."

The Quantum Nature of Reality

Placing this inquiry into a scientific context, quantum physics has revealed that every event in the physical world has at bottom an immaterial source that is synergistically entangled with our psyches.* According to quantum physics, our decisions and choices as conscious observers are crucial to how our world unfolds and manifests. As Max Planck, the founder of quantum physics, said, "I regard consciousness as fundamental. I regard matter as derivative from consciousness. We cannot get behind consciousness. Everything that we talk about, everything that we regard as existing, postulates consciousness."[28] And as the Nobel Prize-winning physicist Erwin Schrödinger stated, "Consciousness cannot be accounted for in physical terms. For consciousness is absolutely fundamental. It cannot be accounted for in terms of anything else."[29]

Part of seeing how the cancer operates in the outside world is to recognize that this seemingly external cancer is coextensive with and reflective of unconscious shadow dynamics that are operating deep within our own psyches.

Psychologically speaking, when we don't recognize and consciously relate to manifestations of the unconscious psyche, we are unwittingly ensuring that these contents will shape our destiny and constellate negatively. In other words, it will get acted out externally in destructive ways. It is *as if* we as a species have collectively dreamed up our unconscious process into full-bodied materialization on the world stage so as to—in true quantum style, *potentially*—awaken us to the part of ourselves that has been in the dark.

The cancer is a revelation of something within us. The cancer is *not* an independently existing, objective entity that is attacking us from outside of ourselves (however convincingly this seems to be

---

*I have recently written a book about this, titled *The Quantum Revelation: A Radical Synthesis of Science and Spirituality.*

the case). To think this way (a thought-form inspired by the cancer), is to cultivate fear and a sense of victimization, which simply feeds the disease. Our feeling victimized carries with it a (false) belief that we are not participating in the genesis of the cancer. Not separate from us one iota, the cancer is an expression of an unknown part of ourselves that is announcing itself to us in projected form via our psyche's influence and connection to the outside world.

Quantum physics has discovered that the physical world—what physicists used to think of as the "real" world—is in actuality a lower-level projection of a higher dimensional reality. Just as in the parable of Plato's cave, if we don't recognize the deeper process that is informing all of the myriad crises in our world, we will have mistaken the shadows on the wall for the substance itself. We will fail to notice the more fundamental reality—in our case, the human psyche out of which the cancer has arisen—that is casting the shadows in the first place. We will then be dealing with mere symptoms instead of the deeper cause.

When we look at human history, we only see the surface of things. What is really happening, the source of what is informing and giving shape to events in our world, eludes the scholarly eye of the historian. The true historical event lies deeply buried, hidden within the psyche of humanity. When we look beneath what is happening on the surface and trace back what events in our world are an expression of, we can see the deeper disorder that is embodying itself through multiple channels in our world. *All of this is inseparable from our own psyche.* This realization is itself an expansion of consciousness, which is the very quantum up-leveling that creates the causes and conditions for the cancer to begin to heal.

To quote McMurtry, "Once the blinkers of the reigning paradigm are shed [and we see the cancer], the bars of the invisible prison fall."[30] This is to say that when we recognize the cancer, the stage is set for the disease to start dissolving back into its empty nature—*as if* it never actually existed in the first place. We can then potentially discover our true nature, which we have never been separate from for a single moment. The purity of our true nature—who we actually are—has always been with us and has never been imprisoned, tainted, or diseased. Once we realize this, our life-force energy that was continually getting unconsciously sucked into feeding the cancerous black hole can then start to be recirculated into nourishing the creative spirit within us. This will enable us to create a world more in alignment with our true nature as interconnected beings who depend upon each other for our well-being.

Once this realization occurs, the cancer shows its other—and hidden—face. Because we would not have woken up without the cancer's *help,* it can be recognized to be the very necessary catalyst for the evolution of our species. Concealed within the seeming poison of the cancer is the needed ingredient that spurs the dynamics of our individual and collective individuation. The cancer is sufficiently dangerous that it is able to confront us with the stark choice: evolve or die.

How amazing: The very cancer that is potentially killing us is teaching us how to heal it. And as an added bonus, it's waking us up in the process.

9

Duped by
the Beast of War

The country I live in, the United States of America, already involved in multiple wars—some overt, others covert—always seems to be threatening to attack another sovereign nation. When I first wrote these words, we were on the verge of attacking Syria, then it became North Korea, then Iran. Who knows who we will be thinking of invading when you are reading this. The whole thing is totally insane; our government's reliance on military solutions, what has been called its "war psychosis," is pathological,* a form of mental illness.† Similar to the insane logic that transpired during the Inquisition to "save souls," there is an intrinsic illogic in waging war to establish peace. Though war is represented as a show of our strength, it is actually revealing the opposite—war shows our weakness, particularly morally.

President Jimmy Carter recently (April 2019) called the United

---

*A distinction needs to be made. I am not talking about wars in which one country rightfully defends itself from outright aggression from another or in the case of fighting fascism (an example would be the Allies fighting Nazi Germany in World War II). The wars in Iraq, Afghanistan, and (possibly) Syria do not fit this category.
†From the ruling elite's point of view, they are just trying to accomplish hegemonic geopolitical objectives and are willing to sacrifice as many innocent people as necessary in order to accomplish their morally depraved goal. Their moral deficiency in having no compunction in doing so is where the mental illness lies.

States "the most warlike nation in the history of the world."[1] Over time, more and more of the funding for the State Department and its diplomacy are being cut, while concurrently more money is being fed into the ever-increasing war machine. Well over half of our discretionary spending is feeding the war machine. Our country spends considerably more on the military than any other country in the world. (In fact, it spends more than the next nine countries with the biggest military budgets combined.) And yet, investing in something like eliminating poverty (via "the war on poverty") is said to be too expensive. In other words, spending to maintain the underlying ideology of separation knows no limits, but investment that acknowledges and strengthens our intrinsic connectedness is seen as an unimportant extravagance.

Our inverted, upside-down values are not something new. Dr. Martin Luther King, in his iconic Riverside Church address in 1967, noted the collapse of the country's antipoverty efforts: "Then came the buildup in Vietnam, and I watched this program broken and eviscerated as if it were some idle political plaything of a society gone mad on war. And I knew that America would never invest the necessary funds or energies in rehabilitation of its poor so long as adventures like Vietnam continued to draw men and skills and money like some demonic, destructive suction tube."

This vampiric suction tube extends itself through the generations as it actively drains and engorges itself on the life force of living—and dying—humanity.

Our country doesn't seem to know how to imagine solutions outside the paradigm of war. The fact that we, as a species, are investing our creative genius to conjure up an endless war that is unceasingly draining us of our most precious resources is complete and utter madness. Our society has truly "gone mad on war."

We should be clear—war is an epidemic of madness. Most wars are pointless, creating hell on Earth, with no benefit to our national interests—or anyone else's either—except for the war profiteers.

Throughout human history, war is the most violent and destructive activity in which we human beings have been engaged. It is an irrational phenomenon that can't be stopped or controlled with rational arguments, for its source is the shared unconscious of humanity.

One of the greatest and most challenging problems facing us today is that our reason alone is no longer sufficient to meet our problems. Once *mass psychology* (what Jung refers to as "a dangerous germ") prevails and fear and emotion reach a certain pitch, the possibility of reason having any effect ceases. Once mass psychology gains enough momentum, a collective possession results that can quickly turn into a psychic epidemic. This psychic epidemic is none other than what is meant by the word *wetiko*.

Our overly intellectual and rationalistic attitude is a sickness. Our overly rationalistic worldview—what Berdyaev refers to as our "rationalistic madness" (*folie raisonnante*) and what Jung refers to as "rationalistic hubris"—has torn our consciousness from its transcendent roots, disabling our ability to respond to numinous symbols and ideas. Oftentimes, behind much over-rationalism is the quest for control. Interestingly, one of the deeper processes going on in the global body politic is the attempt to centralize power and control. We are desperately in need of the illumination of a holy and whole-making spirit, a spirit beyond our accepted reason, logic, intellect, and our habituated, conditioned way of thinking.

Jung described a timeless archetypal force, Wotan, that became activated and infested Germany in the 1930s and 1940s as Nazism. The energy of Wotan—the ancient God of storm and frenzy—could seize and possess people (individually or collectively), inspiring a state of collective fury and transpersonal mania. The archetypal energy of Wotan is an unconscious factor that exists in latent form within the human psyche. Once it becomes catalyzed, it can influence people to fall under its spell and become its instruments. In this sense it is related to how wetiko manifests as a collective psychosis. For once Wotan/wetiko is enlivened, it seizes everything in its path and uproots and overthrows everything that is not firmly rooted. This same force expresses itself today in different forms of corruption, criminality, genocide, dispossession, systemic inequality, war, and the ravaging of natural and emotional worlds. It leads to narco-states, warlords, nonspiritual jihads, and inhospitable worlds that would typically stretch the limits of our imagination except for the fact that it's manifesting as our present reality.

What are all of our cultural achievements worth? What have we really accomplished, being that we are living in a collectively self-created nightmare? When we ask who or what has caused our current nightmare, the answer is none other than the seemingly well-intentioned human spirit. This spirit does everything under the sun to avoid reflecting upon its own state of darkness. We are compulsively driven to do—as if something is "riding" us—what we are all fleeing from in terror. This self-destructive process, wherein we are unwittingly participating in creating the very thing we don't want, is an expression of the traumatized soul of humanity. It not only has the fingerprints of wetiko all over it—it *is* wetiko. In taking a hostile stance toward the darker forces, or trying to escape from them, they come after us—be it outside in the world or within our own minds.

War is a psychic disaster whose origin is to be found within the unconscious psyche of humanity. This is to say that wars are always the result of psychic forces. Most people are more than happy to try to understand the dynamic of war with a smorgasbord of political and economic theories that marginalize or ignore completely the primary role that the psyche plays in creating war. Once there exists enough evidence in outer events to support these theories, it becomes nearly impossible to convince anyone that the source of the disaster is to be found within the human psyche. "The totalitarian psychosis," Jung writes, is "forcing us to pay attention to the psyche and our abysmal unconsciousness of it."[2]

Concerning the creation of war, the things that have the greatest impact are the *imponderabilia,* the invisible and seemingly insubstantial things that we are not able to weigh that pertain to the nature of the psyche. This is a contrary view to the scientific materialist perspective that says that something is real only if it can be physically measured. These unseen immaterial psychic elements are fundamentally continuous and coextensive with our world, interpenetrating it so fully so as to coexist along with it. In some sense we exist within this unseen world, which is revealing itself through the physical world.

Blood Rites

Author Barbara Ehrenreich, in her book *Blood Rites: Origins and History of the Passions of War,* writes, "However and wherever war begins, it persists, it spreads, it propagates itself through time and across space with the terrifying tenacity of a beast attached to the neck of living prey. This is not an idly chosen figure of speech. War spreads and perpetuates itself through a dynamic that often seems independent of human will. It has, as we like to say of things we do not fully understand, 'a life of its own.'"[3]

When I first read Ehrenreich's words, I immediately thought of wetiko. Originating within the psyche, wetiko similarly develops an apparently autonomous and independent life and will of its own. The more I studied Ehrenreich's work, the more I realized that the beast of war is a virulent incarnation of the wetiko bug writ large. The title of her book—*Blood Rites*—connotes the primitive, ritualistic, ceremonial aspect of the act of war, as if something deep within the collective unconscious of humanity is re-enacting itself on the stage of the world theater.

In war our species has created a Frankenstein monster that is running amok. It is wreaking untold havoc all over the planet, as we are swept up in its inexorable momentum, unable to escape from the hell of our own making. It is as if the powers that be, the people who have their hands on the levers of power, have become war addicts whose addictive go-to behavior is to make war—as if war is their drug of choice. This is like someone in the throes of the addictive cycle who, in thirsting to get their next fix, is unwittingly caught by and creating the very Frankenstein monster of the addiction that is killing them.

The late theoretical physicist Stephen Hawking warned in 2014 that artificial intelligence, now being deployed by the military, could become so autonomous—practically a new self-replicating form of life—that it could take off on its own, go rogue, and potentially start a nuclear war by itself. Whether this is merely Hawking's imagination or a possible reality, this vision reflects how the process of wetiko works by taking on a seeming life of its own.

An out-of-control robotic golem, the war machine develops a seeming autonomy that (just like the wetiko virus) generates its own self-perpetuating momentum; war is simultaneously its own cause and effect. War begets nothing but war. "War," in Jung's words, is "a being in itself."[4] War is the ultimate feedback loop: We define ourselves by defining our enemy, who we then try to kill, who now has no choice but to see us as the enemy and subsequently tries to kill us back. This confirms our notion that "the others" are indeed an enemy deserving to be killed, ad infinitum.

This spiral of violence can easily become an endlessly self-generating feedback loop that iterates itself on different scales. This can be seen in modern industrial society in which institutional violence evokes a violent response. This in turn is met with violent repression. The result? Again, this simply feeds the same warring pattern to endlessly repeat itself in amplified form without ever addressing or resolving the underlying problem.[5]

Seen as a cultural trait, war has evolved in the way that it has simply because it is advantageous to and profits from itself. In a self-perpetuating vicious and violent cycle of infinite regress, the only defense against war is war itself. Thus war metastasizes and spreads, steamrolling all peaceful solutions under its relentless, circular, and self-justifying logic. A force of nature unlocked, once the dogs of war are unleashed and Pandora's box of war is opened, there is no coaxing the genie back into the bottle. As we see in the world today in the war against terror, the battlefield has no boundaries. It is to be found everywhere, not just in every corner of the planet, but in outer space and cyberspace, as well as inside of our own minds.

In mathematical studies looking at the outbreaks of wars and national decisions to participate in wars, there are, according to social scientists, strong indications of epidemicity. War spreads in patterns identical to those of disease outbreaks. War is a living flesh and blood example of how human societies can fall prey to systems of behavior that are entirely of our own creation, which can sweep up and devour all involved. This is reminiscent of the legendary resurrected tiger that devours the magician who restored it to life out of its skeletal bones. In war we have fallen prey to the power of our own misguided magic. Jung writes, "More than one sorcerer's apprentice has been drowned in the waters called up by himself."[6]

Failure of Imagination

The first principle of psychological method is that any phenomenon to be understood must be sympathetically imagined. No syndrome can be truly dislodged from its cursed condition until we first move imagination into its heart. Due to its traumatizing nature, many of us don't even know how to think about war. Interestingly, Robert McNamara, Secretary of Defense during much of the Vietnam War, reflecting upon its horrors, writes, "We can now understand these catastrophes for what they were: essentially the products of a failure of imagination." The same phrase—*failure of imagination*—was used during the Bush administration as an excuse for why they weren't prepared for the 9/11 attacks. If war escapes the reach of our imagination, it will dictate, enforce, and establish dominion over all of us, both in our imagination and in our concrete lives. First and foremost an act of an impoverished imagination, war enlists our own imagination to become an agent of negation and destruction.

In modern times, the majority of people apparently find the most decisive and captivating manifestations of power to be in that which destroys, rather than that which creates. This is an expression of the condition of our collective subconscious, which is filled to the brim with un-integrated trauma. The imagination of a people as a whole must be conscripted and reshaped in order to prepare a reluctant citizenry for war. War, and the weapons of collective death that are its accessories, are the products of the greatest creative power operating within the human spirit—the human imagination. And human imagination, it must be added, is capable of getting rid of them. Since our species has invented war, we can also create and manifest peace instead. An impaired imagination, however, unable to even imagine peace, is simultaneously a cause and effect of the proliferation of war. While on one level the war we are involved in uses such things as bombs, the real war is a war on consciousness, which is nothing other than a war on the imagination itself. A debilitated imagination fundamentally weakens humanity, making it easier prey to be manipulated by a predatory elite that profits from war.

Being that the phenomenon of war seems autonomous, I find myself imagining: What if we viewed war *as if* it was a living entity that did have a life and will of its own? In war, it is as if some transhuman/antihuman monstrosity has insinuated itself into the human scene across multiple generations. This warmongering entity is an impersonal, diabolical energy that by all evidence seems to have possessed our species to do its bidding, making all of us its "reps." Our rush to war is a march of folly, as we unconsciously goose-step on the wheel of endless samsaric suffering that we ourselves are creating.

As if in the throes of an addiction, we are seemingly entrapped in the beast of war's iron grip, blindly compelled to become war's instruments of proliferation. The creature of war feeds into and off of the regressed, animal-like part of ourselves, as if it returns us to the state of consciousness of a pea-brained dinosaur. Psychic epidemics like war can only take place when there is a collective lowering of the state of consciousness, an *abaissement du niveau mental*.* Steeped in the fog of war, we become like sleepwalkers in a dream, lemmings headed for the sea.

Besides the dehumanization that is necessary for war to take place, war also contains and potentially catalyzes the polar opposite response in its participants. It is capable of bringing out the most heroic, sublime spiritual qualities of which human beings are capable. Though being in the midst of the horrors of war can take away people's humanity, sometimes soldiers experience the most humane and humanizing moments of their lives. Unlike just about anything else, the nightmare of war can create selfless devotion for one's comrades, calling forth a willingness to sacrifice one's own life for a fellow warrior in the face of death. It is interesting that the act of war—like wetiko—contains encoded within it both the lowest and highest potentialities of humanity.

In our interminable and monomaniacal persistence in error, suffering from an endless inability to learn from our mistakes, it certainly seems as if a demonic entity is pulling the strings of our psyche to influence us to act out in ways that are hell-bent on our self-destruction. To quote eminent theologian and 9/11 truth activist David Ray Griffin, "It does seem that we are possessed by some demonic power that is leading us, trancelike, into self-destruction."[7]

Our battle seems less against "flesh and blood" than against some demonic "powers and principalities," "against spiritual wickedness in high places" (Ephesians 6:12 [KJV]) to which human civilization is in bondage. Along similar lines, theologian Walter Wink writes, "The demonic is an inescapable fact of the twentieth [and the twenty-first] century, perhaps its most characteristic trademark

---

*French psychologist Pierre Janet's term, literally translating as "reduction of mental level." It involves a weakening of the restraints and inhibitions of the ego.

and perverse attainment."[8] The demonic influence of wetiko is the hallmark—the calling card—of our time.

I imagine this malevolent, higher (and lower) dimensional entity feverishly working behind the scenes, manipulatively operating through our unconscious blind spots. It sponsors shadow projections, inspiring our technological advances to create evermore efficient and impersonal killing machines. At the same time, it fans the flames of our fear, greed, and blood lust so as to incite our war fever. And as we wage war on each other, this bellicose wetikoid entity engorges itself on the smorgasbord of our self-created suffering and destruction—or so I imagine.

This dark entity, what Jung refers to as "the dark God," has placed previously unimaginable implements of mass destruction into our hands, set to go off at the push of a button. With this we can ultimately destroy the biosphere itself, the life-support system of the planet. As if performing a sacred "black" mass, the building up of an ever-increasing cache of high-tech weaponry is the preparatory ritual calling forth their inevitable use in a catastrophe that we, as self-entranced, deluded master magicians, are collaboratively conjuring up. Once sufficient weapons of mass destruction are accumulated, the destructive devil within us will be unable to resist putting them to their ill-fated use. It is well-known that weapons of destruction go off by themselves if only enough of them are put together. And yet it is not too late to shed light on this "devil within" and change our course away from the impending disaster.

To the extent we are unconscious of this deeper process in which we have become enlisted, we have no free will and are compulsively forced to act out our destruction through our own inventions. Unfree in our actions, we don't realize that we have become an instrument for—and unknowingly under the thrall of—a destructive will and power greater than our own.

Only something truly alive has the capacity to destroy itself. It is clear we are in the process of destroying ourselves as a species. As if performing a species-wide eco-suicide ritual en masse, we are taking part, whether we know it or not, in a cosmic antisacred ceremony that will leave no one around to experience the end result. Our scientific, technological wizardry has surpassed our wildest dreams. The question is, will our emotional, spiritual, and moral qualities continue to lag far behind, and thus doom us to a morbid future of our own making?

Ehrenreich continues, "If war is analogous to a disease, then, it is analogous to a contagious disease . . . So, to continue the epidemiological metaphor, if war is regarded as an infectious 'disease,' it is caused by a particularly hardy sort of microbe—one capable of encysting itself for generations, if necessary, within the human soul."[9] Interestingly, wetiko, a form of moral insanity, is a disease of the soul—"a particularly hardy sort of microbe." It is contagious, travelling through the vector of our shared unconsciousness through multiple generations.

It is noteworthy that our current generation seems to have lost the capacity for moral outrage. This is a sign that the psychic infection that we are suffering from is slowly eroding the inner psychic infrastructure of our moral imagination. This moral imagination is a critical part of our ethical immune system, and its erosion disables our ability to discern good from evil. We are left dumbed-down, complacent, and paralyzed in the face of a monstrous evil that we ourselves are complicit in via our inability to respond.

Ehrenreich is approaching the phenomenon of war imaginatively—envisioning it as an infectious, contagious disease, an invisible microbe that replicates itself through multiple generations. Her approach is contagious in its own right, as her imaginative musings can activate, inspire, and mobilize our own divinely inspired creative imagination to re-envision our situation in novel and creatively empowering ways.

War is a prosperity-reducing depopulation ritual, a parasite on human life and culture, draining us of as many things as can be imagined—including life itself. Like a parasite, war kills a significant proportion of the host population, and then, in the resulting gaps between wars, immunity from the parasite seems to be conferred. Unfortunately, the gaps between wars have disappeared. We now find ourselves in an endless war, a life-and-death struggle with a seemingly malevolent entity—wetiko being one of its many names—which we ourselves have conjured up. The walls that separate the well-ordered world of ordinary reality from the roiling chaos lurking right below the surface have become very thin. Ultimately speaking, we are fighting with a dark part of ourselves with which we have apparently lost our ability to be in conscious relationship.

The Archetype of War

Viewed as an autonomous entity, war is a self-replicating pattern of behavior, possessed of a dynamism not unlike that found in both living things as well as within the human mind itself. "Self-replicating patterns of behavior" is the way Jung describes the archetypes of the collective unconscious. Informational fields of influence that are atemporal (existing outside of time) and self-organizing, the archetypes of the collective unconscious are the formative templates and blueprints, the very agencies that pattern human perception and give shape and form to both individual and collective human behavior. They are like the invisible stage managers choreographing events behind the scenes of the world theater. This is to say that, though not existing in third-dimensional time and space, they have powerful real-world effects.

War is a living archetypal force that exists within the psyche of humanity; collective psychoses like war are always animated by a constellated archetype, oftentimes informed by deeper religious impulses. A cosmically driven force, once the archetype of war is activated in the collective psyche, like all archetypes, it potentially drafts us into its gravitational field of force. If we remain *unconscious* of the archetypal elements that drive us, however, we won't be able to escape from the downward and destructive pull into its sinkhole. At that point we would be fully possessed by—in the grip of—the archetype, compelled like an automaton to act out its script, forced to its fatal goal.

Having "a life of its own," an archetype reveals its autonomy by the fact that it can swallow up our life such that we become identical with the archetype, embodying it in our actions. When we fall into this circumstance we (arche) typically have no idea that we have been taken over. Unconsciously possessed by an archetype, people's inner development becomes stunted as they develop inhuman qualities.

Even though an archetype expresses itself through individuals—as well as groups—an archetype is impersonal. Enlisted by the archetype to become one of its purveyors, we become a tool in its hand as it takes possession of us like a piece of property, dropping us when we are no longer of use. We have then unwittingly become one of its instruments, enabling the archetype to give shape to itself in our world.

All archetypes are bipolar, which is to say they are ambivalent, having both a potentially negative or positive aspect. If we become *conscious* of the archetypal dimension that is playing out, however, we can mediate, humanize, and channel its enormous energy in a constructive, rather than a destructive way. Whether the emerging archetype turns out to be a blessing or a curse depends on the constitution of the intercepting consciousness. In other words, how the archetype ultimately manifests depends upon how we relate to it.

This self-perpetuating archetypal dynamic is analogous to a self-replicating computer virus or malware that infects a computer and programs it to self-destruct. Like the archetype of war, these computer viruses have no underlying material substance at all, but rather, are programs designed to reproduce themselves. These programs are composed of information (that is immaterial in and of itself) that can be carried and transmitted through material vehicles (such as collective institutions or individual people).

Many of our leaders are themselves just unwitting instruments—patsies—merely playing roles through which this infernal programming can incarnate itself. They look out for what they conceive of as their own interests. Many of them have little or no awareness of the darker aspect of the demonic power that has gripped them and is compelling them to incarnate itself into our world through their agency. America and its military, for example, are being used as an instrument of war to reshape the geopolitical landscape so as to serve the interests of a tiny yet powerful shadowy global cabal that has taken control over significant parts of the U.S. government. Being in the pocket of the cabal, many of our leaders are its mouthpieces.

As if internested iterations of a fractal, the cabal is itself just an intermediary, a pawn doing the bidding of the formless underlying archetype. Speaking of the "enormous forces" that animate the archetype, Sri Aurobindo said, "If the men who fought were instruments in the hands of rulers and financiers, these in turn were mere puppets in the clutch of those [archetypal] forces."[10] Fighting against governments and the psychopathic elite—without taking into account the deeper archetypal level that animates them—will never be successful. This is because the elite are themselves just pawns and puppets of deeper, archetypal forces that possess, and hence, control them.

Once we consciously recognize the deeper archetypal pattern that is informing world events, instead of being compelled to unconsciously re-create ever-amplified versions of the archetype in its destructive form, our expansion of consciousness empowers us to channel the archetype in its more life-affirming form. Imagine that! Jung himself wondered whether the psyche was endowed with consciousness for the very purpose of preventing such destructive archetypal possibilities from happening.

From his writings there is no doubt that Jung recognized the wetiko-like spirit that was having its way with humanity. He felt that modern-day humanity was in desperate need of, in his words, "an exorcism" in order to rescue us from our state of possession by the unconscious. He felt this was the most vital and urgent task facing mankind today.

Looking Glass into the World's Soul

Just like a transpersonal force can literally take over and possess a person and make them its instrument of incarnation—and revelation— this same process can happen on a collective scale as well. A group of people, nations, or an entire species can become seized by a more powerful archetypal energy that compels them to unconsciously, and hence destructively, act it out in the world. In collective events such as wars, we are seeing through a looking glass into the world-soul of humanity as this transpersonal force is being played out on the global stage. In the activity of war, a process that is going on within the collective psyche of humanity—which is to say within each one of us in its own unique way—is getting dreamed up en masse into materialization in the world.

War is an inflammation, an outbreak in the world's body politic reflecting a deeper systemic disease in the underlying psyche of humanity. The future will be decided by changes that take place in the psyche of humanity, which, as Jung points out, is truly the world's pivot.

Interestingly, the book of Revelation talks about a "war in heaven" (Revelation 12:7 [KJV]). The events portrayed in the Bible can be looked at as symbolically encrypted utterances of the soul, pointing to transcendental realities. The "war in heaven" is symbolically representing a living dynamism that is taking place within the collective unconscious of humanity. As long as its inner source is not recognized, however, this split in the psyche is then projected outside of ourselves, appearing in the form of a metaphysical split between the powers of light and the powers of darkness. If, indeed, "the kingdom of heaven is within us," so, too, is the "war in heaven." To quote

Berdyaev, "God and the Devil are at war within the human heart."[11]

When we are not able to contain the warring elements within our own self, this conflict of opposites spills out into the outside world, where it gets acted out—"dreamed up"—in the world theater by way of projection. Most people have their attention drawn to the outer conflict, not the conflict within. Before humanity can truly evolve and ascend to "love and light," we need to come to terms with the warring elements within ourselves.

Interestingly, the splitting of personality that characterizes neurosis results in us appearing to consist of two persons in opposition to each other who are at war with each other. We are composed of a multiplicity of selves. Our inner conflict can be envisioned as being between any pair of internal opposites. Indeed, Goethe's Faust says, "Two souls, alas, are housed within my breast."[12] We think we are simplex and not duplex, imagining ourselves to be innocuous and reasonable creatures. Many of us primarily identify with our light, thinking of ourselves as being good, kind spiritual people, while our other, darker half (our shadow) is anything but. In Faust's words, "You are conscious only of the single urge/O may you never know the other!"[13]

When we spiral downward into, for example, addictive, self-destructive behavior—literally turning on ourselves—this movement is sponsored by, as well as being an expression of and nutrient for, wetiko. Our unified, whole nature becomes split in two, as we simultaneously become our own perpetrator and victim, both sadist and masochist rolled into one. Again, this personal process is also being played out transpersonally, collectively, in the world theater. De Rougemont writes, "We are all in the sinking ship, and at the same time we are all in the ship that has just launched the torpedo . . . there is only one humanity. And that it is this humanity which is launching torpedoes and bombs against itself."[14]

The specter of war breaking out in the greater body politic haunts the collective unconscious of all of humanity. In modern times, the psychopathic Global War on Terror* is everywhere and affects everyone; it is universally traumatizing and is damaging to the soul of humanity. War isn't a phenomenon that only happens halfway around the globe (in Iraq or Afghanistan, for example). War is something that takes place within our very soul. Like a demon, the plague of war can invade humanity's inner world and inspire us to transgress our human limits, carrying us to inconceivable excesses of brutality.

Dissociative Field

Even if our current war is taking place thousands of miles away, just by its mere happening, the act of war creates a dissociative field of trauma that affects all of us and forces everyone to (mal)adapt. Dissociation can readily entrench itself in an entire population, disconnecting us from each other, as well as deadening our hearts as it fragments the inner landscapes of our minds. War dehumanizes everyone, for it requires us not only to dehumanize our enemy, but to anesthetize and dehumanize ourselves as well. An intrinsic part of the dissociative field is a force that opposes and actively resists our seeing the deeper implications of what we are doing to ourselves. The collectively shared dissociation, numbing, denial, and self-deception become self-perpetuating. The dissociative field must, of necessity, be continually maintained lest we wake up to the genocidal enterprise in which we are all participating. To the extent we are feeding this dissociative field through our own dissociation from and within ourselves, we have all become both victims and victimizers of war, complicit in its proliferation. Appearances to the contrary, there are ultimately no winners in war.

---

*The phrase *Global War on Terror* is a contradiction in terms. War *is* terror, so how can terror ever be fought and eliminated by war? The very words *War on Terror* induce a cognitive dissonance in the collective psyche. The fact is that such a war is not intended to ever end, thus serving the insatiable greed of the evil interests who continuously profit from it.

The atrocities that our government is involved in—and we, by proxy, are complicit in—are so horrible that they have to be internally denied. This creates a cognitive dissonance within our minds such that our ability to creatively and responsibly respond is disabled. Many of us simply resist the truth of what's happening. Our looking away reinforces our "need to not know," which then further feeds our dissociation in a diabolical feedback loop of our own making. Complicit in our own self-hypnosis, our moral eyes become blinded in the process. We are a species who has fallen asleep but imagines we are awake.

An entire culture can prefer blindness and America, based on overwhelming evidence, seems to be a nation that has gone blind. Hopefully, as is evidenced by people's increasing outcry against attacking other sovereign nations, increasing numbers of us are seeing through our politicians and mainstream media's feeble to the point of absurd lies and war propaganda purporting that we should attack other countries based on humanitarian pretexts. It would be a true case of "American exceptionalism" that demands true courage if we were to snap out of our dissociation and deal with the shock of multiple realizations: the lie we've been living, the evil we've been complicit in, and the reality we've been avoiding.

The fact that throughout our lifetime there has not been a moment free of one group waging war on another makes war seem normalized, as if it is just the way things are, part of being human. This thought-form is a lie, inspired and fed by the very same energy that animates war itself. If we buy into our feelings of helplessness and believe that we can't do anything about war, we are then its unwitting accomplices.

In actuality we are magicians, powerful beyond measure, having unconsciously misused our own power to bewitch ourselves, having fallen under a curse of our own making. Our task is to break out of our self-induced spell. Holding this possibility in mind, Jung wonders whether one day "even conquest will cease to be the dream."[15]

What will happen, I find myself imagining, as more and more of us, not only ordinary citizens, but actual soldiers in our illegal wars of aggression, wake up? What will happen when the military commanders, generals, senators, presidents, prime ministers, and heads of corporations wake up to how we have been hoodwinked, bamboozled—duped—by the creative genius of our own minds into seeing war as a legitimate means of operating in the world? Ah, what then?

10

Other Lenses Helping Us See Wetiko

Various contemporary spiritual teachers have described wetiko in their own unique and creative ways. The wetiko virus is what Eckhart Tolle, author of the classic *The Power of Now,* calls the "pain-body." Tolle writes, "The pain-body wants to survive, just like every other entity in existence, and it can only survive if it gets you to unconsciously identify with it. It can then rise up, take you over, 'become you,' and live through you. It needs to get its 'food' through you . . . [it] is actually afraid of the light of your consciousness. It is afraid of being found out. Its survival depends upon your unconscious identification with it, as well as on your unconscious fear of facing the pain that lives in you."[1]

The pain-body evokes and then feeds off of our pain, which resonates with its own discordant vibration. Vampiric in nature, this psychic parasite feeds on our very life force. We are sustenance for this seeming entity; we are the ones sustaining it, which is to say we are secretly and unknowingly colluding with it in a way that is ultimately feeding our own destruction.

Tolle continues, "If you don't bring the light of your consciousness into the pain you will be forced to relive it again and again [like a recurring dream] . . . it is an insubstantial phantom that cannot prevail against the powers of your presence."[2] The pain-body/wetiko feeds off of our unawareness of it. Its darkness, however, has no choice but to give way to light, to the power of the presence of our conscious awareness. When we shed light on the pain-body's covert operations within our own mind, Tolle concludes, "It cannot use you anymore by pretending to be you, and it can no longer replenish itself through you."[3] It has a brute compulsion born of terror, fearing at any and every moment that its machinations are going to be uncovered and its food is going to be denied.

Recently Tolle has been emphasizing that there is a highly contagious mental virus that is at the root of the collective psychosis from which our species is suffering. Sound familiar?

Healer and author Michael Brown talks about the same experience in slightly different words. Referring to the state where we are trying to fill the seemingly endless void inside of us and feeling like we can never get enough, he says, "We have become helpless prey in the grips of an energetic experience that is parasitic."[4] "Like an uninvited driver at the wheel of our car,"[5] these parasitic entities feed into and off of, both individually and collectively as a society, our habitual pattern of avoiding our pain. As long as we deny our feelings of pain, we will keep being destructive, for if we don't know our own pain, our unconscious compulsively drives us to create pain in others.

Note the similarity to Tolle's point that the pain-body depends upon our unwillingness to face our pain. Brown continues, "The ride they take our vehicles on is not in our best interest if we seek to evolve."[6] Trespassing our boundaries and taking up residence within us, Brown refers to these seeming entities as "illegal squatters," who have "hijacked" our soul.

Brown talks about the importance of "stalking" these seeming entities' behavior within ourselves so as to recognize them. He writes, "By being able to recognize them we separate their presence from our own."[7] In seeing these seeming entities through the power of our presence, we objectify them, which is to set ourselves apart from them. The part of us that is seeing these seeming entities is other than—and free of—them. A way to understand this—if we have a yellow filter in front of our eyes, we won't be able to recognize the color yellow, as everything will appear yellowish. The point: When we are seeing yellow, the part of us that is seeing yellow is yellow-free. The part of us that is both reflecting and reflecting upon these parasitic energies is who we actually are.

Wetiko as the Topic of Topics

In the Carlos Castaneda books, though called by a different name, the phenomenon of wetiko is considered by the Toltec shamans to be "the topic of topics."[8] Carlos's shamanic teacher, Don Juan, taught Carlos that there was *a predator* (his term for wetiko) that, unbeknownst to us, ruled over us, rendering us docile to its oppression. We become "food" for this predator as it subtly and slyly insinuates and transplants its mind into our mind in such a way so as to surreptitiously enact a covert takeover of our mind while leaving us unaware that anything out of the ordinary has happened.

Identifying with its point of view as our own, we then become instruments through which we unknowingly enact its agenda, assuming that it's our own. Don Juan refers to this as a *foreign installation*, a phrase that connotes images of an alien takeover. These predators live in fear that at any moment their ploy will be discovered and they will be exposed. So whenever we have an inkling of the truth of our situation, they do everything in their power to distract us.[9]

Likewise, in the bestselling book *The Four Agreements* by Toltec teacher Don Miguel Ruiz, the author writes about "a parasite that invades the human mind. From the Toltec point of view, all humans who are domesticated are sick. They are sick because there is a parasite that controls the mind. . . . The food for the parasite is the negative emotions that come from fear."[10] This is a word-for-word description of wetiko, which—as the aforementioned Colin Wilson so aptly imagined—is a parasite of the mind.

Ruiz continues, "The parasite dreams through your mind and

lives its life through your body."[11] When a person's mind is sufficiently colonized by wetiko, the person becomes taken over by this
parasite such that they can be thought of as the instrument through
which this formless disease incarnates itself through human form
into the world. Ruiz concludes that "In all shamanic traditions in
America, from Canada to Argentina, people call themselves *warriors,*
because they are in a war against the parasite in the mind. . . . The
warrior is one who rebels against the invasion of the parasite."[12] We
are all being dreamed up to step into becoming the spiritual warriors
that we truly are—or suffer the consequences of our lack of courage.

The idea of wetiko is, thankfully, beginning to seep into our
national political dialogue. For example, in the Democratic debate
leading up to the 2020 election for president, Marianne Williamson
mentioned a "dark psychic force" (a perfect description of wetiko).
Congresswoman Alexandria Ocasio-Cortez speaks about "a virus
[that] exists on a larger scale beyond just the infected. It also lays
dormant . . . clearly, our nation has not been inoculated."[13]

I take it as a sign of an expansion of our species' consciousness
that talk of dark psychic forces that are conceived of as viruses are
beginning to be seriously talked about. Part of our inoculation
against these darker forces is recognizing what we are up against. To
become fully immunized from the disease is to look in the mirror
and honestly confront ourselves. Thus we distinguish the part of ourselves that is unconsciously colluding with wetiko from the part of
us—the Self—that is forever free of the disease.

Wetiko and Addiction

In trying to point out what is meant by the idea of wetiko, I have
been accused of not having evidence for my wild, "out-there," and
seemingly crazy theory. The irony is that the evidence for what I
am talking about is so overwhelmingly obvious. It is all around us
(as well as inside of us). Thus, it is easy to miss due to its omni-

presence. To use a primary example, wetiko underlies and informs the archetypal process of addiction that is rampant in our world today. This is to say that the essential process at the core of addiction maps onto the key features of the underlying dynamics of wetiko. In shedding light on how addiction works, we can deepen our understanding of wetiko.

Addiction connotes images of substance abuse, but this is only one type of addiction. Many of us are addicted to perspectives, to ideas, to other people, to our suffering, to our "process," to our story, to shopping, to distracting ourselves from looking within, to thinking, or to our sense of a separate self, among many other things.

Jungian psychoanalyst David E. Schoen is the author of the excellent book *The War of the Gods in Addiction*. In it he emphasizes the central role that the psyche plays in the process of how addiction takes over a person. He precisely maps out and describes how the wetiko virus works. In his work on addiction, instead of using the word *wetiko*, Schoen refers to it as the "Addiction-Shadow-Complex," which is composed of the interaction between the addictive behavior, the personal shadow, and archetypal evil.[14]

The addictive behavior opens up the door for the repressed, unconscious aspect of the personal shadow to freely express itself. It thereby insinuates itself into the personality by vampirically feeding on the wellsprings of vital energy that comprise a healthy human being in a mutually reinforcing feedback loop that, over time, can subtly metastasize into the core of the personality. The personal shadow becomes increasingly dependent upon the addictive behavior for its expression, while the addictive behavior feeds off of and is strengthened by the personal shadow.

This unholy alliance opens up the door for the transpersonal forces of darkness—archetypal evil—to eventually, over time, gain the upper hand (i.e., assume control) in such a weakened, debilitated, addiction-ridden psyche, fueling the whole soul-destroying enterprise. As the personal and transpersonal shadow elements align, an insidious self-amplifying cycle is created. This, then, can easily turn into a degenerative downward spiral that greases the path for our potential self-destruction through the addiction (whatever the specific form of the addiction might be). At the core of every addiction is an energy that wants to possess the person; it wants their very life. It is as if there is an evil spirit—the very archetype of evil—at the root of every addiction.

According to Schoen, the Addiction-Shadow-Complex literally takes over, deposes, and displaces the normal ruling ego, replacing it with itself. Schoen writes:

> The Addiction-Shadow-Complex replaces the ruling ego complex with its own ruler, a puppet pseudo-king who serves ultimately only the desires, interests, and agendas of the addiction, which cares nothing for any other values or needs of the person, the psyche or the true Self, or for anyone or anything else . . . there is a permanent hijacking of the entire psychic system; the normal ego complex and all its functions are as if put under a powerful diabolical spell. . . . The addiction then replaces the old system with an entire ruling ego system . . . [it is] an imposter, a liar, a deceiver and charlatan, but now the addicted person, his true Self and healthy ego, are helpless and powerless to fight or even object to the new dictatorship established by the Addiction-Shadow-Complex. . . . The addiction at this point completely possesses the individual person. . . . The prime directive is now the addiction and its agendas; everything else [all of the healthy aspects of the psyche] . . . [are] subsumed by it[15] . . . [the addiction] is then completely in control, calling all the shots, and [the person] is merely a puppet, doing what it dictates.[16]

Here Schoen is describing—word-for-word—the exact process of how wetiko colonizes a human psyche. When someone is taken over by the Addiction-Shadow-Complex/wetiko, it is as if an alien invading power commandeers the executive function of the psyche so as to fulfill its own agenda. This is why the person taken over oftentimes acts in ways that are diametrically opposed to their own best interests. The Addiction-Shadow-Complex/wetiko ultimately destroys its host, as well as itself. Unless interrupted and overcome, it is a living death sentence that can lead to the extinguishing of life.

Trauma and addiction are closely interrelated. Addiction is a living form of the soul-deadening process of trauma. The repetition compulsion of trauma—what Freud called "the death instinct"—can itself be seen as a form of addiction, just as the addict's relapses are a form of repeating their trauma. Both addiction and trauma have a common feature of compulsively repeating and re-creating themselves; at a certain point they become self-generating. Encountering the archetypal evil that drives addiction is traumatizing by its very nature. Trauma is totally implicit in what happens to a person who is addicted; the self-destruction endemic to addiction is traumatic. Addiction is in itself a traumatizing experience.

Oftentimes it's only when the addict hits rock bottom and realizes that they—as a human ego—are helpless and dependent upon a "higher power," that the recovery process starts in earnest. In a letter to Bill W. (the founder of Alcoholics Anonymous), Jung, though talking about alcoholism, could just as well be talking about any addiction, when he writes, "His craving for alcohol was the equivalent, on a low level, of the spiritual thirst of our being for wholeness, expressed in medieval language: the union with God."[17]

Our craving for the addictive substance or behavior is a lower-level thirst for the real thing—in other words, our spiritual wholeness—what Schoen calls "a misplaced worship on the altar of a false God." In trying to find a substitute for a living spiritual experience of fulfillment, the addicted person, in obsessively trying to re-create and repeat the original experience, only winds up perverting it. In his letter, Jung continues, "You see 'alcohol' in Latin is *spiritus,* and you use the same word for the highest religious experience as well as for the most depraving poison."[18] The implication is that hidden encoded within the addictive process is potentially either an experience of living spirit or its opposite: a deadening experience that is toxic to our living spirit.

Jung concludes his letter to Bill W. with the words, "The helpful formula therefore is: *spiritus contra spiritum* [spirit against spirit]."[19] Due to the archetypal Spirit informing the process of addiction, we need a transpersonal (beyond the personal) Spirit with which to treat it—whether we call this an experience of the Self, a Higher Power, Spirit, God, or whatever. Accessing this transpersonal source is paradoxical in that it connects us with something beyond our limited sense of self, while at the same time connecting us with ourselves.

To rediscover the life of the spirit involves offering our ego in service to something greater than ourselves—what Jung would call relativizing the ego in the service to the Self. This can potentially be a life-transforming psycho-spiritual conversion experience, in which we continually cultivate an ongoing, ever-evolving relationship with the Self. After all is said and done, however, we are the ones who ultimately get to choose which master we serve.

11

Scapegoating

How Darkness Hides in the Light

The condition of modern post-industrial life—which equates value with utility—creates social and spiritual fragmentation, thereby strengthening people's internal state of dissociation. This systemic condition—existing in various degrees both outside in the world and within our minds—can create a seeming prohibition from expressing ourselves creatively and authentically. The more suppressed and unconscious people's lives become, the more likely they are to buy into dehumanizing propaganda about those who seem different. Their inner frustration needs a recipient for their negative feelings— a scapegoat—to relieve the ever-increasing pressure within their own psyche. The life force that isn't able to be creatively and constructively expressed by an individual can join forces with others in the same boat, becoming collectively mobilized to channel their suppressed aggression destructively—through acts of violence—onto a convenient scapegoat. Neumann felt that shadow projection is "in fact one of the gravest perils confronting mankind."[1]

The Shadow

A living part of the personality, "the shadow," the darker part of our personality, what Jung calls "our sublunary nature," is at the root of wetiko disease. The psychological process of *projecting* the shadow (scapegoating)—which is the shadow projecting itself outside of itself so that it can remain hidden—is the core underlying dynamic that informs wetiko. Shadow projection is itself none other than the shadow itself in action. "The shadow," to quote Jung, "is always where your eyes are not,"[2] which is to say that the shadow lives and works in and through the blind spots of the unconscious. Understanding the ins and outs of shadow projection therefore helps us to dispell wetiko. To get insight into shadow projecting, it behooves us to revisit the idea of the shadow.

The shadow can be thought of as being the inferior part of everyone's personality, the darker half of the human totality, humanity's worst danger. Fundamentally at odds with the conscious personality, it can't be argued out of existence. The shadow is the part we habitually hide from ourselves. We typically avoid dealing with it as long as we can conveniently project it onto someone else.

One thing for certain is that we are less good than we imagine ourselves to be. Everyone has a shadow, and the less it is consciously embodied in our lives, the darker, denser, and more destructive it is. Our shadow is an unconscious snag that often seems to thwart our best intentions at the most inopportune moments. The shadow is a moral problem that challenges the whole person. Becoming conscious of the shadow is essential for any degree of self-knowledge, which is why the process of shedding light on the shadow is usually met with strong inner resistance. This resistance is typically bound up with corresponding projections, the recognition of which is a moral achievement that is out of the ordinary.

The shadow is the primitive being living within the psyche of modern, civilized humanity. Our sophisticated logic and highest reason means nothing to this figure. The political arena is practically run by the shadow, which is why the power of reason in our political discourse has become disabled, rendered virtually meaningless. We all harbor within ourselves a dangerous shadow figure who is invisibly contributing to the dark goings-on of the political monster in our midst. In other words, the extent to which we are not dealing with our shadow is the extent we are complicit in the evil that is playing out in the world's body politic. Seeing the world through the shadow's lens is to see the problem as being completely outside of ourselves, as if we have nothing to do with what is happening in the world.

We live in a time, however, where it is no longer possible to avoid or postpone dealing with our darker half. We are all destined to come to terms with our shadow. As Jung points out, the only way to avoid the confrontation with the shadow is to live in "eternal darkness." In a very real sense the fate of the world depends upon us opening our eyes to the shadow that, like a dark specter, is looming behind and informing the destructive behavior of modern humanity. Our blindness to our shadow is extremely dangerous. Our blindness to our blindness is one of the chief features of wetiko.

The shadow has two aspects: On the one hand, there is a personal dimension to it, which has to do with our particular wounds and our individual responses to their potentially traumatizing effects. On the other hand, there is also an archetypal dimension of our shadow. This is the part of the shadow that does not belong to us as a person, but is a universal, collective darkness that each of us has to contend with within ourselves in our own way.

The shadow is more than personal and cannot be adequately dealt with unless its archetypal ground is also addressed. The shadow roots the personality in the subsoil of the collective unconscious, where it interfaces with the archetype of the devil—of the primordial forces of darkness. When we split off from our shadow it goes into the unconscious, which strengthens and amplifies the darker powers of the collective unconscious, threatening the psyche with invasion from these archetypal forces. The unconscious itself can then appear to be the devil, which makes it difficult to develop a healthy relationship with the unconscious, to put it mildly.

Though different and important to distinguish, these two aspects—personal and archetypal—of the shadow mutually inform and interpenetrate each other. Many people—under the guise of wanting to get to the real root of the problem—make the mistake of bypassing the personal aspects of their shadow and go right to the impersonal archetypal dimension of the shadow. The personal shadow, however, is the doorway that leads to the mythic, archetypal level of the shadow. In other words, there is no getting away from dealing with our own personal shadow issues.

When we first catch a "dim inkling" of our shadow, we see something uncanny, at odds with the conscious picture we have of ourselves. We typically turn away from such an unpleasant image, but this disreputable person is also an aspect of ourselves. Being a stranger to ourselves, the shadow cannot help but appear uncanny, a bit strange, as it casts itself—and ourselves—in a strange light.

Our shadow desires to be recognized, and like a close sibling, it wants to be with us, to live our life with us. When we reject it, it naturally develops resistances against us, becoming annoyed and irritated with us, turning hostile and venomous. Each time we have revulsion for this inner figure, we are unknowingly reviling ourselves, which evokes this character within us to react as if it was our adversary.

Becoming acquainted with our shadow, however, is a tremendously valuable gift, as it can help us develop a more realistic, two-sided (as compared to one-sided) and all-around picture of ourselves that includes both the light and dark aspects of ourselves. When our darker parts are accepted as part of our totality they can flesh out, reanimate, and enliven us to our core. When we see and begin to embrace our dark side, we become more complete. When we take responsibility for our darker half, we take away the burden of darkness from our unconscious.

As long as the shadow remains unconscious, nothing truly beneficial can emerge from the unconscious. This is because our unrecognized shadow becomes a blight, stopping anything productive from growing out of the soil of the psyche. As soon as we own the shadow that belongs to us, however, the unconscious can resume its naturally creative function.

If we remain unaware of our shadow, however, we are unable to establish real relationships with other people because we have not established an authentic relationship with ourself. Being unconscious of our own shadow compels us to incessantly try to improve other people in our surroundings who carry the projection of our darker parts. We then arrogantly and self-righteously—with the best of conscious intentions—assume we know what other people need to do in order to heal, and we are more than willing to share our seemingly superior insight. Other people's resistance to our benighted efforts are typically interpreted by us as symptoms of the very unconsciousness we are pointing at (a lack of consciousness that is actually our own). This justifies us in doubling down in our efforts to enlighten the other person, invariably resulting in misunderstanding and separation for all involved.

Jung was of the opinion that the only struggle that is really worthwhile is the fight against the overwhelming power drive of the shadow. Coming to terms with the shadow is not an intellectual activity but rather touches us at our core, as it is more a genuine suffering and passion of the whole person. The shadow can only begin to be integrated when it is grasped not merely intellectually, but understood—and experienced—according to its feeling-value. In the realm of psyche, we possess nothing unless we have actually experienced it in reality. Hence a purely abstract, intellectual insight is insufficient, because we know only the words or the idea, but not the essential substance of the thing from the inside.

Encountering and assimilating our shadow is not for the faint of heart. It involves the disillusionment of our illusions about both the world and ourselves. The shadow is a tight passage, a narrow door, the proverbial eye of a needle whose narrow constriction spares no one. It is a portal through which we become initiated to a more fleshed out version of ourselves. Owning our shadow introduces us to both deeper depths and greater heights that live within us unawares.

The shadow is not in itself evil, but there is a capacity in human beings to use the shadow as the doorway for acting out evil. The shadow, however, contains within it an aspect of the Self, the wholeness of our personality. The guardian of the threshold, the way to the Self lies *through* the shadow. Just as the prima materia in alchemy is indispensable in order to make the gold, the shadow is crucial for bringing forth the wholeness of the personality. Without the shadow the process of individuation would never take place, and there would be no reconciliation of the opposites, for the shadow embodies the opposite. This is to say that projecting the shadow outside of ourselves onto a scapegoat actively prevents our individuation, our becoming whole.

Projecting the Shadow

What we don't accept in ourselves, but rather exclude from our self-image and push into the shadows of the netherworld of the unconscious—thereby depriving it of light—becomes toxic. Repressing a content of the psyche renders it poisonous. These repressed shadowy contents build up a charge in the unconscious, becoming contaminated with archaic archetypal energies. The archetypal figure of the devil is the compensatory voice of our own unconscious and the more forcibly we suppress our unconscious the more sinister it appears.

These shadowy forces within ourselves approach us through the circuitous route of projection, which is to say that these shadow energies get dreamed up so as to appear to us in the outside world in the form of an adversarial other. This is to say that the shadow hangs in midair, waiting to be filled out by a living person. The demonization of others is possible only when we fail to recognize the demon within ourselves.

The devil—who is known as the adversary—is in essence our own *other* standpoint. Just as the world formerly teemed with witches and werewolves, it is now full of scapegoats and betes noires. What we avoid, abandon, escape, and turn away from in ourselves will turn against us—both inwardly and outwardly. We have to face our own darkness if we want to have any chance of tapping into the mythic fountain of life. Paradoxically, anyone who can face their own negative aspect overcomes themselves to a great extent.

When we split off from and project the shadow outside of ourselves, we are actually preventing the integration of the whole personality. This is because the shadow contains significant aspects of the Self. In addition, projecting the shadow outward not only deprives us of the capacity to deal with evil, but ensures that we will unwittingly become an instrument of evil. In projecting the shadow outside of ourselves, we are standing in the way of our own light—and are thus "in the dark"—which guarantees that we will become our own evil spirit. This brings to mind the folk saying that the person without a shadow is the devil. Trying to destroy the evil in the world, we become possessed by the very evil we are trying to destroy.

Though the repository of all our inferior and regrettable qualities, the shadow is at the same time the prerequisite for higher consciousness. When we project the shadow we unwittingly deprive ourselves of the possibility of truly expanding our consciousness. The shadow is the block that stops us from hearing and connecting with the sound of God's voice within us, whose sole purpose is to expand our consciousness and wake us up.

When we lose awareness of having a shadow, it is as if we are declaring that a part of us is nonexistent. The darker part of ourselves that we pretend no longer exists while it is buried in the soil of our unconscious grows fat while our soul becomes emaciated as a result. In denying and projecting out our shadow, as if feeding a psychic tapeworm—wetiko—that lives in our body, we are simultaneously nourishing the evil within us while simultaneously starving our true, and potentially healthy and wholesome selves. If we continue to deny our shadow, then our roots can no longer draw the dark nourishment from our depths, and our tree of life will become sickened.

As Hannah Arendt pointed out, every form of totalitarianism is rooted in dehumanization. Shadow projection relies on dehumanizing the recipient of the projection through seeing the worst in them, which justifies hatred, oppression, violence—even genocide—against those perceived as "the other." This is an outer enactment of an intrapsychic process of self-hatred, which only postpones the process of coming to terms with our own hated and rejected parts. Those upon whom the shadow is foisted are typically seen as carriers of infection and are likened to animals, vermin, parasites, microbes, germs, cancers, and bacillus, and so on. They are seen as living poison, and hence need to be destroyed.*

Projecting evil outside of ourselves is the fast road to fascism. It is a very common trope among fascist leaders to refer to the outside enemy with motifs of disease. The *homeland* (a word that carries fascist overtones and, interestingly, entered America's vernacular after 9/11) is considered something that must be kept clean and sanitary. It must be protected from the dreaded "other," which is envisioned as a pathogenic factor that is continually threatening to infect its purity.

The crumbling of social and economic structures releases overwhelming fear and uncertainty. This is a perfect opportunity for a charismatic leader to show up, who can exploit the collectively suppressed emotions of the masses by telling them who to blame for their problems. Although happening inside of an individual psyche, shadow projection can then become collectively mobilized and acted out en masse via various "witch hunts" (to use a politically popular term) against specific individuals or groups.

---

*It should be noted that these are precisely the terms that the Nazis used to characterize the Jews. What the Nazis did to the Jews during World War II was scapegoating writ large—on an industrial scale.

Our leaders can—and often do—manipulate our unconscious propensity to project the shadow outside of ourselves to feed their dreams of power. Manipulating the shadow projections of the masses is one of the most powerful tools of collective mind control used by the power elite. Collective shadow projection is the unmediated acting out of the darkest aspects of the shadow in an expedient and politically correct form that reinforces one's group identity in opposition to some other group that is vilified. War—be it between people, nations, or within our own psyche—is the result. No war can be waged unless the enemy can become the recipient and carrier of our shadow projections.

When we as a nation collectively project the shadow onto another nation or group, it becomes practically a sacred duty to have the most destructive weapons and biggest bombs. It should be noted that the accumulation of arms is itself not just a preparation, but an evocation and a call to war. Due to the mixture of personal and archetypal contents that inform our projections, the recipients of our shadow projections are seen as an amalgam of subhuman and superhuman qualities, the devil incarnate in human form. The figure of the devil, who is "the disintegrator par excellence," can be conceived of as embodying the evil powers of the unconscious. As such, the word *devil* is a very apt name for the autonomous unconscious darker forces of the human psyche.

Shadow projection (also known as *demonization*) is the prime, most essential action of the evil within each one of us. Etymologically speaking, to *demonize* means to open up the recipient of our demonization to the influence of demons. In other words, projecting the shadow onto someone has an effect on them. It calls forth and makes it more likely that the recipient of our shadow projection will indeed manifest the very shadow aspect we are projecting onto them. This simply confirms to us the seemingly "objective truth" of our projection, thereby giving us more evidence to continue to demonize them even more. This then becomes an insidious process of delusion that feeds upon and reinforces itself, ad infinitum.

If we demonize someone, there is a high likelihood that the recipient of our shadow projections will respond in kind, demonizing us right back. This results in the nearly intractable situation of mutual and ceaselessly self-reinforcing shadow projection being relentlessly co-triggered from both sides. Each side is then mirroring the other's dark side, but is entranced by their mirrored reflection so as to think the evil exists "out there," separate from—and other than—themselves. Ironically, though on one level separating them, this diabolical dynamic unconsciously binds the two sides together, which results in the vicious cycle endlessly perpetuating itself.

Both sides are then playing out—in the outside world—the internal process of wanting to get rid of (and potentially destroy) their own darkness. This is the *psychological* process that started the whole dynamic of shadow projection in the first place. This inner process is then acted out in embodied form in the physical world, with others cast in the role of carriers of our own disowned darkness. The whole process is sponsored behind the scenes by wetiko, which feeds and strengthens itself on the polarization (driven by each party's passionate denial of their shadow) in the field.

Though not material substances that can be measured, our projections have a subtle body—with a weight all their own—that has a palpable effect, leaving an impression on the recipient. This is the essence of voodoo, witchcraft, and black magic, wherein a powerful shadow projection—which can be thought of as a psychic projectile*—can make the recipient sick. It is noteworthy that ultimately speaking, all black magic boomerangs and harms the one who practices it. Thus there is an all-around detriment to everyone involved on both sides. In shadow projecting, we influence the recipient of our projection. At the same time we are being reciprocally influenced by them, due to—via our projection—there being a bond of sameness between us.

---

*The Bible mentions "the flaming arrows of the evil one" (Eph 6:16 [CEB]).

"Evil," to quote the Swiss Jungian psychologist Marie Louise von Franz, "starts with lying, that is, with the projection of the shadow."[3] Jung himself simply calls projecting the shadow "the lie."[4] "The devil," to quote Christ, "is a liar and the father of lies" (John 8:44 [ESV]).

Projecting the shadow outside of ourselves is the primordial lie—the father of all lies—in action. The devil is the sponsor of lies, which is to say that the devil—the personification of the forces of darkness—is the inspiration for the process of shadow projecting. "The spirit of darkness" (to use Jung's words) is "the ruler" of our shadow projections. Every time someone projects their shadow, the devil has claimed another victim. Ironically, instead of freeing ourselves from our own evil, shadow projection binds us to it even more.

Coming full circle in our inquiry as to how to heal wetiko, we end up right where we started—with the shadow, which plays a central role in the genesis of wetiko. In other words, it all comes down to the dark, as well as to the light (that casts the shadows in the first place). Light is of little use if it doesn't illumine darkness.

12

René Girard's Take on Scapegoating and the Shadow

French-American philosopher and cultural anthropologist René Girard, author of the classic book *The Scapegoat,* is of the opinion that the origin of human culture is to be discovered in what he calls "the founding murder."[1] This is none other than the psychological process of scapegoating/shadow projecting. Interestingly, Christ—who is the prototypical innocent scapegoat ("the lamb of God" who bears the sins of the world)—refers to the devil as "a murderer from the beginning." This founding murder, what Girard calls "the secret of Satan," must be concealed at all costs, which is to say it must remain unconscious.[2] This founding murder *is* wetiko. This murder is ahistorical and atemporal in that it regenerates itself always and everywhere—informing human *culture* (or lack thereof)—until seen through.

This founding murder and the lie that covers it imprisons humanity in a never-ending, self-replicating feedback loop in which humanity must kill, and continue to kill, in order to not know that we are killing. To quote Girard, "This lie is a double homicide, since its consequence is always another new homicide to cover up the old one."[3] The result is a heart anesthetized and numb to feeling, which enables us to be party to atrocities that we would normally never countenance or even be able to imagine. Speaking about the founding murder, Girard says, "It is an inexhaustible fund; a transcendent source of falsehood that infiltrates every domain and structures everything in its own image, with such success that the truth cannot get in."[4] To the extent we are asleep to this deeper process, we become, in Jung's words, "an unconscious instrument of the wholesale murderer in man."[5] When we are unconscious of the evil within us, it will insinuate itself into the surroundings, where it will work its black magic via the outside world.

Scapegoating/shadow projecting is itself a violent act of self-mutilation. The origin of scapegoating involves a severing and dis-owning of a darker part of ourselves, which we then—in a second act of (energetic) violence—project outside of ourselves onto an "other." We react violently when we encounter an embodied reflection of our shadow in the outer world, wanting to destroy it, for it reminds us of something dark within ourselves that we want to exterminate. This act of external violence is a dramatization of the original inner act of "splitting" (a violent affair in and of itself) off from our own dark-ness. In other words, our inner process of violence toward our own darkness (that is itself inspired by the very darkness we are dissociat-ing from) is being dreamed up and acted out on the canvas of the external world with real-world consequences.

The price we pay for believing in "otherness" is that, in order to justify this belief, we mutilate the universe, rending the seamless wholeness of reality into two seemingly separate domains (the false dichotomy of self and other). Reciprocally co-arising with otherness is fear. If there is an other, there is fear. A question naturally arises: Is *otherness* more threatening in its difference (in its alien quality) or is it more menacing in its sameness (that it's reflecting something back within ourselves)?

The Shadow's Appetite for Violence

Girard felt that humanity was in slavery to violence. He was of the opinion that the scapegoat mechanism has a hold on humanity and is society's best collective defense against coming to terms with its own violence. To quote Girard, "The old pattern of each against another gives way to the unified antagonism of all against one."[6] Girard felt that human culture is based on the deeper archetypal process of conjuring away the pent-up psychological violence intrinsic to humanity's shadow by endlessly projecting it onto new victims. This is to say that human culture is organized around a violent—and thus disingenuous—disavowal of human violence.

The guilt-feelings that co-arise with the very existence of the shadow are discharged in the same way by the individual and the collective—via the mechanism of shadow projection. In an endless cycle, the process of projecting our shadow outside of ourselves—due to its disingenuousness—feeds into our unconscious feelings of guilt, which results in more shadow projection to assuage our guilt. And so the endless cycle continues, feeding on itself. We continually attempt—unsuccessfully—to wash our hands of our guilt and return to innocence by repeating the very thing we feel guilty about. The whole thing is complete madness.

Having someone to project the shadow onto is helpful in a perverse sort of way, as it temporarily shields us from having to look at our own evil or consciously feel our own guilt. Having an adversarial enemy who can be the recipient of our own darkness is on one hand an enormous relief to our conscience (though, on the other hand, unconsciously feeding our guilt), as we then feel like we know who the devil is. In an uncertain world we have a certainty that the cause of our troubles is outside of, rather than within, ourself. The outcast role of the alien other is an important object for the projection of the shadow. Those who carry our evil are seen as alien, just as the (illegal) alien is so often experienced as evil.

Once we demonize others, this self-righteously justifies their destruction without any feelings of conscious guilt or remorse emerging within us. Identifying with what psychiatrist Robert Jay Lifton, in his book *The Nazi Doctors,* calls a "claim to virtue,"[7] we see our actions as laudable rather than sinful. This simply ensures more shadow projection as the destructive cycle continues, ad infinitum. In contrast to Shakespeare's character Iago, who knows he is evil, one of the most dangerous things in the world are people who are instruments of evil and not only don't know they are doing evil, but conceive of themselves as agents of good.

When there is mutual shadow projection between individuals, groups, or nations, each side has an unconscious investment in the other playing out the projected evil so as to prove their own self-righteous innocence. What ensues is a vicious cycle that ensures that neither side has to look at their own darkness. This dynamic fastens the two sides together, as if in their mutual projections there is an elastic band tying them together, and this dynamic becomes self-reinforcing. As such, it gives both parties clear justification to feel victimized by the other as well as continually feeding the diabolical polarization in the field.

In scapegoating, we try to avoid dealing with a darker part of ourselves via the sleight-of-mind of projecting it out into the world, where it becomes hidden in plain sight but cloaked in otherness. The person or group that is carrying our projection then captures our attention (because we unconsciously detect our own repressed and denied attributes in them) and thus becomes the focus of our re-actions. It is paradoxical that in attempting to hide something within ourselves from ourselves, we project it out into the world in front of us. Here it can take over the forefront of our conscious-ness and become an object of fascination, tying us to the very thing we want to get rid of. We become compulsively spellbound by this disowned content for the very reason that it unknowingly belongs to us.

Like a narcotic, shadow projection produces only an apparent and temporary relief, however, invariably demanding more projection of the shadow—more lying and violence—to keep itself in business. The only way to prevent a return of the content of our projections is through their continued projection, a circular process that endlessly loops back and feeds on itself. Once this process gains enough momentum, we will continually be on guard against the slightest apperception of the shadow.

In repression, we are in essence denying a part of our experience of and to ourselves. Intrinsic to denial is an infinite regress, as denial demands denying that we are in denial. Denial is a decision to remain ignorant, deaden our conscience and is, ultimately speaking, to be colluding with evil. This whole process is simultaneously an expression of and results in a splitting of the mind, all of which feeds wetiko.

One of the main ways shadow projection keeps itself alive is through—as if a contagious disease—the known infectious quality of hate. *Heterophobia,* "hatred of the other," feeds into all kinds of fear, racism, and endless projection of the shadow onto those seen as different from ourselves. Our hatred is almost always concentrated on the quality in others that can potentially make us conscious of our own unconscious bad qualities. Considered one of the three poisons by the Buddha (the others being greed/desire and ignorance—all of which are characteristics of wetiko), hatred is the high-octane fuel that powers the very process of shadow projection. Hatred inspires a wish to injure, kill, and destroy, an impulse that can develop an autonomy—and a seeming mind—all its own. Chillingly, it should be noted that "hate crimes" are on the rise.

Hatred of evil delivers us into evil's hands, for it strengthens evil. Instead of opening our heart, increasing our freedom and our appreciation of beauty, hatred spirals us into an increasingly darker world of pain and ugliness. The devil rejoices when he succeeds in inspiring in us feelings of hatred and revulsion toward himself. He attains dominion over us when he tricks us into using his own methods against himself. Leaving nothing untouched, in addition to arousing hateful feelings toward evil, Satan inspires an all-around hatred by inflaming hateful feelings toward the good as well. In Christian theology, the essence of the devil is his hatred of anything wholesome and holy.

To quote novelist and social critic James Baldwin, "I imagine one of the reasons people cling to their hate so stubbornly is because they sense, once hate is gone, they will be forced to deal with pain." One of the things that humanity hates the most is having their precious illusions seen through such that they have to face their unconsciousness that they've been defending. Practically nothing is more hateful to a person than to give up even the smallest little bit of their unconsciousness. This is why many people react violently when others reflect back their unconscious shadow.

Speaking at a 1987 symposium called Understanding Evil, American historian and religious studies scholar Jeffrey Burton Russell said "A powerful, centered, destructive, focused force of hatred exists within us—in our minds. I know this from experience. This notion certainly resembles the traditional idea of a hateful personality that everywhere seeks to destroy and annihilate—what Goethe called *der Geist der stets verneint* ('the spirit which always denies')."[8] We are all fated to come to terms with a *seeming* entity that lives inside of us that is against us stepping into the light of our true nature. I choose my words carefully here. I say *seeming* because it manifests as if it is an actual entity, but is it a split-off part of ourselves or an actual entity that is other than ourselves? This is a doorway into the question of who we are.

Our projections transform the world into a replica of our own unknown face. In projecting our own evil outside of ourselves, we transform the outer world into an embodied mirrored reflection of the unknown visage of our own evil. There is a primitive instinctual tendency in us to shut our eyes to evil and expel it to some foreign location, similar to the scapegoating rite in the Hebrew scriptures. Scapegoating is related to shutting our eyes (becoming blind) to evil. Collective scapegoating is a dangerous situation, in that the disturbance (whose origin is within ourselves) is now attributed to an evil will outside of ourselves. This invariably leads to collective delusions, one-sidedness, violent conflicts, and war—in other words, destructive mass psychoses. Wetiko is just such a mass psychosis.

What It Would Mean to Lose Our Shadow

Due to our proclivity to project the shadow outside of ourselves, humanity is in danger of losing our shadow altogether. To lose our shadow means our shadow falls into the unconscious. In other words, the unconscious has become dominant over the conscious mind. A world without shadows, instead of having three dimensions, would be a superficial, flat, two-dimensional world without depth. Losing—dissociating from—our shadow would be catastrophic, for our shadow adds substance to both the world and ourselves; it makes us truly human. People who lose their shadow become a mere façade with nothing behind it. Jung makes the point that people who lose their shadow open themselves up to falling prey to what the devil symbolizes.

When we lose our shadow, instead of being—and embodying— who we are, we become a caricature of ourselves, made up of how we imagine other people see us. We then become interested in managing other people's perceptions of our image. We become increasingly identified with this image—our persona—at the cost of who we really are. We can then become unconsciously absorbed by and identical with the character that we are presenting, the role that we want people to see us as, which limits the scope of our genuine self-expression. The shadow can never fully disappear so that no one can see it, however. Somewhere the shadow will seep through one's mask, no matter how much we try and make it invisible.

In losing—splitting from—our shadow we are also ensuring that our shadow will confront us in projected form through and as the outside world. The more we lay claim to the moral high ground, the more the Self will appear to us as something dark and menacing. As Jung points out again and again, the split-off parts of the unconscious are projected outside of ourselves, where they get "dreamed up" such that we encounter them in—and as belonging to—the outside world.

Once collective shadow projection becomes the order of the day, it becomes systematized, inevitably resulting in collective paranoia. The repressed aggressive impulses that underlie the shadow projection become projected out and reappear in the fear of persecution by the recipients of our projection. We then preemptively and insanely try to kill others out of fear of them attacking us first,* thus endlessly strengthening the spiral of fear, abuse, and madness.

Shadow of the Lord

According to Girard, the figure of Satan (one of whose inner meanings is "the shadow of the Lord") is the name and the source of all the various forms of lying that take place in the human world. The violence inherent to scapegoating isn't just "the work of Satan," to quote from James G. Williams's foreword to Girard's book *I See Satan Fall Like Lightning*, "it *is* Satan."[9]

Girard ties scapegoating to the true mystery of Satan (a.k.a. wetiko), referring to it as "his most clever trick." Girard calls scapegoating "the satanic principle," considering it the source of Satan's astonishing power. It is not for nothing that Satan, a personification of the archetype of the shadow, is known as "the accuser." In shadow projecting, we are accusing the other of what we ourselves are secretly doing. Accusing others of doing what we ourselves are doing—as if we're looking in a mirror and responding to our own reflection as if it is other than ourselves—is one of the chief features

---

*This point is exemplified when Himmler declared that the Jews "want to destroy us." This worldview allowed the Nazis to claim that in their attempted genocide they were acting out of self-defense against what was perceived as a threat of annihilation.

of wetiko. In accusing—and then attacking—the other, we become blinded. It's a good idea before we rail at others to reflect upon whether the judgment we are so happy to throw on them should really be reserved for ourselves.

Satan sponsors the project(ion) of the shadow onto the (innocent) recipient—creating a split in the community—and then, in a sleight of hand that goes unnoticed, inspires the victim to be condemned and expelled from the community to seemingly restore balance and harmony. In other words, Satan creates the problem by fomenting disorder, sowing scandals, and then at the height of the crises that he himself provokes, offers the solution. This invariably just further feeds the lie that is the source of the problem in a self-generating cycle that poisons the community. This process continues forever until seen through.

Collective scapegoating is a form of organized violence in the service of social tranquility, in that it tranquilizes (puts to sleep) its adherents. Once the scapegoat—who is seen as the cause of the community's problems—is exiled, a sense of peace is initially restored. This peace serves as evidence confirming the guilt of the scapegoat, further entrenching the apparent truth of the lie that underlies and foments the whole process.

Just like individuals have an ineradicable tendency to get rid of their own evil by foisting it upon someone else, it is the nature of political bodies to always see the evil in their adversary or the opposing party. When scapegoating happens collectively, the identity of the scapegoat is based on no evidence other than the unshakable unanimity of the collectivity's own consensus. This collective colluding with each other's illusions (etymologically, the word *collusion* has to do with "the sharing of an illusion")—a form of group-think—is based on the irrational illogic of the herd, what I refer to as "wetiko-logic" (or "wetiko-illogic"). To the extent that we are unaware of the scapegoat mechanism that covertly operates through our world, we are all complicit in collectively perpetuating it. We are then all murderers of Christ. All the while we imagine ourselves alien to—and innocent of—all violence.

This primordial self-division intrinsic to the scapegoating process is referred to in the Bible as "Satan driving out Satan," as if the devil is casting out Beelzebub (Mark 3:23–7 [NIV]). In a project doomed to failure from the beginning, darkness is trying to get rid of itself. This is the very act that generates, and is generated by the darkness in the first place. Projecting the shadow, while seeming to rescue us from the evil threatening us within, is the act that produces the very evil from which we are attempting to rid ourselves.

The Integration of Evil

Without the integration of evil, there is no totality; we will never attain our wholeness. But how can evil be integrated? Jung realized that there was only one possibility: to become aware of it and to raise it to the level of consciousness, which itself is a crucial and necessary step in assimilating it. To integrate evil means to become conscious of it as a numinous factor within the unconscious, as we consciously take it up as our cross. Integrating our darker unconscious aspects into the light of consciousness—becoming conscious—is the definition of individuation, the process of becoming whole. Becoming conscious of an unconscious content is a *coniunctio Solis et Lunae*—"a conjunction of sun and moon"—symbolic of a coming together of the opposites.

The process of individuation and the development of consciousness necessarily requires the withdrawal of as many of our projections as we can possibly muster. This necessarily means to withdraw our shadow projections, which involves recognizing and accepting "the other" in ourselves. Once we recognize and withdraw our projections, we can no longer blame other people for our problems.

Becoming aware of and owning our own darkness empowers us to deal with the darkness in the world. To deal with our own darkness is to be making a real contribution to the world. In Jung's words, to own our shadow is to have "succeeded in shouldering at least an infinitesimal part of the gigantic, unsolved social problems of our day."[10] Whenever any of us, as individuals, integrates an aspect of our shadows, it instantaneously registers and has a nonlocal effect on the whole universe. This adds a bit more light to the universe as a whole, which gets reflected throughout time and space.

Speaking in theological terms, Jung writes in *The Red Book,* "God suffers when man does not accept his darkness."[11] In psychological terms, this translates to the fact that if the conscious ego doesn't try to integrate the shadow it results in deep suffering for the individual and a failure to actualize the Self. Not accepting our own shadow isn't merely a passive act, but initially starts out as an active, deliberate response. Once we become habituated to turning away from our shadow, however, this knee-jerk reaction falls into the unconscious and becomes chronic—becoming our default mechanism, our modus operandi—such that we don't even notice it.

We need to own our own shadow, while at the same time, however, not identify with it, which would be to make a grave mistake that ultimately feeds wetiko. The shadow belongs to us. It is our responsibility, and yet it is not who we are. If we identify with it, we can easily fall into the abyss of despair, depression, and worthlessness, which can not only be dangerous, but potentially fatal. Discriminating between the shadow and who we are—our true nature that embraces and transcends our shadow—opens the doorway for the shadow, rather than obscuring our light, to flesh it out and reveal it.

Girard's founding murder is repeated—reproduced again and again, over, as, and throughout history—oftentimes (if not always) taking as its victim the person who has revealed it (think of Christ), whose liberating message everyone refuses to understand. The one who is in essence simply holding up a mirror and reflecting back to us our own violence is typically silenced, thereby serving as living evidence for the very process they are pointing at. The messenger is killed, so to speak, in what becomes a collectively sanctioned symbolic murder.

The intrusion of a mirror that reflects truth (mirrors, after all, show us our true face) can't help but to shine light on the darkness. Holding up a mirror and reflecting the group's unconscious shadow is an act that is seen by the collective as subversive. This is because it disturbs its comfortable, familiar illusions, which depend upon a lie. When someone points out the shadow they are, ironically, typically viewed by people who aren't seeing the shadow (and are hence unconsciously acting it out) as being blind. It is very dangerous to reflect back to people their unconscious shadow—in doing so, we run the risk of being demonized ourselves.

"The devil," as it says in the Bible, "has always hated the truth" (John 8:44 [NLT]). Only those who are themselves living a lie become upset when someone speaks the truth.

The more the violence that underlies the scapegoat mechanism tries to conceal its secret—by forcibly suppressing its being exposed— the more it reveals itself. Ironically, in this very process the reflection of our underlying violence that the collective tries to stifle is thereby confirmed as true. This is to say that the revelation is one and the same as—and is validated by—the violent reaction and opposition to the revelation. Seeing this equivalency between the revelation and our violent resistance to the revelation (which is evidence confirming the very revelation it is reacting against) is the doorway through which the revelation can actually take hold and blossom within our mind, thereby liberating us from the lie.

Girard's founding murder—the unconscious act of scapegoating— is disclosed and symbolically revealed through the crucifixion. God uses the violent death of his envoy as the occasion of a new and supreme revelation. God/Christ—out of his infinite love for us— allowed himself to be murdered/crucified in order to make the entire cycle of satanic violence that we are unconsciously participating in visible, conscious, and hence, eventually inoperative. In the crucifixion, the darker powers, in silencing the one who was outing them, believed themselves to be victorious, but in their violent actions they had unwittingly exposed—and revealed—themselves, and hence, prepared their own grave.

The secret underlying the satanic principle had never before been so explicitly revealed. In the crucifixion, the display is the victory itself—it is the unveiling and symbolic representation of the violent origin and nature of culture. The darker powers are not put on display because they are defeated; they are defeated because they are put on display. Our job is to recognize what is being symbolically revealed to us. This is not a passive realization, but one in which we are invited to actively participate via our re-cognition.

In waking up to our complicity in the violent process that has been unconsciously informing the history of our species, we can begin to realize our power to put a stop to this ongoing murder. To the extent that humanity doesn't recognize the revelation that is coming through Christ's voluntary sacrifice of himself, however, we continue our fall into bondage as a result of unknowingly participating in the founding murder—a murder that holds us prisoner.

Misguided "Goodness"

The most horrible acts of persecution are often committed in the name of the fight against persecution. The ones who are scapegoating believe they are self-righteously supporting the truth while in actuality they are living and propagating an egregious lie. Under this self-created delusion, people enact the most appalling and inhuman atrocities with the self-assurance of being on the side of good, oftentimes having a completely clear conscience. Doing evil is one thing. What makes it truly diabolical—and crazy-making—is representing it (both to oneself and others) as being good.

Scapegoating illustrates how the darkness uses people who are overly identified with the light as its secret outposts. The more we split off from our shadow and one-sidedly identify with our light side, the more we are unknowingly strengthening the darker forces of the unconscious. The more we consciously try to be overly positive, good, and wonderful, the more the shadow descends into the under-world and develops a will to be evil and destructive. Because they deny their shadow, such marvelously good people invariably become possessed by darker forces beneath their conscious awareness.

In addition to the dark shadows, one of the places darkness can hide is in the light itself. Overly identifying with our light nature and projecting out our darkness are interrelated aspects of a deeper singular process. People who hold themselves in overly high regard, thinking they possess incredible virtues, always have someone in their environment who carries all of their (split-off) evil.

It is noteworthy that, symbolically speaking, Christ is the arche-typal scapegoat. This symbolically illustrates how scapegoating and the incarnation of the highest value (Christ) are secretly related and actually go together. In other words, scapegoating—the activity of evil—and the holy have everything to do with each other. The sacred is locked up in and through the process of scapegoating. Withdrawing our shadow projections from the outside world, finding the darkness within ourselves, owning it but not identifying with it—like modern-day alchemists—we liberate the spirit that was imprisoned in matter. This Holy Spirit is then available to serve us, becoming "on call" for creative inspiration 24/7. Liberated from its bondage in the physical world, the spirit breathes a sigh of relief as it fulfills the very divinely mandated mission for which it was created—or so I imagine. And we, from our side, experience the relief of a lifetime.

Taking back within ourselves the projection of our own darkness is to realize that we are our own worst enemy, that we contain within ourselves what we are fighting against in the outside world. This is to become aware that we are both the one thing and the other. We are both of the opposites, the light and the dark, the good and the bad, the divine and the human. When we perceive the shadow and light part of ourselves simultaneously, we are seeing ourselves from two sides and thus arrive at the middle, which is where the Self, the wholeness of our personality, is to be found.

Projecting the shadow is simultaneously the way we try to distance ourselves from our own violence while, ironically, being a violent act itself. Instead of trying to avoid our inner violence through projection, intellectual tricks, or rationalizations, we need to consciously experience the dark part of ourselves as much as possible. Knowing our violence from the inside snaps us out of having to be both victim and perpetrator of violence. By owning our violence, we possess it rather than it possessing us. We then are no longer unconsciously driven to compulsively act out our violence, either on ourselves or on others.

Withdrawing our shadow projections and owning our own darker half adds depth, breadth, and substance to us. Confronting our own darkness is not a fun experience. On the contrary, it can be quite terrifying to behold the abysmal depths of darkness of which we are capable. Embracing our darkness, however, paradoxically becomes the doorway for us to choose to step more decisively into embodying the full grandeur of our light. Embracing our darkness doesn't magically turn it into light, but rather, kindles a light that illumines the darkness from within the darkness itself.

Being consciously identified with being decent, nice people, it is always the others who are capable of doing horrific acts—never us. But the fact that we ourselves are people who could potentially do these things is what escapes us, is what we are unwilling or unable to face. In being incapable of facing our own potential capacity for evil—personified in the inner figure that Nietzsche calls "the ugliest man"—we thereby tragically disable the only power we have to do anything about the problem of evil, which lies in our ability to deal with it within ourselves.[12]

We all have a darker half. We can all become potential criminals under the right circumstances. We are all inseparably interconnected and partake of the shared collective unconscious of humanity—in both its dark and light aspects. None of us stands outside of humanity's dark collective shadow.

We can't be substantial and have gravitas without casting a shadow. Being whole means having both a light and a dark side. When we become conscious of our shadow, we remember that we are simply a human being who is just like others in our human condition. Becoming conscious of our own darkness dispels our sense of being better (or worse) than anyone else. This recognition connects us with the rest of humanity—as we are all recognized to be in the same boat. We discover that the people we've been projecting the shadow onto are not who we thought they were. They are now deemed to be ordinary, flawed human beings, just like ourselves. This realization fulfills what very well might be our deepest need—overcoming our sense of separation—while engendering a felt sense of our interconnectedness and love for others. The result is an increase in genuine compassion, both for others as well as the darker part of ourselves. As indigenous people would say, we have become a human being.

Once we've attained the privileged status of becoming a human being, instead of demonizing each other, we can then make our highest priority what it should have been all along: helping each other to awaken and step into our immense untapped creative potential and brilliance. Recognizing the dreamlike nature of reality, a recognition that contains the insight that there are vast domains of undreamt of possibilities available to us, we can learn to sync up with each other and put our shared lucidity together and *dream ourselves awake*. To say it differently: We can conspire to co-inspire each other (a true conspiracy theory) to greater heights of lucidity.

Scapegoating only functions based on ignorance, blindness, and a persecutory unconsciousness. In Christ's words, those who scapegoat "know not what they do" (Luke 23:34 [KJV]). Its power is dependent on a lie, which is why the lie must remain hidden at all costs. When the lie underlying the scapegoating mechanism is exposed, the spiral of violence is disrupted, wetiko loses its power over us—and the spell is broken.

PART III

The Coronavirus and the Wetiko Virus

In this next section, I write about the coronavirus pandemic from the dreaming point of view (seeing it as a phenomenon that we have all dreamed up in our world), and interpreting it, like I would a dream, symbolically. I do so in order to decipher the deeper levels of symbolic meaning that are encoded within it so as to be able to receive the potential lessons and gifts that it's offering us.

13

Covid-19 Is a Symbol of a Much Deeper Infection

With the coronavirus pandemic it is as if the immaterial wetiko virus has *taken on* corporeal form. It is a true game changer to recognize that the physical virus is a materialization in our world—a REVELATION—of the immaterial and heretofore invisible wetiko virus that exists deep within the collective unconscious of humanity. What is playing out with the Covid-19 pandemic, with all the various political, social, and financial reactions to it, as well as what it brings up inside of our minds, can help us—in true quantum style, potentially—to see wetiko.

Multiple Vectors of Transmission

It is a limited and overly one-sided materialistic viewpoint that conceives of Covid-19 as solely being a physical virus. Having multiple facets of operation and channels of influence, the virus is multidimensional in its impact. It is affecting our world in practically every way imaginable. Besides its obvious physical aspect, Covid-19 also has a psychological vector of transmitting itself into our minds (via our unconscious reactions of fear, stress, anxiety, etc.). The "mental" vector of the virus spreads much more quickly, as it is exponentially more contagious than its biological counterpart. It propagates itself through the channel of our shared unconscious blind spots and fears.

If we become enchanted by the forms of the outer world, entranced in thinking the virus is merely physical, we forget the outer world's inseparable interconnection to the world within us—which splits our mind in two. We then become dissociated within—and from—ourselves, a state that forecloses on our being able to be of help to anyone, including ourselves. We have then unwittingly fallen under the thrall of the psychological aspect of the virus. This is where the physical aspect of the coronavirus and the psychological aspect of the wetiko virus intersect and join hands, as if parts of a greater psycho-physical body.

Like an entity with many tentacles, in addition to its physical and mental components, Covid-19 also has an interpersonal, behavioral vector of transmission. In other words, in affecting our minds (and thus, how we think and feel), Covid-19 impacts our behavior. This in turn influences how we interact with each other and the world around us. This is to say that the virus deeply impacts the underlying social matrix that fashions human culture, leaving no stone unturned in its effects upon our world.

The virus has a countless legion of effects. In addition to making people physically sick, some of whom die, the virus makes people afraid, creates enormous stress, changes governmental policies around the world, impacts the financial markets, inspires power grabs and profiteering from all sorts of unsavory people and institutions, feeds into and provides a pretext for totalitarian agendas, affects how often we leave our homes, influences what we think about, where we place our attention, and what we wear when we go out in public, transforms the way we interact with each other, and renders our future completely uncertain. Indeed, it might either destroy our civilization or herald a new historical epoch. Covid-19 has so gotten into our heads that it has even intruded, in one form or another, into many people's dreams.

Recognizing that Covid-19 has multiple vectors of transmission opens up our vision to begin to see how—just like a symbol in a dream—the virus is revealing something deeper than itself. Like wetiko, Covid-19 is a field phenomenon, which is to say it doesn't exist as an isolated entity that independently exists on its own, walled off from the environment. Rather, it exists in relation to and as an expression of the field in which it arises. When we get right down to it, the boundary between where the virus ends and the world begins becomes indistinguishable.

Even though on one level Covid-19 is a physical virus that has seemingly invaded our world, being a field phenomenon means that all of its myriad effects and repercussions throughout every area of our lives are not separate from the virus itself. The virus has an energetic body that extends itself out into the world. Its effects in our world are its expression, the spore prints of its subtle body, so to speak. The irony is that the effects of the virus's subtle body in our world are anything but subtle. Encoded within the physical pathogen are hidden catalysts that trigger us in ways that are beyond the merely physical.

Rather than distancing ourselves from what has been triggered within us—social distancing from ourselves—if we are able to bear, carry, and utilize this uncomfortable and sometimes excruciating tension in a conscious way, we can potentially ignite the creative spirit within us to be set aflame with the light of divine inspiration. In these instances, when traced back to its source, the credit for our creativity falls at the feet of the virus.

The Fusion of Consciousness and the Physical World

The virus triggers reactions to itself within the human psyche, reactions that are not separate from the virus but are part of its "operational body" (i.e., how the virus surgically operates on us). Just as the rays of the sun are not separate from the sun but are its energetic expression, all of the ripple effects of the virus into our world (and within our minds) are appendages of the nonlocal energetic body of the virus that are continuous and coextensive with the virus itself. It greatly behooves us to step out of our dualistic mindset, expand our limited and fragmented vision, and see the actual true nature of the virus from a more wholistic perspective in which we begin to recognize the inseparability between the physical world and consciousness.

For example, if the moon's reflection appears in the ocean, the image of its reflection in the water can't be separated out from either the moon, the ocean, or the mind that perceives the reflection. They are all part of one whole quantum system. The moon isn't *causing* the reflection any more than the ocean (or our mind) is. All of these interrelated factors are interdependently reciprocally co-arising with each other so as to produce the resultant effect (the image of the moon's reflection in water that is arising within our minds). To think of them as separate parts interacting with each other is a cognitive error preventing us from seeing the deeper, whole system that is openly revealing itself through their shared interplay.

Or think of the ocean's waves. The ocean isn't in any way separate from its waves; the waves are its unmediated expression. The ocean isn't *causing* the waves, the waves aren't the *effect* of the ocean—the waves *are* the ocean.

If we wish to heal the virus—in all of its myriad psycho-physical aspects—we need to see its true multidimensional nature. Just like a human being (and other sentient beings) have different "bodies"—physical, mental, emotional, astral, etheric, energetic, etc.—so too **does** the virus. In order to discover the cure for it, we first have to get into focus what exactly we are dealing with. It is a limited and myopic viewpoint that only sees the virus in its physical aspect. This point of view is an expression of how deeply under the spell we are from the prevailing materialist point of view. In order to be seen in its true form, the virus is demanding us to open our eyes and expand our vision. The coronavirus (a virus that we can see under a microscope) and all of its various effects in the world are actually lower-level psycho-physical emanations of the formless wetiko mind-virus.

The myriad effects on our behavior that the virus has activated throughout human global society are based on our *reactions*—both conscious and unconscious—to its presence in our world. Our reactions are, in turn, mediated through and shaped by the human psyche, which is the medium of operations for wetiko. This points to the fact that the wetiko mind-virus is influencing our reactions and hence our behavior, both individually and collectively. At the quantum level—which is to say at the reality level—mind and matter interpenetrate each other so fully as to reveal themselves to be indivisible. The physical virus and the psychological virus are not two separate things interacting. Instead they are inseparable aspects of a greater whole unified quantum field in which mind and matter are one.

The effects of the virus on our world can only be separated out from the virus in thought. This means that the idea that the virus is separate from its effects is just that—an idea—with no basis in reality. The idea that objects exist separate from their effects is an expression of the same unconscious conceptual blind spot that spawns our sense of self that thinks it exists separate from others and the environment. At the quantum level there is no difference between what something is (its being) and what effects it has (its doing). This essentially replaces the world of material substances with a world populated by actions, events, and inseparable processes in ever-flowing or constant movement.

When we contemplate the biochemical, physical virus under the microscope of our mind from a whole systems point of view, it becomes impossible to differentiate the physical virus from the psychological virus. This is because they both reciprocally feed into and off of each other. It is thus impossible to tell where one ends and the other begins. In informing and coordinating our unconscious reactions to Covid-19, the wetiko mind-virus is like the stage manager behind the scenes, influencing our psychological state and thereby orchestrating our behavior from beneath our conscious awareness. Cloaking itself under the cover of the global pandemic, the wetiko mind-virus is then able to materially incarnate—take on physical form—by influencing our internal reactions to the physical virus.

To view the virus from a whole systems point of view is to recognize that the virus and its ecosystem (which in our case happens to be the whole planet) are one seamlessly interconnected whole quantum system with no separable parts anywhere to be found. The virus and its myriad effects in our world and within our minds, when all seen together as interrelated aspects of a greater whole, are both literally and symbolically the revelation of something deeper. This something deeper is the wetiko mind-virus.

Covid-19 as Symbol

Again, in the coronavirus pandemic the formless spirit of the wetiko virus has taken on corporeal, full-bodied form and become visible. Analogous to the shadows on the wall of Plato's cave (which we mentioned earlier), the physical outbreak of the coronavirus is like a lower-dimensional shadow projected into our world cast from an archetypal or higher dimensional realm. Studying the shadow (the coronavirus pandemic) within its proper context—relative to what it is an emanation and re-presentation of—helps us begin to understand the deeper higher dimensional process (the wetiko virus) that is revealing itself through the pandemic.

In his recent article, "Searching for the Anti-Virus: Covid-19 as Quantum Phenomenon," the global activist Martin Winiecki writes, "*Wetiko*—often referred to as a mind virus—propagates the deep-seated illusion of seeing oneself desperately confined to the cage of a separated ego. From this perspective of isolation, others appear either as competitors or as prey. In a worldview in which fear is the basic condition, fight and exploitation seem rational, empathy ridiculous and sentimental. . . . Wetiko has numbed our hearts, blurring our ability to perceive both the sacredness and the pain of life, both outside and inside ourselves. Innumerable beings are perishing due to this chronic inability to feel empathy."[1] It is our very ignorance and the fear that accompanies the physical virus that is the food for the wetiko mind-virus.

Winiecki asks, "What if Covid-19 weren't a danger independent from our minds and souls . . . [something] we've collectively summoned into existence? An embodiment of something buried deeply in the realms of the collective subconscious that we haven't, so far, been able to comprehend? A living symbol of a much deeper infection?"[2] What if, as Winiecki suggests, we have unconsciously called forth and summoned—"dreamed up"—Covid-19 as a symbol to potentially reveal the much more dangerous underlying infection (wetiko) that exists within the collective unconscious of humanity? We as of yet haven't been able to see this because it is taking place deep within the dark depths of our unconscious. It is notable that recognizing that the world is speaking symbolically (i.e., just like a dream) is the viewpoint that literally connects us with a more fundamental level of reality.

Winiecki wonders, "How has the specter of Covid-19 been able to haunt 7.5 billion people and bring the world to a standstill in no time at all? Because the narrative massively resonates with something latent that is both teeming and deeply suppressed in people's subconscious."[3] Similar to how a symbol in a dream resonates with, speaks to, and invokes something in the dreamer, it is not an accident the "specter of Covid-19" has been able to "haunt" humanity. It is only able to have this profound effect on us collectively because it is touching something that is alive and actively at work deep within our unconscious.

Winiecki's article came out the same day I published my article "Quantum Medicine for the Coronavirus." This got my attention;

we were clearly thinking along similar lines. To quote Winiecki, "Much more than just a difficult trial for humanity, the Covid-19 outbreak also holds the possibility for collective healing from the predatory mass infection of Wetiko. We can make sense of it as a global somatization—or symbolic simulation—of the underlying Wetiko disease."[4] In other words, Covid-19 is a symbolic yet also full-bodied representation on the world stage of the underlying immaterial wetiko mind-virus that is playing out behind the scenes.

The Power of Dreaming to Our Rescue

Our night dreams—which are clearly a manifestation of the unconscious—can teach us how to proceed. Though an illusion of the mind, our dreams potentially reveal the nature of reality and the role we play in it. The way to unwrap the freely offered gifts that our dreams are lavishing on us starts with our creative imagination. This makes sense, for our creative imagination is the source of our dreams.

As if making a magical elixir, there is a way of combining two of our intrinsic faculties—our unconscious dreaming/imaginative powers and the ability of our conscious mind to reflect upon these creative powers. Through self-reflecting (i.e., reflecting upon itself and its creations), the mind processes information. It thereby potentially gains insight into the internal dynamics of the mental projections that are shaping our moment-to-moment experience. This can potentially unlock a profound realization about the role we play in the arising of our experience—an insight lying dormant within us that has been yearning to be brought into the light of day.

When we are unconscious of something, the unconscious content will literally become symbolized and get "dreamed up" in our dreams again and again in a variety of (dis)guises (oftentimes in a series of recurring dreams). This will continue until we begin to recognize what the symbol is representing and touching within us.

In psychology speak, we can then own this content as belonging to us. In this, we are able to integrate within ourselves what it is reflecting to us, thereby expanding our consciousness and enlarging our sense of self.

For example, when we are unaware of an unconscious content—such as the part of our mind that is under the thrall of wetiko—it hides in identification with us. To say this differently, we become unconsciously identified with it. In other words, when we aren't seeing wetiko, it has taken on our form such that it becomes the lens through which we see the world, which renders its existence invisible to us. People who are afflicted with wetiko have no idea there's anything askew within them, always seeing the problem as outside of themselves.

In a dream, the psyche has projected itself seemingly outside of itself and then observes and interacts with itself as if it is something other than and separate from itself, forgetting that what it is reacting to is its own creation. If the psyche becomes absorbed in this process—falling asleep to what it is creating as it is creating it—it becomes conditioned by its reactions in a way that constricts and limits its infinite creativity. In so doing, it uses its profound creative potency against itself, entrancing—and casting a binding spell—upon itself. The good news is that encoded within this very process is the possibility of seeing through it, whose origin is within our own minds. This is to recognize the dreamlike nature of the situation we are in and become lucid—which changes everything.

When an inner, unconscious, and destructive content of the psyche such as wetiko gets dreamed up and appears in the outer world in physical form—such as in its revelation of itself via the Covid-19 pandemic—something is becoming available to us that, if recognized, can free us from the tyrannical hold the previously unconscious content (wetiko) had on us.

Once we become aware that the manifestation of the physical virus in our world is mirroring back to us a more fundamental underlying mental virus, we can self-reflectively put our attention on what within us is triggered by the external virus. By doing so, the unconscious energy that was bound up (as if being held hostage) in the compulsive re-creation of the mind-virus becomes available to be channeled constructively and expressed creatively in a way that, instead of keeping us stuck, serves our individuation and continual evolution.

Realizing the correlation between the Covid-19 outbreak and the wetiko mind-virus is to begin to recognize the dreamlike nature of our predicament. Here, just like a dream, our inner situation is actively mirrored by and reflected through the outer world. Recognizing the connection between the inner and outer dimensions of our experience sheds light on the crucial and active role that the psyche plays in the creation of our experience.

Recognizing the role of our psyche in all of this isn't a passive realization, however, but being a realization that takes place within the psyche itself, simultaneously activates and unlocks the very creative nature of the psyche that we are recognizing. In other words, this realization isn't abstract, intellectual, or theoretical. Rather, it is a felt-sense that directly connects us with and helps us access the enormous creative power each of us—knowingly or unknowingly—carries within us. This insight by itself is just the beginning, however, for we are then called to carry and embody our inner realization into the outer world in our own uniquely creative way.

Our world has become surreal beyond belief. Who would have imagined—in their wildest dreams—that it would have changed so dramatically in so short a time? In his recent article, Winiecki concludes, "If there's one thing that Covid-19 has taught us, it is that dramatic shifts of collective behavior can actually occur overnight." Seen through the eyes of symbolic awareness, Covid-19 reveals to us just how fluid, impermanent, and malleable the underlying structures of our world are, as well as how unpredictable and dreamlike our ever-changing experience of the world really is. Seeing the dreamlike nature of our universe helps us to realize that it is not just the coronavirus that is revealing the more fundamental and dangerous wetiko mind-virus. In addition, we can also realize that the entire universe is itself a continuous living revelation offering us everything we need in order to wake up, if only we have the eyes to see.

14

The Coronavirus Contains
Its Own Vaccine

Living through a global pandemic can feel surreal, as if we are living in a dreamworld. Though it can feel like we are living through a collective nightmare, there are precious gifts encoded within the experience that should not be overlooked. Of course it is imperative to deal with the physical outbreak of the virus by every means at our disposal. And yet, it would be a tragedy beyond measure if we focused our attention merely on its external manifestation while marginalizing what the pandemic is touching—and revealing—within us about ourselves.

An invisible specter in the field, the coronavirus is creating havoc in our world, disrupting business as usual as it ripples—both in our world and within our psyches—throughout the globe. To quote Jung, "Everything could be left undisturbed did not the new way demand to be discovered, and did it not visit humanity with all the plagues of Egypt until it finally is discovered."[1] The coronavirus can be envisioned as a modern-day plague of Egypt. It is a living revelation that is dying to show us something about who we are and our place in the universe. What it is revealing to us about ourselves is crucially important for us to know. Our very survival depends upon receiving its message.

We hear every day the phrase *We are all in this together*. In the late 1950s, Jung wrote words that are as relevant today as they were then, "We are in the soup that is going to be cooked for us, whether we claim to have invented it or not. . . . We are threatened with universal genocide if we cannot work out the way of salvation by a symbolic death."[2] In other words, we are fated to suffer an unconscious literal death if we don't consciously go through a symbolic death. This symbolic death has everything to do with finding "the new way" that is demanding to be discovered by our current worldwide plague.

As we go through a species-wide dark night of the soul—the mythic night sea journey—our illusions about the world we live in—and ourselves as well—are being *shattered*. Seeing through our illusions is a symbolic death of the self that was wed to—and lived by—illusion. Being disillusioned—having our illusions dispelled—is to become sober, stepping out of our intoxicated state. Being disillusioned is truly mortifying, a real death. It is the dying of an overly one-sided—and bogus—image of who we are (remember—one of wetiko's other names is "ME disease," i.e., a misidentification of who we think we are).

Our species has gotten drafted into an archetypal death/rebirth experience. In symbolically dying to a part of ourselves that is no longer serving us, another part of us is being reborn. We as a species have been drawn into the cycle of the death and rebirth of the gods. Said another way, having become part of a deeper mythic, archetypal, and alchemical process of transformation, we are going through a cosmic death/rebirth experience of a higher order.

The divine process of transformation is typically experienced as punishment, torment, an experience of death and then transfiguration. This divinely sponsored process is subjectively experienced by the human ego as torture.* However, if we don't personalize the experience, identify with it, or get stuck in its nightmarish aspect—a great danger—but allow this deeper process to refine us as it moves through us, it can lead to a transfiguration of our very being.

---

*In alchemy, the torturing of the prima materia was an allegory of Christ's passion.

If we remain unconscious when a living archetypal process is activated within us, this inner process will physically manifest itself externally in the outside world. Here, as if by fate, it will get unconsciously dreamed up and acted out in a literal, concrete and oftentimes destructive way. Instead of going through an inner *symbolic* death, for example, we then *literally* kill each other, as well as, ultimately, ourselves. If we recognize, however, that we are being cast to play a role in a deeper cosmic process, instead of being destined to enact it unconsciously, and hence, destructively, we are able to consciously and creatively "incarnate" this archetypal process as individuation.

Whether consciously or not, since the advent of the coronavirus we are all in a state of grieving. The world we knew, as well as a false part of ourselves, is dying. Our sense of who we think we are—imagining we exist as a separate self, alien to and apart from other separate selves as well as the rest of the universe—is an illusion whose expiration date has now been reached. If not recognized as illusory, this illusion can become reified and become a lethal mirage. Either our illusion (of existing as a separate self) expires, or we do. As the poet Rumi would say, we need to "die before we die."

Seen as a dreaming phenomenon, we have collectively dreamed up a global pandemic, a modern-day plague of Egypt, an invasion by a mysterious microbe from which no one is immune, to help us dispel the primary illusion of the separate self and assist us in facing the reality of who we are in the greater scheme of things. We can—in potential—unite as one to overcome our common enemy, which on one level is the coronavirus, but on a deeper level is our ignorance of our interconnectedness with each other.

The coronavirus is the medicine that can help us get over ourselves and realize that the most vital and urgent task for humanity is to see through what Einstein famously calls an "optical delusion of consciousness"—the illusion of the separate self. To see through the illusion of the separate self is at the same time to take away the power that fear has over us (as well as to empower ourselves). For the experience of separation and fear (of "the other") mutually co-arise, reciprocally reinforcing each other.

The coronavirus feeds off of and engenders fear—within us, all around us, and everywhere in between. Fear is contagious. When it develops enough collective momentum, it feeds on itself, taking on a seemingly autonomous and independent life of its own, driving a downward spiral into the darkness of the underworld. As fear propagates itself throughout the field, it unleashes the terrifying and fearsome powers of darkness. This then inspires more fear in a never-ending, crazy-making feedback loop. When fear becomes rampant, we become more susceptible to being controlled by external forces.

Our day-to-day lives have changed and become so surreal. Yet if we manage to step out of and not be caught by our fear, it has actually become much easier to recognize the dreamlike nature of reality. Hence it has become easier than it was before the pandemic's arrival to become lucid in the waking dream of life. It is *as if* we are living in a dystopian Philip K. Dick sci-fi novel or movie in which our world has turned upside down and inside out. What could be more dreamlike than that?

It is noteworthy that recognizing the dreamlike nature of our shared reality is a realization that dispels fear. Realizing the dreamlike nature is to recognize that we are *dream characters*—embodied reflective aspects—of each other. We all exist relative to—are related to—each other in a seamless interdependent web of mutual connectivity. This realization carries within it an implicit intuition that otherness and separation are ultimately illusory mental constructs. There is no separate self anywhere to be found when we realize the dreamlike nature of the universe.

When we get right down to it, the coronavirus elicits fear, as well as—by revealing reality's dreamlike nature—also potentially dispelling the very fear it triggers. It is up to each one of us which of these parallel universes—one riddled with fear; the other, dreamlike beyond belief—we invest our attention in, and hence, create. If we choose the universe ridden by fear, we will undoubtedly be doomed to a tragic fate. If we recognize that the universe is in fact a collective dream, however, and choose to consciously step into the dream, we discover that the universe is malleable. This is to say that we have a hand (or two) in creating it. As we come to understand this, we begin to realize our intrinsic creative power, another one of the gifts offered us by the coronavirus outbreak.

We're All Connected

American journalist I. F. Stone was right when he said, "Either we learn to live together or we die together." The lesson of the pandemic is clear. Due to our interconnectedness, a health problem in any part of the world can rapidly become a health problem for everyone around the globe. Our world has shrunk. We truly live in a global village. Our tolerating, turning a blind eye toward, or worse yet, engendering disease in any place in the world is at our own peril. This new way of seeing the interrelated unity of humanity can be called "holographic awareness." Just like every fragment of a hologram contains the whole hologram, each of us contains encoded within us the whole, which is to say that if any of us are sick we all are affected.

The coronavirus pandemic is a form of collectively shared trauma to which no one is immune. The coronavirus doesn't create an aftershock, it itself is the shock. The virus is multidimensional—having a micro and macro aspect—in that it doesn't just shock our system, it shocks "the system." No one among us is untouched by its shattering impact, both upon our lives and within our psyches. When we are shaken up by trauma, however, it can—potentially—be the impetus for a long-dreamed of transformation within our soul, as our inner constitution can be rewritten in a way that helps us to become free.

The coronavirus, by so shaking up our world, our ordinary routines as well as our psyches, is potentially "a lucidity stimulator" undreamed of until now, potentially catalyzing us to greater heights of lucidity. But being like a dream, how the coronavirus pandemic manifests within our minds—as nightmare or lucidity stimulator—depends upon whether or not we recognize what it is revealing to us about ourselves, and what we do with what it has triggered within us. The coronavirus can help us to remember that it is within ourselves that our true power and agency lies—another of its many gifts.

It is of the utmost significance that the coronavirus is a quantum phenomenon, in that it contains within itself both death-creating poison as well as its own medicine. Encoded in the virus is its own vaccine. As interdependently connected cells in a greater living organism, each of us is being demanded by the coronavirus to realize how we can synergistically cooperate together so as to resist and overcome its invasion. Though itself continually mutating, the coronavirus is, when push comes to shove, forcing us to expand our consciousness. As such, the coronavirus—like wetiko—is a powerful catalyst for human evolution.

As Jung reminds us, a "new way"—which he likens to an undiscovered vein that lives within the greater body politic of humanity that connects us all—is "demanding" to be discovered. This unknown vein within us is a living part of the psyche that connects us with the creativity of our mutually shared collective consciousness. It connects us with each other, with our wholeness, and thereby heals our fragmentation (both within ourselves and amongst each other).

This is the gift concealed within the disease that not only helps us to heal the disease, but heals us as well.

Does the Coronavirus Inspire Optimism or Pessimism?

As a writer, I've noticed something very interesting in the coronavirus outbreak regarding people's reactions to my writings on the subject. Since the virus has taken hold of our consciousness (as we focus our attention on it), I've been pointing out that the global pandemic—and our unconscious reactions to it—can be seen to be a revelation of something deep within our unconscious, which it greatly behooves us to know. People's reactions to what I'm writing about have become as interesting to me as the revelation encoded within the pandemic. It's as if people's reactions to what I'm shining light on are themselves part of the revelation at which I'm pointing.

Though a suffering-filled nightmare on one level, I have been pointing out that the coronavirus pandemic also has many gifts encoded within it. For example, helping people more deeply realize our interdependence (our literal "oneness"), a realization that generates compassion, as well as helping us to realize the dreamlike nature of our universe (helping us become lucid in this shared waking dream). This realization also helps us to step out of fear and unlock our intrinsic power, agency, and creativity—all of which are in the service of potentially awakening the human species from our collective slumber. And yet, when I send out my writing, in addition to the responses from people who really appreciate and draw inspiration from what I'm saying, the responses from people who take issue with what I'm pointing at have really gotten my attention.

The people who disagree with what I'm saying point out, in essence, the undeniable insidious power grab (with the fingerprints of wetiko all over it) that is taking place behind the scenes while we are distracted by the pandemic. This involves the sinister restructuring of the economy and of the government, the centralization of power and control, the militarization of our society, the transfer of wealth and power, the implementation of a totalitarian agenda—all designed to strengthen the grip of the corrupt corporate banking oligarchy that has us increasingly under its thumb. This has been called disaster capitalism. In times of catastrophe, while most everyone is distracted by the crisis, certain people or institutions seize an opportunity to profit at the expense of everyone else's suffering. Call it what you will, this is a very real phenomenon that is definitely taking place under our masked noses. It doesn't serve us to turn a blind eye to this malevolent darkness that is increasingly becoming visible in our world.

It has been reflected back to me that, with a roof over my head and food in my belly, it is easy for me to write about the many gifts hidden within the virus, as I am in a privileged position—a perspective with which I don't disagree. To quote one of my readers (who happens to be a very accomplished spiritual teacher),

> For those who have lost their jobs and are struggling to get by from one day to the next; for the low-income workers who have to work, putting themselves and their families at risk; for the doctors and nurses without sufficient protective gear fighting on behalf of an overload of patients; for those in Italy and Iran and Spain and still other countries where the virus hangs like a dark terror over their heads; for people in Spain, whose aged parents are being taken off respirators so that these can then be used for younger patients—for all these it would take a tremendous swivel at the seat of consciousness to see the virus as a bearer of gifts.

I can't disagree at all with this reader's point. For people who are losing their source of income and/or their own health or the very lives of their loved ones, to hear someone proclaiming the many gifts that the pandemic bears can sound like so much new age, feel-good, magical thinking nonsense. And yet, their reaction, though justified and steeped in truth, is revealing something about how to navigate the nature of the conversation into which we have all been drafted.

Their reaction begs the question: Should I not be pointing out the very real potential gifts that are encoded within the pandemic? Is it unfeeling and insensitive of me to do so? And yet, just like my reader's point of view, the perspective that the coronavirus carries a revelation within it also has a truth to it that is undeniable. Shedding light on this paradoxical dilemma can become a key that unlocks an important insight within our minds.

What would make a "tremendous swivel at the seat of consciousness" take place other than something—like the recent pandemic—that is truly shocking? The fact that an event causes mass suffering doesn't preclude that it can also contain within it a transformative gift. Oftentimes events like these are the necessary catalyst to transform both individuals and our species as a whole. Isn't this the deeper meaning of the Christian myth—that we can't have the Resurrection without the Crucifixion? And isn't this the meaning of the Four Noble Truths of Buddhism?* The idea is that our world is pervaded by suffering, but that encoded within the suffering is the possibility of discovering its root cause so as to alleviate it. The greater the suffering, the greater the incentive to uncover its source. The fact that there is a potential revelation hidden within our suffering—that reveals to us how to end our suffering—is the basis of the whole Buddhist path.

Our narratives—the stories we tell ourselves about what is happening in our world—are the interpretive frameworks through which we make sense of our world. Internally consistent and self-reinforcing from within their own viewpoint, these narratives have a spellbinding effect upon our minds. This makes it hard to take in evidence that is contrary to our viewpoint. Each of us has a particular narrative that we invest in as being objectively, unimpeachably true, what can be called our "narrative bias."

The Danger of Not Seeing the Bigger Picture

Some of us understandably feel despair and pessimism because of the dark agenda that is undeniably being implemented not just behind the scenes, but on the main stage of the world for all who have eyes

---

*In the appendix please find the Four Ignoble Blindnesses of Wetiko.

to see. There is very convincing real-world evidence to justify the pessimistic point of view of their narrative bias. Others of us can hold out the possibility that a deeper good might be emerging out of the collective nightmare that we are living through. This is a viewpoint that seems naive and ridiculous from the perspective of the people whose narrative bias is pessimistic.

If someone has fallen prey to pessimism, thinking that they are helpless to change the trajectory of our species' suicidal behavior, they will see the world through a lens that draws evidence to confirm their pessimistic viewpoint. This results in them being even more convinced of the validity of their viewpoint and the objective nature of what they are seeing in an infinitely regressing, self-generating samsaric cycle that is of the nature of a self-fulfilling prophecy. They wouldn't be so pessimistic if our world wasn't manifesting so darkly, and our world wouldn't be manifesting so darkly if they weren't so pessimistic. It is important to note that wetiko both inspires and feeds off of an overly pessimistic attitude.

The question naturally arises: In their pessimistic viewpoint, are they just being sober-minded "realists," having a justified response to the reality of our situation? Or have they become entranced by the creative genius of their own mind to call forth reality in an image confirming their pessimistic viewpoint? It should get our attention that there is something flawed in our logic if the accomplishment from winning a debate about the truth of our pessimism is that we are screwed. It is noteworthy that if someone becomes entrenched in their pessimistic point of view, they have become unwittingly complicit in creating their own worst nightmare.

On the other hand, I've noticed that when I point out the darker agenda to people who are identified with an overly one-sided, spiritual, and optimistic point of view, they get upset. They don't want to put their attention on the shadowy goings-on in our world. This might be for fear of thinking they'd be feeding the darkness by focusing their attention on it. Or perhaps they might sense that they'd get overly stressed out, anxious, and depressed if they took in the darkness, in which case they couldn't be of help to anyone. By holding onto an overly optimistic, light-filled viewpoint, however, while marginalizing the darker, more frightening point of view, they are avoiding relationship with their own inner darkness. They thereby unwittingly make it more probable that the very darker reality that they are denying will actually manifest. Similar to over-pessimism, wetiko simultaneously inspires and feeds off of an overly optimistic attitude.

And yet these two polar opposite points of view—though seemingly contradictory and mutually exclusive—can both be seen to be potentially valid depending on the reference point through which they're viewed. The pessimistic viewpoint sees us creating hell on Earth, and the optimistic point of view imagines that the pandemic will bring in a new, more grace-filled world. All of the possible universes exist in a state of quantum superposition, like multiple transparencies overlaid on each other, and which potential reality actually manifests depends upon our creative response (or lack thereof).

There is a psychological phenomenon that happens when we see an aspect of the truth. This is that oftentimes we fall prey to imagining that what we are seeing is the whole truth, instead of realizing that we are only seeing one of its many multitextured facets. Seeing a partial truth but being certain that we are in possession of the whole truth can actually serve to obscure us from seeing a more comprehensive truth. (This is a process that, once again, wetiko both inspires and feeds off of.) We ourselves then unknowingly become our own agents of obfuscation.

Many people, based on their narrative bias, are identified with one point of view, which is not only seen as true, but is conflated with THE TRUTH itself. This is often done to the exclusion of the contrary viewpoint, which is not only deemed to be false, but oftentimes seen as something dangerous and/or evil. One of the results of this is to divide and separate us among ourselves based on whichever particular *reality tunnel* (to use author Robert Anton Wilson's phrase) we inhabit in the moment. People who are interpreting the world the way we see it validate the rightness of our point of view and are seen as allies. People who view things differently than us are typically seen as "others." They are seen as having a deluded perspective and are deemed a threat to our version of reality, which creates a sense of judgment and separation from those who hold a different viewpoint.

Becoming divided among ourselves is part of the psychological effect of the virus that we are unwittingly colluding with through our fixed views. When we become divided and polarized, we are more easily manipulated and controlled (divide and conquer) by outside forces. If we become stuck in our viewpoint we are actually enabling the virus to propagate itself at our expense. This is to say that the psychological aspect of the virus depends on our cognitive prejudices to keep itself in business, so to speak.

Just like a dream compensates a one-sidedness in the dreamer, oftentimes the counter-narrative to our own may contain some facet of truth, some important piece of the bigger picture. This, if recognized, can enhance and flesh out our perspective. The exception, of course, is when someone's narrative is simply deluded and out of touch with reality, a result of the pervasive brainwashing propaganda that seems to be everywhere in our world today. If we are able to find even the smallest grain of truth in the opposing viewpoint, however, it can help us to dispel our sense of separation from the other person who seems to be holding a contrary perspective to our own, which increases our compassion.

In our world today it is as if people are inhabiting two parallel universes, with no intersection of viewpoints between the two. It behooves us to access a metaperspective such that we can see the differing viewpoints of both parallel universes simultaneously, without solely identifying with—and hence, being caught by—one or the other.

Creating and Maintaining a Metaperspective

What I notice in myself is an ever-growing capacity to simultaneously hold a metaperspective from which both seemingly opposing points of view are seen as potentially true. I am not turning a blind eye or marginalizing either of the two extremes, nor identifying with one at the expense of the other. This is to step out of the limited two-valued, binary logic—which sees things as either true or false—into the more expanded four-valued quantum dream logic, which is able to see things as both true and false at the same time. I see both the potential nightmare as well as the potential lucid dream, so to speak. And though it can be painful to hold the tension of these opposites, I continually cultivate the ability—like going to the gym to build up my psycho-spiritual muscles—to hold both possibilities in my mind's eye and see what spontaneously emerges out of the creative tension this elicits in my psyche.

Consciously holding the tension of the opposites within our own awareness without splitting off and identifying with either of the opposites (either optimistic or pessimistic) is an intrinsic superhero power that we all possess, knowingly or unknowingly. Interestingly, holding the tension of the opposites is experienced as—and symbolized by—a veritable crucifixion of our limited egoic identity. Is this to be genuinely imitating Christ and, as he counseled his followers to do, carry our own cross?

Humanity has been hobbled by our narrative biases. Instead of locking down on one narrative, the ability to have a comprehensive, omniperspectival view of the world—where instead of seeing only a partial view of what might be happening, we are more able to see the big picture—is a critically important evolutionary capacity that we are each being called to develop.

If, due to our narrative bias, we identify with one of the opposites as being true and the other as being false, however, we dissociate within ourselves. This disconnects us from our wholeness and forecloses on our ability to access genuine compassion. Abnegating our ability to be of benefit to a world so greatly in need of our help, we then become unwittingly complicit in participating in the unfolding world catastrophe, which would be truly tragic.

We can be of maximum benefit to both ourselves and the world at large when we are intimately connected with our intrinsic wholeness, whose natural perspective is not fixed in any particular dogmatic viewpoint or fixed narrative but sees things from as many points of view as we are able to imagine.

15

Quantum Medicine for the Coronavirus

One of the real dangers of the current pandemic is for us to feel helpless—overwhelmed with despair, impending doom, and pessimism—a state that cuts us off from our agency and creative power. With all that's happening in the world today, I am personally aware of a real sense of foreboding; from one very convincing perspective our future looks bleak. I have to confess that there is part of me (thank God it's only a part and not the whole of me), that can fall into a real sense of despair based on the overwhelming evidence, on so many fronts, that we are screwed.

The way our world is manifesting—even before the advent of the coronavirus—seems nightmarish beyond belief. Add in the global pandemic and the nightmare takes on an even denser seeming reality than before. When I see the dire nature of our situation, it is easy to feel that any talk about global awakening and the evolution of our species is utter pablum, the ravings coming from the fevered imagination of someone who is deeply in denial regarding the depth of evil manifesting. And yet I also see that something is being revealed to us through the darkness that can—in true quantum style, potentially—change everything.

The source of the problems confronting humanity are fundamentally not economic, political, or technological, but rather are to be found within the human psyche. To quote Stanislav Grof, "In the last analysis, the current global crisis is a psychospiritual crisis;

it reflects the level of consciousness evolution of the human species. It is, therefore, hard to imagine that it could be resolved without a radical inner transformation of humanity on a large scale and its rise to a higher level of emotional maturity and spiritual awareness. . . . Radical psychospiritual transformation of humanity is not only possible, but is already underway."[1] This is an important point to consider: There is undeniable evidence that an expansion of consciousness in the human species is not only a remote possibility but is already taking place. Grof concludes, "The question is only whether it can be sufficiently fast and extensive to reverse the current self-destructive trend of modern humanity."[2]

I am what holocaust survivor Victor Frankl would call a "tragic optimist," (or in my words, a "pessi-optimist"). Being a pessi-optimist, I see with open eyes and am deeply affected by the tragic and unbearable suffering, the unspeakable evil and mind-rending horror that is unfolding in our world. This causes me immense pain and distress. At the same time, however, as if having an uplifting pessimism, I am still able to find the good in our world, create a sense of meaning, and see glimmers of light in the darkness. This ability allows me to grow and evolve (what has been called post-traumatic growth) in ways in which I might not have been able to previously.

Light from the Field of Quantum Physics

Strangely enough, the hardest of the hard sciences—quantum physics—comes to our aid to serve as medicine to protect us from the psychological danger of becoming absorbed in our despair. By revealing that we live in a thoroughly quantum universe, quantum physics is placing the keys to our future in our own hands. The question is, Do we know how to use the gift that is being freely offered to us? A little insight into the essence of what quantum physics reveals to us about the nature of our world and how we operate within it can be the best antidepressant imaginable.

Quantum physics is empirically showing us the malleable and dreamlike nature of our universe. As quantum physics has revealed, our act of observing the universe influences the universe that we are observing. This is to say that our act of observation is creative. We are not passive witnesses of our world, but—whether we know it or not—active cocreators with it. What this means is that we hold enormous power in shaping our world.

Quantum physics points out that even if something is incredibly, ridiculously unlikely, it can still manifest "in reality" in this very moment. Highly unlikely is not quite the same as impossible. An infinitesimally small or "nonzero" probability is radically different than something that is impossible; we should be very careful what we assign to the trash bin of the impossible. The implications of this, both in "the real world" and within our minds, are truly uplifting and inspiring.

In questioning and shedding light on the boundary between the possible and the impossible, quantum physics is expanding the realm of the possible to previously unimaginable degrees. In a time such as ours, filled with lies, propaganda and disinformation it becomes nearly impossible to tell what is true or false. It thus greatly behooves us to at least be able to say what is within the realm of possibility.

To be clear, there is still a small chance—even if it's an "incredibly, ridiculously unlikely" chance—that enough of humanity might wake up in time so as to be able to change our species' trajectory before we destroy ourselves. This doesn't have to be all of us, but a sufficient number—think of the *hundredth monkey phenomenon* (when enough monkeys learn a new behavior, it is energetically accessed by the collective monkey population). Or the symbolic 144,000 in the book of Revelation—that acts as so much yeast in the dough to help the bread (of humanity) to rise, so to speak. That our species is waking up is not solely a remote possibility, but a desperately needed real one, an imperative that is demanded by circumstances.

Sometimes the unconscious (the dreamer of our dreams) puts us in a seemingly helpless, dangerous, and unsustainable situation so as to force us to become lucid and find gifts within ourselves that we didn't know we had. When a sufficient number of us who are waking up to our creative potency connect with each other, it is within the realm of possibility for us to discover that we can collectively put our realization together in a way that can literally change the way the world operates and does business. This isn't some new age woo-woo theory, but is the very real power that we, as a species, unknowingly wield. When we begin to collaboratively realize this consciously, all bets are off as to what is possible. The only limits are in our imagination, or rather, in our lack thereof.

I continue to feel that we have been here before. To let my imagination run wild for a moment (or two)—the image is that we are having a recurring dream. We have been at this same turning point in the historical evolution of our species countless times, and again and again we have destroyed ourselves as a species. It takes billions upon billions of years (which in dreamtime is no time at all) to regenerate ourselves. Here we are, back at the same choice point. Are we going to once again enact collective suicide, or this time are we finally going to get the message and recognize our interdependence? Are we going to come together as interconnected cells in a greater organism and avert the impending self-created catastrophe so as to collectively evolve as a species?

It is noteworthy that the meaning of the word *catastrophe* in ancient Greek is "a turning point." We have reached a point of necessary transformation in the evolution of our species. As quantum physics points out, due to the uncertain, indeterminate, and probabilistic nature of our experience, the choice is truly ours regarding how things transpire.

It is within the realm of the possible for enough people to snap out of their self-limiting spell so as to come together in lucidity and dream up a more grace-filled world that better reflects and is in alignment with who we are discovering ourselves to be relative to—and as relatives of—each other. The revelations emerging from quantum physics undeniably imply that it is crazy to not invest our creative energy into envisioning that we can "come together" so as to turn the tide of self-destructive madness that is overtaking us, and just as crazy to imagine that we can't. If we aren't investing our creative imagination in ways that enable us to heal, evolve, and wake up, then what are we thinking? As always, the real solution gets turned back onto—and into—ourselves.

I Had a Dream—of Covid-19— What Does It Mean?

When the unconscious becomes a living experience for enough people, it often heralds a new creative epoch for humanity. Covid-19 has not only intruded into our day-to-day world, making it surreal beyond belief, but has insinuated itself into many people's night dreams as well. When life becomes so dreamlike, it can potentially activate our creative imagination—this has certainly been true for yours truly.

I find myself imagining: What if a client came into my office and shared the following dream: Within a matter of weeks their world shifted suddenly. A potentially deadly virus had gotten on the loose and was killing people and making countless others sick, creating a global pandemic. Rampant fear was quickly consuming the globe. Due to the contagious nature of the disease, people became afraid to get too close to each other. Many countries around the world locked down their citizens, restraining their movement. Everybody began to wear masks. The future seemed completely uncertain. I could go on, but I think you get the idea—this person's dream was exactly what is happening in our world today. The question arises, How would we interpret this dream?

Dreams are the unmediated expression of the unconscious; Freud called them "the royal road" to the unconscious. Our dreams at night are one of the psyche's major compensatory, self-regulating mechanisms. When we get out of balance, off-center, or one-sided, the unconscious sends us dreams to help us reconnect with the part of ourselves we've lost touch with. To try to understand what the symbols in our dream are saying to us is a type of self-reflection. Symbols reflect something unconscious within us, which, even if only dimly recognized, can potentially activate the part within us with which the symbol resonates.

Dreams are multidimensional, having various levels of meanings encoded within the fabric of the dream, all of which have value. It's not a question of which interpretation is true—they can all be (relatively) true simultaneously. These multiple levels of meaning can actually complement and illuminate each other, helping to unlock the gifts encoded within the dream. When these different levels of meaning are seen together as interrelated aspects of a greater whole, a deeper picture—the full meaning of the dream—can begin to emerge. This is to say that there is no "one size fits all" way of interpreting dreams, in that the unconscious custom tailors a dream to uniquely suit the current psychological state of the particular dreamer. If a variety of people have the same dream, it could conceivably mean different things to each one of them.

For example, one person might be having a dream of the coronavirus pandemic and the feature that stands out in their dream is how everyone is coming together and helping each other. Their dream has an uplifting spirit behind it. In another person's dream, the pandemic might represent the advent of the apocalyptic end-times and be a nightmare. Their dream might be pushing them down—depressing them—into the darkness of the underworld. Being a projection of the unconscious, the unconscious projects itself into and reveals itself through the inkblot of the dream. The dreamscape is a reflection of what is going on deep inside the psyche of the individual dreamer.

Getting back to my client, I notice that in his particular dream there are certain features that stand out as he tells me his dream.

He seems not overly scared of the actual physical virus. He mentions that, being by nature introspective and hermetic, he doesn't mind the sheltering in place that's happening in the dream, as it gives him more time to do his creative, spiritual work. What really gets my attention, however, is that he has a charge when he describes what seem to be "darker forces" (his words) that are exploiting the pandemic to gain more of a foothold in the world. When I ask him about this, he says that there's a sense of fascist, totalitarian forces in his dream that are insidiously creeping around the planet so as to centralize power and control over the rest of us. As he describes what he is seeing in the dream, he doesn't sound overly paranoid or like a crazy conspiracy theorist, but on the contrary, very sober-minded and clear-seeing. He very insistently describes the multiple power grabs that he sees happening in his dream. He mentions that this is the part of the dream in which he feels the most disturbed and afraid.

As I questioned him about his dream, he kept on saying that there seemed to be a sense of collective mind control being perpetrated throughout the dream, as if the majority of the dream characters in his dream had "drank the Kool-Aid" and fallen under "a spell" (these are his phrases). It was becoming increasingly more difficult to discern *truth*—what was really happening—from made-up fiction.

He mentioned that in the dream, like an ongoing soundtrack in the background, there was a particular narrative or story that was being broadcast into people's minds by the mainstream media. What really "freaked him out" (his exact words) was when he began to realize that anyone who had a counter-narrative to the agreed upon consensus reality version of what was happening was literally deplatformed, censored, and silenced. He seemed really upset by this. When he told me this part of his dream, it sent chills down my spine.

How do we interpret this dream? I always start by putting the ball back in the dreamer's court, so to speak. When I ask him what he thinks his dream means, he immediately begins talking about how triggered he was about the censorship. This reminded him of how earlier in his life he was "silenced" from speaking his truth. I relate, based on my own experience. I realize that most, if not all of us, have a similar version of this process—of having our vocal chords severed. In this, our unique expression of who we are is not only not welcome, but is actually deemed a threat and shut down. This made me realize that even though his dream was his personal process, he was also touching on a shared universal archetypal dimension of experience common to us all. This is one of the amazing things about dreams: that they could be, and often are, reflecting both personal and archetypal levels of experience simultaneously.

I always try to notice where in a person's dream—and in their telling of the dream after they awaken—they have the most energy. In this person's process, it was around the censorship that was happening, which was related to the haunting sense of totalitarianism that was propagating itself around the globe. When I questioned him about this, not only did this bring up fear in him, which was palpably present in the room, he also mentioned that it made him feel helpless. This, in turn, elicited deeper feelings of hopelessness and despair. It felt like we were really touching a deep place in his unconscious.

Doing dreamwork with my client, I began to associate, which helps me to get out of my (rational) mind and to more deeply connect with my unconscious. I remembered that I had, synchronistically, just written something that seemed to address his dream. I was quickly able to find what I had written and read it aloud to him: "When we are not in touch with our intrinsic creative power, the external power of the state is more than happy to pick up our unconscious agency for us and use it against us for its own ends. If we marginalize our own internal authority, we dream up external totalitarian forces to limit our freedom and create our experience for us, as we see throughout the world today."

He seemed startled by my words. He immediately says, "That's it!" He then tells me that the gnawing feeling he had when he woke up from the dream was that he wasn't in touch with a part of himself. He was having the dawning realization that this missing part was his creative power and agency. As he said this, it was like I was watching a lightbulb being turned on inside of his head. He was beginning to realize that the dream was reflecting back to him the part of himself that was preemptively shutting him down—silencing him—for a variety of different reasons.

As if giving voice for the first time to something that he had been unconsciously acting out in his life, he then began listing one after another the reasons for his self-silencing: his fear of not being good enough, his being afraid it wouldn't come out perfectly, of not knowing how to start, feeling resistance, feeling afraid he would be judged. In other words, all the usual stuff that every creative person has to deal with. I didn't even have to say anything. All I was doing at this point was simply holding space and witnessing him taking in and being affected by the deeper meaning and incredible gift of his dream. We both had a feeling that we were participating in something sacred.

As if waking from a dream, at that moment I snap out of my imagination, which seemed as real as real can be. I immediately notice I feel refreshed, as if something within me had started to move. Still partially in the dreamworld of my imagination, however, my vision reminded me of something that Jung had written. I find myself making a beeline to a particular volume of Jung's Collected Works (*The Spirit in Man, Art, and Literature*). Then, as if drawing an oracular tarot card, I open to a page where he is writing about the moment when someone connects with and becomes an instrument for the creative spirit to move through them. This primordial experience, Jung writes, "evokes in us all those beneficent forces that ever and anon have enabled humanity to find a refuge from every peril and to outlive the longest night."[3] Seeing these words feels like it completes my vision (as well as this book), as if the universe itself is offering us the solution—the creative spirit— to the crisis we are currently facing.

Epilogue

In times of great social and political upheaval such as we see in the world today, whatever has been suppressed by the prevailing agreed upon attitudes builds up in—and disturbs—the collective unconscious, accumulating enormous energy that needs to be channeled somewhere. If these contents of the activated unconscious remain suppressed, however, there is a great danger that the unconscious will get into the driver's seat of our vehicle. There it will, so to speak—destructively, instead of constructively—act out in the world what has been blocked from healthy expression and thereby rendered unconscious. Then we will be truly dreaming a nightmare, as we see in the converging world crises that are engulfing us at this current moment in history.

Oftentimes humanity is not saved from a crisis by the products of our conscious intellect, but rather the saving grace comes from something being revealed to us that emerges unexpectedly as a result of the crisis. Revelations—which can be likened to timeless treasures waiting to be discovered in time—come in many forms and in many ways. Sometimes they first emerge seemingly outside of ourselves through—or are triggered by—some external event in the world like the coronavirus outbreak. Ultimately speaking, however, the deepest revelation is something that lies hidden within the nature of our soul awaiting discovery. We have to reveal it out of and from within ourselves, which is a self-sanctifying act needing no outside validation.

Awakening Treasures

There are treasures buried within us, concealed within our unconscious. These hidden gems are like precious jewels or diamonds in the rough that are encoded within the fabric of the unconscious psyche. They can be conceived of as existing in a higher dimension relative to our conscious mind, and as such, are typically invisible to our intellect. These treasures, having lain buried and dormant in the collective unconscious of our species from time immemorial, are typically awakened in times of great need and duress.

When the time is ripe, our intuition—due to its connection to our unconscious—divines and begins to "see" the heretofore formless revelation that is gestating in the alchemical cauldron of the unconscious. Our task then becomes how to bring forth and creatively express the revelation in a form that helps it come to fruition as we realize it more clearly within ourselves.

The potential revelation can be conceived of as an innovative force of nature alive in the unconscious. This force is thirsting to incarnate both within our minds and into our world. As if a living entity gestating in the womb of the collective unconscious of humanity, this soon to be revelation will draft a suitably creative person—someone who is sensitive to and resonates with the potential revelation—to become the instrument through which the newborn revelation clothes itself. In this, it takes on a particular individualized form and enters into our third-dimensional world.

Our spirit, the sentient presence that animates us, is by its very nature creative. The very center of our being is an unknown creative energy that forges us in its likeness, one way or another (with our cooperation or not). As human beings we are a creative force thirsting for conscious realization. Our creativity isn't as a mere hobby, a sideline, something that we should just indulge in on our days off. The creative spirit is an essential part of our being, the life-giving oxygen for our soul. Creative expression is not merely the embellishment of the forms of life, but the very dynamic of the life force itself taking new forms. The mysterious secret of our being can only be realized via participating in the creative act itself. Knowing is an act of creation in itself; if we want to know creativity, we have to be creative. There are no holy scriptures for this creative activity—we are left to our own devices. Being creative means to partake in our innate god-like spiritual freedom.

We can conceive of the creative instinct as a timeless, living impulse implanted in the human psyche that moves through the generations. The inspired individual participates within their own soul in the same creative process that takes place outside of themselves in nature. The creative person follows an unknown directive, a higher authority, what Jung would call the Self, the wholeness and guiding force of the deeper personality. People who are inspired by the creative spirit are oriented toward the invisible, toward a mysterious something that wants to become visible and reveal itself. The creative artist is giving utterance to the authentic and direct revelation of the *numinosum,* which raises their function to the level of the sacred. "The creative principle," Erich Neumann writes, is typically venerated "as the hidden treasure that in humble form conceals [and, I might add, simultaneously reveals] a fragment of the godhead."[1]

Listening to the Voice Inside

Wetiko is a "daemonic" energy, which is to say it is a transpersonal energy—beyond the merely personal—that can take over a person (or a group of people). The "daemon" can be envisioned as an indwelling force that can't be nailed down because of its nomadic nature, taking up residence in those who are receptive to its call. Etymologically speaking, the inner meaning of the word *daemon* is our guiding spirit, inner voice, internal teacher, muse, spiritual ally, wish-fulfilling genie, and genius. The daemon connects us with our calling, and helps us find our vocation, our mission in life, why we are here on the planet.

The original meaning of the word *vocation* has to do with being addressed by a voice. In listening to our inner voice—what Jung calls "the voice of the inner man"—we are at the same time given the sacred responsibility to outwardly speak in the world the voice that is uniquely ours to speak—our true authentic voice. The paradox is that in speaking the voice that is most our own, this voice does not belong to us. Rather it is the voice of all of humanity that resounds in us. The truly creative person, be they poet, writer, dancer, or painter, for instance, is that courageous someone, Jung writes, "voicing aloud what others only dream."[2] In other words, a creative person gives living form to something that exists in the formless and seemingly insubstantial ethers.

The demonic is the creative in *statu nascendi,* "not yet realized," or "made real" by a conscious ego. This is to say that hidden encoded within the darkness of wetiko is our unexpressed creativity. When the creativity that naturally bubbles forth within us is suppressed, however, it feeds the poisonous aspect of wetiko. The malady that our species is collectively suffering from is, in essence, the fact that we are not connecting with, mobilizing, and expressing our creative nature. Once our creativity is repressed, the daemonic aspect of wetiko becomes *demonic,* our creativity turns back on itself and manifests destructively—be it within ourselves or out in the world.

To have eyes and not see—to be blind—is an unmistakable symptom of an occlusion to the call of the creative spirit. The figure of the artist is the one who opens humanity's eyes, teaching us how to see. The black-hole aspect of wetiko is a creativity-destroyer by its very nature, so we need to generate and mobilize as much ingenuity as possible in order to contend with it. Paradoxically, wetiko both spurns and spurs our creative impulses. The blazing fire of a soul set aflame with its own destiny, burning with the passion of following its deeper calling, fulfilling its mission in life, puts a stake through the heart of the inner vampiric figure of wetiko. The more we pursue what we love, what gives meaning to our lives, the more we allow our creative nature to express itself and the more we "kill" the inner figure of wetiko.

Revelation is not something that the conscious ego could have invented by itself, but can only organically arise out of the tension between a stable consciousness and a charged unconscious. To consciously endure this innate creative tension necessarily involves a state of suffering. Describing the creative individual, Neumann writes, "Only by suffering, perhaps unconsciously, under the poverty of his culture and his time can he arrive at the freshly opening source which is destined to quench the thirst of his time."[3]

In our own individual suffering of the daemonic energies that pervade and make up the collective unconscious, the spirit within us intimately experiences the profound depths of the woundedness of the collectivity and the time in which we live. Spiritual practitioners and true artists are able to find within their own subjective experience, however, a unique and utterly original response to their wound. As if organs of the collective body politic of humanity, sensitive, spiritually attuned, and creative people are the alchemical retorts in which the poisons, the antidotes, and the psycho-spiritual medicines for the collective are distilled.

The Healing Power of the Creative Spirit

It is no badge of honor or measure of sanity to adapt to a world gone mad. Instead of trying to adapt to the world's insanity, a person who is awakening remains open to the world—and open to their wounds—such that a regenerative and curative power arises from within their own dark depths in response. This healing power is the creative spirit. The creative impulse is simultaneously an individual and collective phenomenon, which is to say that when any of us becomes a channel for this spirit, it serves all of us.

A creative person's healing power lies in their willingness to not cling to fixed ideas—of who they are or of the world at large—but to allow themselves to be shaped and informed by new experiences of the world. Then, in turn, they are able to translate and craft these experiences into novel "art"-iculations. This involves a receptivity to authentically and imaginatively respond to the reciprocal interactions and continual collisions—with the inevitable wounding—between ourselves and the world. The litmus test for our creativity is our inspired response—or lack thereof—to these experiences.

The hidden treasure, the great revelation that is hidden within our unconscious—also referred mythically as "The Treasure Hard to Attain"—is the creative spirit itself. When tapped into, this spirit is a seemingly inexhaustible source of inspiration within us that issues forth a stream of revelations like a spring bubbling upward from the depths of our unconscious. This living current—our greatest resource—helps us to connect with our source. Whenever it manifests, this vital spirit appears as a revelation in which we are participating as the instrument through which it incarnates in time and space. Our creativity transforms the world so as to find our place in it. To quote philosopher Martin Heidegger, "A work of art is something new in the world that changes the world to allow itself to exist."[4]

Our species is desperately in need of the guidance and aid of the boundless creative forces latent within the depths of our unconscious to help us find new ways to resolve the myriad interwoven aspects of our multiple world crises. Creative expression is the zero point at which consciousness and the unconscious momentarily become a generative unity. Only at the point in which the stream of unbridled inspiration emerges from the darkness of the unconscious and enters the light of consciousness, and is thus both at once—darkness and light—is the creative spirit made real in time. As resourceful individuals, it is our job to harness the raw impulses arising from the depths of the unconscious into a form that serves our world. This "creative point," to again quote Neumann, is "the buried treasure which is the water of life, immortality, fertility, and the after-life all rolled into one."[5]

It is not the conscious ego that will change the world, but rather, sufficient numbers of people who develop a relationship within themselves between their conscious and unconscious parts who then connect with one another—deepening each other's inspiration in the process. As long as we remain unaware of the contents of our unconscious—therefore not being able to be the conscious architects of our inner landscape—our ability to transform the outer world will be limited.

Given that our widespread systemic crises are the result of a deficiency in human consciousness, it becomes obvious that it is only through an expansion of consciousness that we will be able to navigate the tight passage before us. Consciousness can evolve and develop, however, only where it preserves and cultivates a living connection with the creative powers of the unconscious. Just as our view of the world is a decisive factor in shaping the unconscious, the forces activated in the unconscious reciprocally transform our conscious perspectives. In its collective archetypal dimension the unconscious contains the wisdom and experience of untold ages and could serve as a guide par excellence for us during these troubled times.

Certain individuals gifted with particularly strong intuition sense the moving currents taking place in the collective unconscious and are able to translate these changes into communicable language (verbal and/or nonverbal). These original expressions can potentially spread rapidly—going viral—and have such powerful transformative power because parallel changes have been taking place in the unconscious of other people. Contagious in its effects, genuine creative expression emerging at the right moment can "virally" spread via the unconscious of our species in ways that can ignite latent, creative energy lying dormant in the collective unconscious of humanity. This can bring forth and actualize hidden possibilities (both within us and in the world) into the light of conscious awareness, which is a process that has the power to effect real change in the world.

A new idea is itself an expression of a creative act. Certain ideas can assist us in remembering something that we had forgotten we had forgotten. A new idea—such as wetiko—can set up a chain reaction in people's minds that can potentially unleash previously unimagined insight and creativity. As part of their design, mind-expanding ideas are meant to be shared with others so as to fully activate their nonlocal benefit and blessing. These ideas endlessly increase in potency the more they are shared among us. Like a key unlocking a door or like a charm that breaks a spell, a new symbolic idea can unleash the dormant creative spirit imprisoned within us. A revolutionary idea has the potential to catalyze revolutions in thinking; a shift in a single idea can precipitate a shift into a new epoch.

The creativity of the unconscious psyche—which is an agency in a state of never-ending re-creation and re-formation—continually transforms our experience of reality as well as itself. As an artist of life, we are what Neumann refers to as a "bearer of the divine miracle," actively and endlessly participating in re-creating ourselves anew, revealing ourselves—to ourselves—through the bringing forth of our gifts to the world. Only in these acts do we actualize our wholeness. Acting out of our wholeness is like kryptonite to the seeming superpowers of wetiko. In being creative we not only find refuge from the dangers of wetiko, but we discover the true revelation that is none other than ourselves. Each new act of creativity brings with it an element of self-discovery. We must create in order to know ourselves.

When human beings are deprived of their freedom and power of expression, however, they will unconsciously express themselves in the drive for power. This only feeds the will to power of the demonic and destructive shadow, with the baneful consequences we see in the world today. Being oppressed in our expression, instead of stopping us cold, however, can potentially—if we so choose—fuel our creative fire, forging in us an "inner necessity" to connect with the living primal generative spirit that lives within us. The authentic creative spirit—if it's the real thing—can't be discouraged or kept down for long, for then it wouldn't be creative.

Artists as Molders of the Collective Unconscious

To quote poet Allen Ginsberg, "The warfare's psychic now. Whoever controls the language, the images, controls the race." Instruments of war in the hands of generals are extremely dangerous. In the same way, nothing is more dangerous and potentially world-transforming than implements of creative expression in the hands of artists. They are the molders of the unconscious psychic life of humanity, the mythmakers of their age. It is the artists—and we are all artists—who are the healers of the world.

Rather than letting our perceptions be managed and manipulated by the powers that be and their propaganda organs, we as sovereign beings can connect with our own perceptions and create our own unique and authentic experience of the world and a refreshed experience of ourselves. What a radical—and truly liberating—idea!

Healing wetiko entails each of us becoming an empiricist—there is no getting around this. In this we must simply inquire directly into the nature of our present moment experience, without giving credence to what any outer authority is telling us is true. Ultimately speaking, we ourselves are the arbiters of our own experience. By our very nature, we are interpreters of our experience and generators of meaning. This is a process that affects our experience of both ourselves and of the universe at large. Realizing our own creative agency is where we find ourselves, which is the beginning of the cure for wetiko as well as the cure itself.

Once we creatively express our nature, it is nature itself that is doing the talking. Then there's nothing to do but listen and respond in kind to our unique and individual call.

The Four Ignoble Blindnesses of Wetiko

A Play on the Four Noble Truths of Buddhism

1. You are blind to your own blindness, or doubly blind. You're blind and you do not know you are blind and in fact imagine that you can see clearly and come to believe that you can see more clearly than those who are clear-sighted. You then become unaware of what it is to be sighted, as you have no reference point for comparison.

2. You are blind to the very existence of wetiko and its malign effects within your mind. You do not see how you are unwittingly colluding with wetiko's pernicious effects and thereby you are unaware of how you are having negative or ill effects upon others and the world.

3. You are blind to your own light, which is to say that wetiko blocks you from seeing both your own darkness as well as your own light. You are blinded to and incapable of seeing your true nature and identify instead with a false imposter of who you truly are.

4. You are blind to the fact that wetiko is a revelation. Being blind
   to your blindness, being blind to the existence of wetiko, and
   being blind to your own light necessarily results in being blind
   to wetiko's revelatory function. Wetiko is potentially revealing
   your own creative genius, power, and agency. Recognizing that
   wetiko is a revelation is to realize that wetiko contains encoded
   within it not just its own medicine and cure, but a blessing, for
   it is helping you to wake up to the dreamlike nature of the universe and to remember who you actually are.

Notes

Foreword

1. See Braud, *Distant Mental Influence* (Charlottesville, Va.: Hampton Roads, 2003); Dossey, *One Mind: How Our Individual Mind Is Part of a Greater Consciousness and Why It Matters* (Carlsbad, Calif.: Hay House, 2013); Kafatos and Nadeau, *The Conscious Universe: Parts and Wholes in Physical Reality* (New York: Springer, 2000); Radin, *The Conscious Universe* (San Francisco: HarperSanFrancisco, 1997); and Radin, *Entangled Minds: Extrasensory Perception in a Quantum Reality* (New York: Paraview/Simon & Schuster, 2006), 19, 21–24, 137–40, 270.

2. Levin, "The Power of Love," Interview in *Alternative Therapies in Health and Medicine* 5, no. 4 (1999): 78–86; Levin, "A Prolegomenon to an Epidemiology of Love: Theory, Measurement, and Health Outcomes," *Journal of Social and Clinical Psychology* 19 (2000): 117–36.

3. Abe, Ichinomya, Kanai, and Yamamoto, "Effect of a Japanese Energy Healing Method Known as *Johrei* on Viability and Proliferation of Cultured Cancer Cells in vitro," *Journal of Alternative and Complementary Medicine* 18, no. 3 (March 2012): 221–28.

4. Dossey, *Be Careful What You Pray For* (San Francisco: HarperSanFrancisco, 1997).

5. Bengston and Krinsley, "The Effect of the 'Laying on of Hands' on Transplanted Breast Cancer in Mice," *Journal of Scientific Exploration* 14, no. 3 (2000): 353–64.

6. See Schrödinger, *My View of the World* (Woodbridge, Conn.: Ox Bow Press, 1983), 31–34; Schrödinger, *What Is Life?/ Mind and Matter* (London: Cambridge University Press, 1969), 139, 145; Eddington, *The*

Nature of the Physical World (New York: Macmillan, 1928), 338; Bohm, quoted in Renée Weber, *Dialogues with Scientists and Sages* (New York: Routledge & Kegan Paul, 1986), 41.

Introduction. Wetiko in a Nutshell

1. Jensen, *Songs of the Dead*, 46.
2. Griffin, *Christian Faith and the Truth Behind 9/11*, 143.
3. For more on active imagination, please see the glossary in *Dispelling Wetiko*, 297.
4. To better understand archetypes, please see the glossary in *Dispelling Wetiko*, 300.
5. *The Collected Works of C. G. Jung*, vol. 10, para. 523.
6. Laing, *The Politics of Experience*, 73.
7. Forbes, *Columbus and Other Cannibals*, xix.
8. Duran, *Healing the Soul Wound*, 21–22.
9. For a further discussion of nonlocality see the glossary in *Dispelling Wetiko*, 315.

1. It's All in the Psyche

1. Ortega y Gasset, *The Revolt of the Masses*.
2. *The Collected Works of C. G. Jung*, vol. 10, para. 523.
3. Hillman and Shamdasani, *Lament of the Dead*, 159.
4. Neumann, *Art and the Creative Unconscious*, 163.
5. *The Collected Works of C. G. Jung*, vol. 10, para. 471.
6. Quoted in *The Collected Works of C. G. Jung*, vol. 9, part 2, para 342. (There is a footnote in Jung's text that reads: *Ennead*, VI, 9, 8—Guthrie trans., p. 163, slightly mod.)
7. In *The Collected Works of C. G. Jung*, vol. 9, part 2, para 342.
8. De Rougemont, *The Devil's Share*, 44.
9. De Rougemont, *The Devil's Share*, 115.
10. Ladha and Kirk. "Seeing Wetiko."
11. Kirsten Roya Azal, "Dispelling Shaytan (Wetiko)," *The Art of Islamic Healing* (blog, no longer available).
12. Siri Guru Granth Sahib, 466, line 18.

2. The Kabbalah's Remarkable Idea

1. Raine, *Blake and Tradition*, 220.
2. Berdyaev, *The Destiny of Man*, 183.

3. Scholem, *Origins of the Kabbalah*, 149–50.

4. Drob, *Symbols of the Kabbalah*, 329.

5. Laing, *The Politics of Experience*, 75.

6. Jung, "An Eightieth Birthday Interview," 271–72.

7. In *The Collected Works of C. G. Jung*, 14:8, fn 26.

8. Neumann, *Depth Psychology and a New Ethic*, 144.

9. To learn more about prima materia, please see the glossary in my book *Dispelling Wetiko*, 316, or go to "Glossary of Terms" (in drop down menu under "Articles") on my website www.awakeninthedream.com.

10. The Zohar, 4:125.

11. De Rougemont, *The Devil's Share*, 39.

12. Wirtz, *Trauma and Beyond*, 338.

13. Jung, *The Red Book*, 115–20.

14. Berdyaev, *Freedom & the Spirit*, 185.

15. Berdyaev, *The Meaning of the Creative Act*, 154.

3. The Masters of Deception

1. Wesselman, *The Bowl of Light*, 224–37.

2. Wesselman, *The Bowl of Light*, 224–37.

3. Laing, *The Politics of Experience*, 73.

4. Penn-Lewis, *War on the Saints*, 11.

5. Wesselman, *The Bowl of Light*, 224–37.

6. Wesselman, *The Bowl of Light*, 224–37.

7. De Rougemont, *The Devil's Share*, 14.

8. De Rougemont, *The Devil's Share*, 51.

9. *The Collected Works of C. G. Jung*, vol. 12, para. 460.

10. *The Collected Works of C. G. Jung*, vol. 9, part 2, para. 75.

11. *The Collected Works of C. G. Jung*, vol. 9, part 2, para. 75.

12. Siri Guru Granth Sahib, 229.

13. Penn-Lewis, *War on the Saints*, 156.

14. Penn-Lewis, *War on the Saints*, 156.

15. Robinson, *The Nag Hammadi Library*, 117.

16. Robinson, *The Nag Hammadi Library*, 122.

17. *The Collected Works of C. G. Jung*, vol. 9, part 2, para. 67.

18. Campbell, *Spiritual Disciplines*, 254.

19. *Pistis Sophia*, III, ch. 115, 247ff.

20. Laing, *The Politics of Experience*, 35.

21. Wesselman, *The Re-Enchantment*.

22. Wesselman, *The Bowl of Light,* 224–37.
23. Arendt, *Responsibility and Judgment,* 111.
24. Holmquist, "Bonhoeffer on the 'Stupidity' That Led to Hitler's Rise."
25. Ladha and Kirk, "Seeing Wetiko."
26. Woodruff and Wilmer, *Facing Evil,* 48.
27. Neumann, *The Origins and History of Consciousness,* 391.
28. Wesselman, *The Bowl of Light,* 224–37.
29. Wesselman, *The Bowl of Light,* 224–37.

4. Sri Aurobindo and the Hostile Forces

1. Aurobindo, *Letters on Yoga: Volume 1,* 465.
2. Aurobindo, *Letters on Yoga: Volume 1,* 466.
3. Dalal, *The Hidden Forces of Life,* 87.
4. Aurobindo, *Letters on Yoga: Volume 4,* 772.
5. Aurobindo, *On Yoga II,* 1655.
6. Aurobindo, *The Hour of God.*
7. Aurobindo, *Letters on Yoga: Volume 1,* 466.
8. Aurobindo, *Letters on Yoga* (University of Virginia), 1753.
9. Aurobindo, *Letters on Yoga: Volume 1,* 466.
10. Aurobindo, *Letters on Yoga* (University of Virginia), 1733.
11. Aurobindo, *Letters on Yoga* (University of Virginia), 1736.
12. Dalal, *The Hidden Forces of Life,* 8.
13. Dalal, *The Hidden Forces of Life,* 121.
14. Aïvanhov, *Man's Two Natures, Human and Divine,* 120–21.
15. Aurobindo, *The Integral Yoga,* 283.
16. Aurobindo, *On Yoga II,* 1674.
17. Donnelly, *Founding the Life Divine,* 182.
18. Aurobindo, *Life, Literature, Yoga: Some Letters of Sri Aurobindo,* 15.
19. Aurobindo, *Letters on Yoga* (University of Virginia), 1755.
20. Dalal, *The Hidden Forces of Life,* 55.
21. Aurobindo, *Letters on Yoga* (University of Virginia), 1759.
22. Aurobindo, *The Integral Yoga,* 278.
23. Aurobindo, *On Yoga II,* 1673.
24. Aurobindo, *The Mother with Letters on the Mother.*
25. Dalal, *The Hidden Forces of Life,* 6.
26. Aurobindo, *Letters on Yoga* (University of Virginia), 1734.
27. *The Collected Works of C. G. Jung.*
28. Aurobindo, *On Yoga II,* 1647.

29. Aurobindo, *Letters on Yoga* (University of Virginia), 1755.

30. Aurobindo, *Letters on Yoga* (University of Virginia), 1759.

5. The Mind Parasites of Colin Wilson

1. Lachman, in foreword for Colin Wilson, *The Mind Parasites* (2005 edition), 13.

2. Zimmer, *Parasite Rex,* 82–83.

3. Zimmer, *Parasite Rex,* 245.

4. Wilson, *The Mind Parasites,* 75.

5. Wilson, *The Mind Parasites,* 76.

6. Wilson, *The Mind Parasites,* 83.

7. Wilson, *The Mind Parasites,* 89.

8. Wilson, *The Mind Parasites,* 90.

9. Wilson, *The Mind Parasites,* 90.

10. Wilson, *The Mind Parasites,* 105.

11. Penn-Lewis, *War on the Saints,* 12.

12. Wilson, *The Mind Parasites,* 88.

13. Wilson, *The Mind Parasites,* 103.

14. *The Collected Works of C. G. Jung,* vol. 10, para. 437–39.

15. Wilson, *The Mind Parasites,* 89.

16. Wilson, *The Mind Parasites,* 89.

6. The Enlightened Madness of Philip K. Dick

1. Doyle, in Jackson and Lethem, *The Exegesis of Philip K. Dick,* afterword, 899.

2. Jackson and Lethem, *The Exegesis of Philip K. Dick,* 553.

3. Jackson and Lethem, *The Exegesis of Philip K. Dick,* 778.

4. Herron, *The Selected Letters of Philip K. Dick,* 267.

5. Herron, *The Selected Letters of Philip K. Dick,* 96.

6. Jackson and Lethem, *The Exegesis of Philip K. Dick,* 404.

7. Jackson and Lethem, *The Exegesis of Philip K. Dick,* 294.

8. Jackson and Lethem, *The Exegesis of Philip K. Dick,* 403.

9. Jackson and Lethem, *The Exegesis of Philip K. Dick,* 517.

10. Herron, *The Selected Letters of Philip K. Dick,* 146.

11. Jackson and Lethem, *The Exegesis of Philip K. Dick,* 693.

12. Jackson and Lethem, *The Exegesis of Philip K. Dick,* 473.

13. Dick, *The Divine Invasion,* 18.

14. Dick, *Philip K. Dick*, 97.
15. Laing, *The Politics of Experience*, 74.
16. Jackson and Lethem, *The Exegesis of Philip K. Dick*, 405.
17. Jackson and Lethem, *The Exegesis of Philip K. Dick*, 357.
18. Dick, *The Divine Invasion*, 182.
19. Jackson and Lethem, *The Exegesis of Philip K. Dick*, 405.
20. Sutin, *The Shifting Realities of Philip K. Dick*, 310.
21. Jackson and Lethem, *The Exegesis of Philip K. Dick*, 828.
22. Jackson and Lethem, *The Exegesis of Philip K. Dick*, 319.
23. Jackson and Lethem, *The Exegesis of Philip K. Dick*, 391.
24. Jackson and Lethem, *The Exegesis of Philip K. Dick*, 391.
25. Jackson and Lethem, *The Exegesis of Philip K. Dick*, 291.
26. Jackson and Lethem, *The Exegesis of Philip K. Dick*, 178.
27. Jackson and Lethem, *The Exegesis of Philip K. Dick*, 402.
28. Jackson and Lethem, *The Exegesis of Philip K. Dick*, 328.
29. Jackson and Lethem, *The Exegesis of Philip K. Dick*, 608.
30. Jackson and Lethem, *The Exegesis of Philip K. Dick*, 473.
31. Jackson and Lethem, *The Exegesis of Philip K. Dick*, 346.
32. Jackson and Lethem, *The Exegesis of Philip K. Dick*, 323.
33. Jackson and Lethem, *The Exegesis of Philip K. Dick*, 414.
34. Jackson and Lethem, *The Exegesis of Philip K. Dick*, 316.
35. Raine, *Blake and Tradition*, 243.
36. Berdyaev, *The Destiny of Man*, 182.
37. Bonhoeffer, *The Cost of Discipleship*, 160.
38. Jackson and Lethem, *The Exegesis of Philip K. Dick*, 263.
39. Jackson and Lethem, *The Exegesis of Philip K. Dick*, 596.
40. Sutin, *The Shifting Realities of Philip K. Dick*, 262.
41. Sutin, *The Shifting Realities of Philip K. Dick*, 263–64.
42. Jackson and Lethem, *The Exegesis of Philip K. Dick*, 554.
43. Jackson and Lethem, *The Exegesis of Philip K. Dick*, 289.
44. Jackson and Lethem, *The Exegesis of Philip K. Dick*, 596.
45. Sutin, *The Shifting Realities of Philip K. Dick*, 251.
46. Jackson and Lethem, *The Exegesis of Philip K. Dick*, 222.
47. Jackson and Lethem, *The Exegesis of Philip K. Dick*, 277.
48. Jackson and Lethem, *The Exegesis of Philip K. Dick*, 327.
49. Jackson and Lethem, *The Exegesis of Philip K. Dick*, 419.
50. Jackson and Lethem, *The Exegesis of Philip K. Dick*, 277.
51. Jackson and Lethem, *The Exegesis of Philip K. Dick*, 316.

52. Sutin, *The Shifting Realities of Philip K. Dick,* 308.

53. Sutin, *The Shifting Realities of Philip K. Dick,* 285.

54. Sutin, *The Shifting Realities of Philip K. Dick,* 309.

55. Jackson and Lethem, *The Exegesis of Philip K. Dick,* 391.

56. Sutin, *The Shifting Realities of Philip K. Dick,* 295.

57. Jackson and Lethem, *The Exegesis of Philip K. Dick,* 332.

58. Jackson and Lethem, *The Exegesis of Philip K. Dick,* 315.

59. Jackson and Lethem, *The Exegesis of Philip K. Dick,* 222.

60. Jackson and Lethem, *The Exegesis of Philip K. Dick,* 332.

61. Jackson and Lethem, *The Exegesis of Philip K. Dick,* 414.

62. Jackson and Lethem, *The Exegesis of Philip K. Dick,* 278.

63. Sutin, *The Shifting Realities of Philip K. Dick,* 296.

64. Jackson and Lethem, *The Exegesis of Philip K. Dick,* 222.

65. Jackson and Lethem, *The Exegesis of Philip K. Dick,* 290.

66. Jackson and Lethem, *The Exegesis of Philip K. Dick,* 294.

67. Jackson and Lethem, *The Exegesis of Philip K. Dick,* 317.

68. Sutin, *The Shifting Realities of Philip K. Dick,* 291.

69. Herron, *The Selected Letters of Philip K. Dick,* 79.

70. Jackson and Lethem, *The Exegesis of Philip K. Dick,* 413.

71. Jackson and Lethem, *The Exegesis of Philip K. Dick,* 702.

72. Jackson and Lethem, *The Exegesis of Philip K. Dick,* 278.

73. Jackson and Lethem, *The Exegesis of Philip K. Dick,* 404.

74. Jackson and Lethem, *The Exegesis of Philip K. Dick,* 75.

75. Jackson and Lethem, *The Exegesis of Philip K. Dick,* 75.

76. Jackson and Lethem, *The Exegesis of Philip K. Dick,* 272.

77. Jackson and Lethem, *The Exegesis of Philip K. Dick,* 76.

78. Sutin, *The Shifting Realities of Philip K. Dick,* 289.

79. Jackson and Lethem, *The Exegesis of Philip K. Dick,* 612.

80. Jackson and Lethem, *The Exegesis of Philip K. Dick,* 692.

81. Jackson and Lethem, *The Exegesis of Philip K. Dick,* 692.

82. Sutin, *The Shifting Realities of Philip K. Dick,* 296.

83. Jackson and Lethem, *The Exegesis of Philip K. Dick,* 692.

84. Dick, *Valis,* 56.

85. Jackson and Lethem, *The Exegesis of Philip K. Dick,* 692–93.

86. Jackson and Lethem, *The Exegesis of Philip K. Dick,* 877–78.

87. Jackson and Lethem, *The Exegesis of Philip K. Dick,* 878.

88. Jackson and Lethem, *The Exegesis of Philip K. Dick,* 296.

89. Jackson and Lethem, *The Exegesis of Philip K. Dick,* 877.

90. Jackson and Lethem, *The Exegesis of Philip K. Dick,* 878.

91. DePrez, "An Interview with Philip K. Dick."

7. Are We Humans Terminally Insane or Just Waking Up?

1. Levy, *Dispelling Wetiko,* chapter 13.

2. *The Collected Works of C. G. Jung,* vol. 6, 313.

3. Ortega y Gasset, *The Revolt of the Masses.*

4. Neumann, *Depth Psychology and a New Ethic,* 26.

5. Lewis, *The Screwtape Letters.*

6. Jung, *Letters,* 33.

7. *The Collected Works of C. G. Jung,* vol. 11, para. 962.

8. *The Collected Works of C. G. Jung,* vol. 10, 588.

9. Diedrich, *Sitting Bull: The Collected Speeches,* 75.

10. Berdyaev, *The Destiny of Man,* 183.

11. Jung, *Mysterium Coniunctionis,* CW 14, para. 192.

12. Jung, *Mysterium Coniunctionis,* CW 14, para. 192.

8. A Cancer of the Soul

1. McMurtry, *The Cancer Stage of Capitalism,* 4.

2. *The Collected Works of C. G. Jung,* vol. 16, para. 196.

3. De Rougemont, *The Devil's Share,* 72.

4. Dostoyevsky, *The Brothers Karamazov.*

5. Steiner, *The Karma of Untruthfulness.*

6. McMurtry, *Value Wars,* 88.

7. Solzhenitsyn, "Nobel Lecture in Literature 1970."

8. Solzhenitsyn, "Nobel Lecture in Literature 1970."

9. Solzhenitsyn, "Nobel Lecture in Literature 1970."

10. Solzhenitsyn, *Gulag Archipelago.*

11. Wallace, "Wallace Defines 'American Fascism.'"

12. Arendt, *The Origins of Totalitarianism.*

13. Wallace, "Wallace Defines 'American Fascism.'"

14. Wallace, "Wallace Defines 'American Fascism.'"

15. Wallace, "Wallace Defines 'American Fascism.'"

16. Wallace, "Wallace Defines 'American Fascism.'"

17. Wallace, "Wallace Defines 'American Fascism.'"

18. Wallace, "Wallace Defines 'American Fascism.'"

19. McMurtry, *The Cancer Stage of Capitalism,* 24.

20. McMurtry, *The Cancer Stage of Capitalism*, 48.

21. Ladha and Kirk, "Seeing Wetiko."

22. McMurtry, *The Cancer Stage of Capitalism*, 108.

23. McMurtry, *The Cancer Stage of Capitalism*, 10.

24. McMurtry, *The Cancer Stage of Capitalism*, 34.

25. McMurtry, *The Cancer Stage of Capitalism*, 80.

26. McMurtry, *The Cancer Stage of Capitalism*.

27. McMurtry, *The Cancer Stage of Capitalism*, 91.

28. Planck, "Interviews with Great Scientists."

29. Schrödinger, *Collected Papers*, 334.

30. McMurtry, *The Cancer Stage of Capitalism*, 20.

9. Duped by the Beast of War

1. Quoted in Brett Wilkins, "Jimmy Carter: US 'Most Warlike Nation in History of the World,'" Common Dreams (website).

2. *The Collected Works of C. G. Jung*, vol. 16, para. 442.

3. Ehrenreich, *Blood Rites*, 132.

4. Jung, *Dream Symbols of the Individuation Process*, 265.

5. See Camera, *Spiral of Violence*.

6. *The Collected Works of C. G. Jung*, vol. 9, part 1, para. 31.

7. Griffin, *Christian Faith and the Truth Behind 9/11*, 123.

8. Wink, *Unmasking the Powers*, 41.

9. Ehrenreich, *Blood Rites*, 133.

10. Dalal, *The Hidden Forces of Life*, 6.

11. Berdyaev, *Freedom & the Spirit*, 170.

12. Quoted in *The Collected Works of C. G. Jung*, vol. 16, para. 470.

13. Quoted in *The Collected Works of C. G. Jung*, vol. 16, para. 470.

14. De Rougemont, *The Devil's Share*, 187.

15. *The Collected Works of C. G. Jung*, vol. 11, para. 787.

10. Other Lenses Helping Us See Wetiko

1. Tolle, *The Power of Now*, 30–31.

2. Tolle, *The Power of Now*, 31.

3. Tolle, *The Power of Now*, 31.

4. Brown, *Being Our Companion*.

5. Brown, *Being Our Companion*.

6. Brown, *Being Our Companion*.

7. Brown, *Being Our Companion*.

8. Castaneda, *The Active Side of Infinity,* 218.
9. Castaneda, *The Active Side of Infinity,* 220.
10. Ruiz, *The Four Agreements,* 109.
11. Ruiz, *The Four Agreements,* 110.
12. Ruiz, *The Four Agreements,* 111.
13. Quoted in Ewan Palmer, "Alexandria Ocasio-Cortez Says White Supremacy Is Like a Virus and It's America's 'Original Sin': 'It Never Went Away. It Was Just Dormant,'" Newsweek (website), August 8, 2019.
14. Schoen, *The War of the Gods in Addiction,* 40–41.
15. Schoen, *The War of the Gods in Addiction,* 41–42.
16. Schoen, *The War of the Gods in Addiction,* 74.
17. Jung's letter to Bill W., in Schoen, *The War of the Gods in Addiction,* 19–20.
18. Jung's letter to Bill W., in Schoen, *The War of the Gods in Addiction,* 19–20.
19. Jung's letter to Bill W., in Schoen, *The War of the Gods in Addiction,* 19–20.

11. Scapegoating

1. Neumann, *Depth Psychology and a New Ethic,* 50.
2. Jung, *Visions,* 1110.
3. Von Franz, *Projection and Recollection in Jungian Psychology,* 120.
4. Jung, *Letters,* 168.

12. René Girard's Take on Scapegoating and the Shadow

1. Girard, *I See Satan Fall like Lightning,* xv.
2. Girard, *I See Satan Fall like Lightning,* 125.
3. Girard, *Things Hidden Since the Foundation of the World,* 161.
4. Girard, *Things Hidden Since the Foundation of the World,* 162.
5. *The Collected Works of C. G. Jung,* vol. 11, para. 86.
6. Girard, *Violence and the Sacred,* 82.
7. Lifton, *The Nazi Doctors: Medical Killing and the Psychology of Genocide.*
8. Woodruff and Wilmer, *Facing Evil,* 48.
9. Williams in Girard, *I See Satan Fall like Lighting,* xxi.
10. *The Collected Works of C. G. Jung,* vol. 11, para. 140.
11. Jung, *The Red Book,* 310.
12. Nietzche, *Thus Spoke Zarathustra.*

13. Covid-19 Is a Symbol of a Much Deeper Infection

1. Winiecki, "Searching for the Anti-Virus: Covid-19 as Quantum Phenomenon."
2. Winiecki, "Searching for the Anti-Virus: Covid-19 as Quantum Phenomenon."
3. Winiecki, "Searching for the Anti-Virus: Covid-19 as Quantum Phenomenon."
4. Winiecki, "Searching for the Anti-Virus: Covid-19 as Quantum Phenomenon."

14. The Coronavirus Contains Its Own Vaccine

1. *The Collected Works of C. G. Jung,* vol. 17, para. 323.
2. *The Collected Works of C. G. Jung,* vol. 18, para. 1661.

15. Quantum Medicine for the Coronavirus

1. Grof, "Healing Individuals, Transforming the Collective, Saving the Planet."
2. Grof, "Healing Individuals, Transforming the Collective, Saving the Planet."
3. *The Collected Works of C. G. Jung,* vol. 15, para. 129.

Epilogue

1. Neumann, *Art and the Creative Unconscious,* 168.
2. *The Collected Works of C. G. Jung,* vol. 6, 323.
3. Neumann, *Art and the Creative Unconscious,* 98.
4. Heidegger, *The Origin of the Work of Art.*
5. Neumann, *The Origins and History of Consciousness,* 212.

Bibliography

Aïvanhov, Omraam Mikhaël. *Man's Two Natures, Human and Divine.* Frejus Cedex, France: Editions Prosveta, S. A., 1989.

Arendt, Hannah. *The Origins of Totalitarianism.* London: George Allen and Unwin, 1955.

———. *Responsibility and Judgment.* New York: Schocken Books, 2005.

Aurobindo, Sri. *The Hour of God: Selections from His Writings.* New Delhi, India: Sahita Akademi, 1995.

———. *The Integral Yoga: Sri Aurobindo's Teaching and Method of Practice, Selected Letters of Sri Aurobindo.* Compiled by Sri Aurobindo Ashram. Twin Lakes, Wisc.: Lotus Press, 1993.

———. *Letters on Yoga.* Charlottesville: University of Virginia, Sri Aurobindo Birth Centenary Library, 1970 (digitized 2010).

———. *Letters on Yoga: Volume 1.* Pondicherry, India: Sri Aurobindo Ashram, 2015.

———. *Letters on Yoga: Volume 4.* Pondicherry, India: Sri Aurobindo Ashram, 2015.

———. *Life, Literature, Yoga: Some Letters of Sri Aurobindo.* Pondicherry, India: Sri Aurobindo Ashram, 1967.

———. *The Mother with Letters on the Mother.* Twin Lakes, Wisc.: Lotus Press, 2012.

———. *On Yoga II: Letters on Yoga.* Pondicherry, India: Sri Aurobindo Ashram, 1958.

Berdyaev, Nicolas. *The Destiny of Man.* New York: Harper & Row, 1960.

———. *Freedom & the Spirit.* San Rafael, Calif.: Semantron Press, 2009.

———. *The Meaning of the Creative Act.* New York: Collier Books, 1962.

Bonhoeffer, Dietrich. *The Cost of Discipleship.* New York: Macmillan Company, 1969.

Brown, Michael. *Being Our Companion,* ebook.

Camera, Helder. *Spiral of Violence.* London: Sheed & Ward, 1971.

Campbell, Joseph, ed. *Spiritual Disciplines. Vol. 4 of Papers from the Eranos Yearbooks.* Princeton, N.J.: Princeton University Press, 1985.

Castaneda, Carlos. *The Active Side of Infinity.* New York: HarperCollins, 1998.

Dalal, A. S., ed. *The Hidden Forces of Life: Selections from the Works of Sri Aurobindo and The Mother.* Pondicherry, India: Sri Aurobindo Ashram, 2012.

DePrez, Daniel. "An Interview with Philip K. Dick." *Science Fiction Review* 19 (November 1976).

de Rougement, Denis. *The Devil's Share: An Essay on the Diabolic in Modern Society.* New York: Meridian Books, 1956.

Dick, Philip K. *The Divine Invasion.* New York: Mariner Books, 2011.

———. *Valis.* New York: Mariner Books, 2011.

———. *Philip K. Dick: The Last Interview and Other Conversations.* Edited by David Streitfeld. New York: Melville House, 2015.

Diedrich, Mark, ed. *Sitting Bull: The Collected Speeches.* Rochester, Minn.: Coyote Books, 1998.

Donnelly, Morwenna. *Founding the Life Divine: The Integral Yoga of Sri Aurobindo.* New York: Rider, 1955.

Dostoyevsky, Fyodor. *The Brothers Karamazov.* New York: Farrar, Straus and Giroux, 2002.

Drob, Sanford. *Symbols of the Kabbalah.* Northvale, N.J.: Jason Aronson, 2000.

Duran, Eduardo. *Healing the Soul Wound.* New York: Teachers College Press, 2006.

Ehrenreich, Barbara. *Blood Rites: Origins and History of the Passions of War.* New York: Metropolitan Books, 1997.

Forbes, Jack. *Columbus and Other Cannibals.* N.Y.: Seven Stories Press, 1992.

Girard, René. *I See Satan Fall like Lightning.* Maryknoll, N.Y.: Orbis Books, 2001.

———. *Things Hidden Since the Foundation of the World.* Stanford, Calif.: Stanford University Press, 1987.

———. *Violence and the Sacred.* New York: Continuum, 2005.

Griffin, David Ray. *Christian Faith and the Truth Behind 9/11.* Louisville, Ky.: Westminster John Knox Press, 2006.

Grof, Stanislav. "Healing Individuals, Transforming the Collective, Saving the Planet." *The Inner Door—A Publication of the Association for Holotropic Breathwork International* 19, no. 1 (February 2007).

Herron, Don, ed. *The Selected Letters of Philip K. Dick: 1908–1982.* Nevada City, Calif.: Underwood Books, 2009.

Hillman, James, and Sonu Shamdasani. *Lament of the Dead: Psychology After Jung's Red Book.* New York: W. W. Norton, 2013.

Holmquist, Annie. "Bonhoeffer on the 'Stupidity' That Led to Hitler's Rise." Intellectual Takeout (website). Updated April 8, 2016.

Jackson, Pamela, and Jonathan Lethem, eds. *The Exegesis of Philip K. Dick.* New York: Houghton Mifflin Harcourt, 2011.

Jensen, Derrick. *Songs of the Dead.* Crescent City, Calif.: Flashpoint Press, 2009.

Jung, C. G. *The Collected Works of C. G. Jung.* Translated by R. F. C. Hull, Gerard Adler, and Sir Herbert Read. Edited by Gerard Adler, R. F. C. Hull, Lisa Ress, William McGuire, Michael Fordham. 20 vols. Princeton. N.J.: Princeton, 1961–89.

———. *Dream Symbols of the Individuation Process: Notes of C. G. Jung's Seminars on Wolfgang Pauli's Dreams.* Princeton, N.J.: Princeton University Press, 2019.

———. "An Eightieth Birthday Interview." In *C. G. Jung Speaking*, edited by W. McGuire and R. F. C. Hull, 271–72. Princeton, N.J.: Princeton University Press, 1977.

———. *Letters.* Vol 1. London: Routledge, 1973.

———. *Psychological Reflections.* Princeton, N.J.: Princeton University Press, 1970.

———. *The Red Book: Liber Novus—A Reader's Edition.* New York: W. W. Norton, 2009.

———. *Visions.* Vol 2. Princeton, N.J.: Princeton University Press, 1997.

Ladha, Alnoor, and Martin Kirk. "Seeing Wetiko: On Capitalism, Mind Viruses, and Antidotes for a World in Transition." *Kosmos: Journal for Global Transformation* (website). Updated Spring, 2016.

Laing, R. D. *The Politics of Experience.* New York: Ballantine Books, 1967.

Levy, Paul. *Dispelling Wetiko.* Berkeley, Calif.: North Atlantic Books, 2013.

———. "Quantum Medicine for the Coronavirus," Awaken in the Dream (website), 2020.

Lewis, C. S. *The Screwtape Letters*. New York: HarperOne, 2001.

Lifton, Robert Jay. *The Nazi Doctors: Medical Killing and the Psychology of Genocide*. New York: Basic Books, 2017.

McMurtry, John. *The Cancer Stage of Capitalism: From Crisis to Cure*. London: Pluto Press, 1999.

———. *Value Wars: The Global Market Versus the Life Economy*. London: Pluto Press, 2002.

Narby, Jeremy. "Confessions of a White Vampire." Granta (website). Accessed May 15, 2021.

Neumann, Erich. *Art and the Creative Unconscious*. New York: Pantheon Books, 1959.

———. *Depth Psychology and a New Ethic*. New York: G. P. Putnam's Sons, 1969.

———. *The Origins and History of Consciousness*. New York: Pantheon Books, 1964.

Nietzsche, Friedrich. *Thus Spoke Zarathustra*. New York: Penguin Classics, 1961.

Ortega y Gasset, Jose. *The Revolt of the Masses*. New York: W. W. Norton, 1994.

Penn-Lewis, Jessie. *War on the Saints*. New York: Thomas E. Lowe, 1988.

Pistis Sohpia: Challenge to Early Christianity. Translated by G. R. S. Mead. Secaucus, N.J.: University Books, 1974.

Planck, Max. "Interviews with Great Scientists." *The Observer*. January 25, 1931.

Raine, Kathleen. *Blake and Tradition*. Vol 2. Princeton, N.J.: Princeton University Press, 1968.

Robinson, James M., ed. *The Nag Hammadi Library*. New York: HarperOne, 1988.

Ruiz, Don Miguel. *The Four Agreements*. San Rafael, Calif.: Amber-Allen Publishing, 1997.

Schoen, David E. *The War of the Gods in Addiction: C. G. Jung, Alcoholics Anonymous, and Archetypal Evil*. New Orleans, La.: Spring Journal Books, 2009.

Scholem, Gerhom. *Origins of the Kabbalah*. Translated by R. J. Zwi Werblowsky. Princeton, N.J.: Princeton University Press, 1987.

Schrödinger, Erwin. *Collected Papers*. Vol. 4, *General Scientific and Popular*

Papers. Vienna: Austrian Academy of Sciences. Friedr. Vieweg & Sohn, Braunschweig/Wiesbaden, 1984.

Solzhenitsyn, Aleksandr. *The Gulag Archipelago*. New York: Vintage Publishing, 2018.

———. "Nobel Lecture in Literature 1970." The Nobel Prize (website).

Steiner, Rudolf. *The Karma of Untruthfulness*. Vol. 1. London: Rudolf Steiner Press, 1988.

Sutin, Lawrence, ed. *The Shifting Realities of Philip K. Dick: Selected Literary and Philosophical Writings*. New York: Pantheon Books, 1995.

Taibbi, Matt. *Griftopia: Bubble Machines, Vampire Squids, and the Long Con That is Breaking America*. New York: Spiegel and Grau, 2010.

Tolle, Eckhart. *The Power of Now*. Novato, Calif.: New World Library, 1999.

von Frantz, Marie Louise. *Projection and Recollection in Jungian Psychology*. La Salle, Ill.: Open Court, 1982.

Wallace, Henry A. "Wallace Defines 'American Facism.'" *New York Times,* April 9, 1944.

Wesselman, Hank. *The Bowl of Light: Ancestral Wisdom from a Hawaiian Shaman*. Boulder, Colo.: Sounds True, 2011.

———. *The Re-enchantment: A Shamanic Path to a Life of Wonder*. Boulder, Colo: Sounds True, 2016.

Wilson, Colin. *The Mind Parasites*. Rhinebeck, N.Y.: Monkfish Book Publishing, 2005.

Winiecki, Martin. "Searching for the Anti-Virus: Covid-19 as Quantum Phenomenon." Kosmos Journal for Global Transofrmation (website), April 13, 2020.

Wink, Walter. *Unmasking the Powers*. Philadelphia, Pa.: Fortress Press, 1986.

Wirtz, Ursula. *Trauma and Beyond: The Mystery of Transformation*. New Orleans, La.: Spring Journal, 2014.

Woodruff, Paul, and Harry A. Wilmer, eds. *Facing Evil: Light at the Core of Darkness*. LaSalle, Ill.: Open Court, 1989.

Zimmer, Carl. *Parasite Rex: Inside the Bizarre World of Nature's Most Dangerous Creatures*. New York: Simon & Schuster, 2000.

The Zohar. Vol. 5. Translated by Harry Sperling and Maurice Simon. London: Soncino Press, 1949.

About the Author

 A creative artist, Paul Levy was born in 1956 and grew up in Yonkers, New York. In the mid-seventies he attended the State University of New York at Binghamton (now called Binghamton University), receiving degrees in both economics and studio art. While an undergraduate, he was hired by Princeton University to do research in economics.

In 1981, catalyzed by an intense trauma, Paul had a life-changing spiritual awakening in which he began to recognize the dreamlike nature of reality. During the first year of his spiritual emergence, he was hospitalized a number of times and was told he was having a severe psychotic break from reality and (mis)diagnosed as having a chemical imbalance. He was informed that he had what was then called manic depression (now called bipolar disorder) and that he would have to live with his illness for the rest of his life and would need to take medication until his dying breath. Little did the doctors realize, however, that he was taking part in a spiritual awakening/ shamanic-initiation process, which at times mimicked psychosis but in actuality was a spiritual experience of a far different order that was completely off the map of the psychiatric system. Fortunately, over time he was able to extricate himself from the psychiatric establishment so that he could continue to unfold his inner process of awakening.

After the trauma of his shamanic breakdown/breakthrough, Paul became a certified art teacher and taught both painting and drawing for a handful of years to people of all ages. Intensely interested in the work of C. G. Jung, in 1988 he became the manager of the C. G. Jung Foundation Book Service in New York, as well as the advertising manager for the Jungian journal *Quadrant*.

In 1990 Paul moved to Portland, Oregon. In 1993, after a dozen years of working on himself so as to integrate his nonordinary experiences, he started to openly share his insights about the dreamlike nature of reality by giving talks and facilitating groups based on the way that life is a shared waking dream that we are all cocreating and dreaming together. A pioneer in the field of spiritual emergence, Paul is a wounded healer in private practice, helping others who are also awakening to the dreamlike nature of reality. He is the founder of the Awakening in the Dream community in Portland, Oregon.

Paul is the author of *The Quantum Revelation: A Radical Synthesis of Science and Spirituality, Dispelling Wetiko: Breaking the Curse of Evil, Awakened by Darkness: When Evil Becomes Your Father,* and *The Madness of George W. Bush: A Reflection of Our Collective Psychosis*. A Tibetan Buddhist practitioner for more than thirty years, Paul has intimately studied with some of the greatest spiritual masters of Tibet and Burma. He was the coordinator of the Portland chapter of the Padmasambhava Buddhist Center for over twenty years.

His website is **www.awakeninthedream.com**;
his email is **paul@awakeninthedream.com**.

A Statement from the Front Cover Artist

For thirty years, I have been drawn to the sacred art I have encountered while living throughout Asia. Whether it is the underlying geometry of a Tibetan thangka or the complex iconography of a Taoist temple painting, I have often found myself transfixed by images that are meant to be unpacked and decoded. So it's no surprise that I leapt at the chance to work with Paul Levy on the cover of *Wetiko* because it represented a chance to create just such an image with an author whose work and wisdom I greatly admire.

What I could not have anticipated was that our collaboration would evolve into a profound dance. There were epiphanies for both of us as we dreamed our way together through the journey of bringing this cover into being. Each of its elements describes the alchemical process through which the energy of wetiko is transformed into creativity and new beginnings.

For me, the process of "co-dreaming" this cover with Paul was a model of the transformative energy of openness and generosity that is not only a hallmark of all the best collaborative work, but also an essential part of the approach we all must take to effect the collective awakening our world so desperately needs. I am grateful to have had this opportunity to contribute to this profound project.

SETH TAYLOR,
WWW.SETHTAYLORSTUDIO.COM

Index

Books of Related Interest

Egregores
The Occult Entities That Watch Over Human Destiny
by Mark Stavish

Precognitive Dreamwork and the Long Self
Interpreting Messages from Your Future
by Eric Wargo

Energy Vampires
A Practical Guide for Psychic Self-protection
by Dorothy Harbour

Dark Light Consciousness
Melanin, Serpent Power, and the Luminous Matrix of Reality
by Edward Bruce Bynum, Ph.D., ABPP

The King in Orange
The Magical and Occult Roots of Political Power
by John Michael Greer

Entity Possession
Freeing the Energy Body of Negative Influences
by Samuel Sagan, M.D.

Cleansing Rites of Curanderismo
Limpias Espirituales of Ancient Mesoamerican Shamans
by Erika Buenaflor, M.A., J.D.

Indigenous Healing Psychology
Honoring the Wisdom of the First Peoples
by Richard Katz, Ph.D.

INNER TRADITIONS • BEAR & COMPANY
P.O. Box 388 • Rochester, VT 05767
1-800-246-8648
www.InnerTraditions.com

Or contact your local bookseller